MUSICAL DEVELOPMENT AND LEARNING

Related titles

Colin Durrant and Graham Welch:
Making Sense of Music: Foundations for Music Education

Joanna Glover and Stephen Ward (eds):
Teaching Music in the Primary School (Second Edition)

Michael Gray:
Song and Dance Man III

Peter Lang, Yaacov Katz and Isabel Menezes (eds):
Affective Education: A Comparative View

Gonzalo Retamal and Ruth Aedo-Richmond (eds):
Education as a Humanitarian Response

Witold Tulasiewicz and Tony Adams:
Teaching the Mother Tongue in a Multilingual Europe

Kangmin Zeng:
Dragon Gate: Competitive Examinations and their Consequences

Frontiers of International Education
Series Editor: Colin Brock

MUSICAL DEVELOPMENT AND LEARNING

The International Perspective

Edited by
David J. Hargreaves and Adrian C. North

continuum
LONDON • NEW YORK
www.continuumbooks.com

CONTINUUM
The Tower Building   370 Lexington Avenue
11 York Road   New York
London SE1 7NX   NY 10017–6503

First published 2001
Reprinted 2002

British Library Cataloguing-in-Publication Data
A catalogue record for this book is available from the British Library.

ISBN 0-8264-6042-9

Typeset by BookEns Ltd, Royston, Herts
Printed and bound in Great Britain by Biddles Ltd,
www.biddles.co.uk

Contents

Contributors

Myung-sook Auh
Faculty of Education
University of Technology, Sydney
Australia

Peter Dunbar-Hall
Sydney Conservatorium of Music
University of Sydney
Sydney
Australia

Gerry Farrell
Department of Music
City University
London
United Kingdom

Heiner Gembris
Institute for Musicology
Martin-Luther-University of Halle-Wittenberg
Halle/Saale
Germany

Marina Gulina
Faculty of Psychology
St Petersburg State University
St Petersburg
Russia

David J. Hargreaves
Faculty of Education
University of Surrey Roehampton
London
United Kingdom

Wojciech Jankowski
Fryderyk Chopin Academy of Music,
Warszawa
Poland

Gary McPherson
School of Music and Music Education
University of New South Wales
Sydney
Australia

Kacper Miklaszewski
DUX Recording Producers
Warszawa
Poland

Graça Mota
Escola Superior de Educação
Instituto Polytécnico do Porto
Porto
Portugal

Tadahiro Murao
Department of Music
Aichi University of Education
Kariya City
Japan

Adrian C. North
Department of Psychology
University of Leicester
Leicester
United Kingdom

Alda de Jesus Oliveira
Federal University of Bahia
Salvador
Bahia
Brazil

Bengt Olsson
School of Music and Musicology
University of Göteborg
Göteborg
Sweden

Kathy Primos
School of Music
University of the Witwatersrand
Johannesburg
South Africa

Rudolf E. Radocy
Division of Music Education and Music Therapy
The University of Kansas
Lawrence
Kansas
United States of America

Johannella Tafuri
Conservatorio di musica 'Martini'
Bologna
Italy

Maris Valk-Falk
Estonian Academy of Music
Tallinn
Estonia

Robert Walker
School of Music and Music Education
University of New South Wales
Sydney
Australia

Graham F. Welch
Institute of Education
University of London
United Kingdom

Bernadette Wilkins
Faculty of Education
University of Surrey Roehampton
London
United Kingdom

Cheung-shing Yeh
Education Department
Curriculum Development Institute
Government of Hong Kong

Preface

There has been a considerable increase of interest in the psychological basis of musical thinking, behaviour and development over the last two decades, and this is of vital interest and importance to music educators. *The Developmental Psychology of Music*, by one of us, was published in 1986 and was one of the first attempts to map out the psychological foundations of music education. This book has been used extensively by music educators in various different countries, and the success of other recent titles in the same area reflects the increasing importance of music psychology in education.

Undergraduate and postgraduate degree courses in music education naturally include the study of curriculum content, pedagogical methods and other practical aspects of music teaching, but the psychological basis of music learning is gaining increasing prominence. Richard Colwell's *Handbook of Music Teaching and Learning* (1992) is an encyclopaedic work which comprehensively reflects the state of the art of North American music education in 1992. A new edition is currently being prepared. The importance of psychological studies is clearly apparent in many of its chapters: educational practice and psychological theory have an increasingly close and symbiotic relationship, and many research developments in the last decade should have direct implications for the classroom.

One clear trend in this proliferation of research activity is the diversity and increasing availability of music itself, and of the situations in which it is experienced and 'consumed'. Technological developments such as the Walkman, DVD, home video players and the internet mean that the range of styles of music available to most people in the industrialized world is vast, as is the range of situations in which it is present. The importance of the *social and cultural context* of musical behaviour is becoming increasingly recognized, and our previous book,

The Social Psychology of Music (1997), attempted to map out some of the main ways in which this is happening.

In the case of music education, it is clear that the social and cultural conventions and traditions of different countries, particularly of their educational institutions, play a key role in shaping the nature of musical development. In some cases this might stem from particularly strong pedagogical traditions, such as the Kodály method in Hungary or the Orff and Suzuki 'methods', which originate from Germany and Japan respectively, but which have much wider application. In other cases the influence is attributable to more general aspects of educational policy such as the degree of reliance on published schemes of work or the role of assessment.

These specific conditions which shape music education in each country – details of curriculum content and objectives and the specific methods and attitudes of the teachers involved – clearly have a direct influence upon children's musical development and learning and this book aims to explore these influences. If we broaden the scope of 'music education' to take into account those activities and experiences which take place *outside* the classroom, then it becomes even more important to consider the influence of different cultural traditions and environments on musical development, as well as those of peers, parents, local organizations and other external influences.

Our original aim in compiling this book was, therefore, to present a range of international experts with some core issues concerning musical development and learning and to ask them to explore these from the point of view of the policies, practices and cultural traditions in their own countries. National differences profoundly affect the nature of music learning, the content of music teaching, the research problems that are addressed (if any) and the methodologies that are used in doing so. It seemed to us that no book as yet has focused on this obvious issue, and so our aim is to redress the balance.

We contacted prominent authors from in fifteen countries and invited them to contribute chapters structured around three broad issues: 'aims and objectives'; 'contents and methods'; and 'student issues'. We also asked them to consider some more detailed suggestions about the possible contents of each. Under 'aims and objectives' we asked them to consider the three issues of composing, performing and listening in music learning; notation and music reading; and specialist and general music education. Under 'contents and methods' we asked them to consider national curricula; IT and music technology; the role of assessment; world and popular music; and multicultural issues. Under 'student issues' we asked them to consider gender issues in music learning; the gifted pupil; music learning outside the classroom; and careers in music.

Our authors were invited to explore how their own nation or region's approach to music education influences the nature of students' musical learning and development with respect to these three broad issues. They were not expected to provide a comprehensive coverage of each issue, nor indeed to follow our outline systematically, but rather to select those of particular salience in their own geographical area. Our intention was to maintain an acceptable balance between, on the one hand, the inevitable diversity of approaches and salient national issues and, on the other, the need to 'steer' each contributor in order to ensure that the book possessed an acceptable level of coherence.

We were delighted by the general enthusiasm with which the distinguished authors accepted our invitation, clearly welcoming the chance to put forward their own nation or region's perspective to an international audience. As we expected, they varied considerably in the extent to which they followed our suggestions, but all agreed cheerfully to submit themselves to detailed negotiations with us as to the planned contents of their chapters, and also in the subsequent drafting and redrafting, which was inevitable, given the diversity of the subject matter and the obvious fact that the majority of the contributors are not native speakers of English. In the event, we were most impressed by the dedication and care our authors brought to these tasks.

In retrospect, it has been a privilege and a valuable learning experience for us to have collated, co-ordinated and tried to make some overall sense of the diversity of attitudes, skills, interests and specialized knowledge that our contributors have brought to the book. Some concerns are common to all of those involved with promoting musical development and learning regardless of national background, and our concluding chapter deals with these in terms of four broad issues: the specific historical, political and cultural background of each country; curriculum issues (national curricula, specialist and generalist music education); aims and objectives (the purpose of music in the curriculum, pupil- and teacher-centred approaches); and music learning inside and outside schools.

Although these common concerns undoubtedly exist, the global diversity of national traditions and circumstances and the sheer variation in the size and population of different countries and regions make it inevitable that no survey can ever be comprehensively cross-cultural. Given the inevitable constraints on space, any coverage is bound to be selective to some degree, and so we made the decision to identify potential contributors in those areas in which music education policy is an active concern. We also made the conscious decision to describe broad patterns of musical learning and development in populations as a whole rather than to deal in any systematic fashion with particular pedagogical methods or techniques.

Numerous people have been extremely helpful, in differing ways, in ensuring that this book finally came out. We would like to express our particular thanks to Nigel Foreman, Marina Gulina, Anthony Haynes, Regina Konstantinova Klochkova, Kristin Sarv, Yoshiko Sugie, Robert Walker and Bernadette Wilkins.

References

Colwell, R. (ed.) (1992) *Handbook of Research on Music Teaching and Learning*. New York: Schirmer/Macmillan.

Hargreaves, D. J. (1986) *The Developmental Psychology of Music*. Cambridge: Cambridge University Press.

Hargreaves, D. J. and North, A. C. (eds) (1997) *The Social Psychology of Music*. Oxford: Oxford University Press.

CHAPTER

1

Africa

Kathy Primos

It is impossible to consider music learning and development in Africa without being drawn into historical, cultural and political issues. The pervasiveness of western culture, the legacies of colonialist structures, the effects of globalization and the desire to regain and maintain African traditions have become major issues in the field of education. Throughout the continent there has been an uneasy co-existence of African and western traditions; traditions which, together with popular culture, carry fundamentally different approaches to music learning. This chapter explores the implications for music learning and development in the context of these issues; first, in terms of sub-Saharan Africa as a whole and then, more specifically, in the South African situation.

Africa

Music learning in the African tradition

Music pounds deep in the heart of every African; it is considered to be of the purest spiritual essence – a part of a person's social and spiritual being; a vehicle for healing mind, body and spirit, and inseparable from life experience. Storytelling, message carrying, children's games, ceremonial and gender-related functions and family and community rituals all incorporate music as an essential tool for social interaction and human development. Used as a socially acceptable vehicle for self-expression, personal messages or problems can be communicated musically without fear of offence to the community. Its spiritual nature means that exponents may use it to 'tune in' to the spirits of their ancestors. Thus, they should be worthy and respectful of music's powers.

Musical activities in the African tradition are learned orally and stored in the memory; however, they are not memorized for exact reproduction, but as a framework for creating future performances. An African approaches tradition as a way of experiencing and managing the present – what Nzewi (1997, p. 43) describes as 'circular futurity'. There is no search for correct reproduction, only for correct re-creation. The correctness is judged by non-musical factors, such as its contribution to 'humanness'. The Nguni term for this is *ubuntu*. Ubuntu is a prevailing spirit in which everyone acknowledges their existence only in terms of their oneness with others. It is deep-seated in all traditionally rooted Africans and creates a unique unity of persons across the continent. The way in which they make and use music closely reflects this *ubuntu* spirit. Everyone brings their personal contribution to the whole musical fabric and united event, be it in a leading role or as part of group interaction.

Musical skills are essential for the social development of the African child. Typically, women sing a welcome to the baby as it is born into the community. 'The newly born is rocked in the parent's arms to a song ... and, soon, the child begins to fling its arms and legs in response to these' (Amoaku, 1998, p. 23). Joe Ngozi Mokwunyei (1998, p. 437) describes how, in Ghana and Nigeria, mothers sing to soothe a crying or wakeful child:

> Children are also exposed to familiar cultural rhythms when women make music out of their daily/regular chores such as pounding, weeding, and sweeping... [ultimately they will have] learnt rhythms that include the hemiola and other cross rhythms which in other cultures are considered complicated.

There is a pulsation in the music that is shared by all, and interactive rhythmic patterns are woven into the texture by the participants. It gives rise to lithesome movement which, unlike the western classical tradition for example, expresses accentuated pulsations with upward thrusts of the body.

Learning of musical skills is simultaneously blended with other forms of expression: 'the integration of music, movement, drama, poetry and visual art, is the key to the developing child artist' (Amoaku, 1998, p. 23). In addition to singing games, children are encouraged to make up their own songs to suit their own purposes. Musical creativity is thus not only encouraged at an early age but is also an expected part of a child's personal and social development. Unless a specific situation makes it inappropriate, children are encouraged to participate in adult musical activities:

all children invariably learn to sing and dance, although as with every human endeavour, they do so at different rates. Consequently, almost everyone becomes at least an adequate enough singer and dancer to participate in communal African life ... almost everybody at least attains the competence of an amateur in African music and musicianship. (Mokwunyei, 1998, p. 438).

While songs can be shared across nations, or remain specific to certain villages or families, the right occasion is needed in order to perform certain music. It would be considered inappropriate, for example, for wedding, initiation or funeral songs to be sung elsewhere or at another time. Singing and instrumental playing are often gender-bearing activities. Women may be forbidden to play certain instruments and may be confined to an accompanying role or to singing and dancing (Agak, 1998, p. 3).

Western education and African music

Christian missionaries brought western education to Africa, setting up educational institutions throughout the continent. The influence of the Christian church on music learning among Africans cannot be underestimated. The use of Curwen sol-fa notation in their music teaching also had an extraordinary impact and today remains a favoured system of notation for many African choral composers and singers. Hymn singing is probably the single most indelible colonial influence on African music, with its rigid beat, four-part SATB harmony and homophonic texture. From the nineteenth century, African composers began to emerge whose music was heavily influenced by such church music. A good example of this would be Enoch Sontonga's *Nkosi sikelel'i Africa* (1897). It is now sung across the continent, is part of South Africa's national anthem and attests to the authentic Africanization of the style. The barriers set up by the missionaries between African traditions and Christian worship are not so rigidly retained today. James Flolu (1996) describes how new musical styles have begun to emerge through the integration of church music and indigenous Ghanaian music.

Across sub-Saharan Africa, in spite of the political independence of African nations, the legacy of colonial governance still retains its influence in formal music education. Where English is used as an educational medium, certificated music teachers are likely to have followed the graded learning processes of the British, public music examination systems and may have entered tertiary music education in a local or overseas western-oriented university or college institution. Fela Sowande, Akin Euba, J. H. Kwabena Nketia and Khabi Mngoma – renowned African musicians and scholars – all followed this learning route. The influence of the western paradigm on African musicians and scholars, and in institutions of music learning, has been pervasive and has caused much concern (Flolu, 1998). Ways in which Africans learn their musical culture are fundamentally different from western perceptions of musical development. Meki Nzewi is an outspoken critic of the imposition of western learning and thinking processes on African musicians and scholars. 'There is a strong need to redesign the orientation and content in curricula for African music education in Africa ... in order to impart authoritative African philosophical thoughts as well as unique principles of creativity'(Nzewi, 1997, p. 13). It is now common for African music to be included in the curricula of African schools, colleges and universities, but 'there still exists a distressingly wide gap between the school music programme and the local culture environment' (Flolu, 1998, p. 184). Nevertheless, there is a strong lobby of support for maintaining western music, its learning systems and notation.

Urbanization

While traditional music practices are still maintained in the rural areas, many Africans have become urbanized – some for several generations now – and must sometimes travel long distances to take part in ceremonies and rituals. Some of those people no longer subscribe to the same traditions and there is pressure upon them to drop such traditions. Christians, for example, consider the rituals to be pagan and unacceptable to modern Africans. During the apartheid era, South Africans were encouraged to practise their own music separately; viewed as a political ploy to prevent blacks from entering the modern world, it fostered strong resistance from political activists. Today there are those who continue to reject their traditions, while others regret the separation. To retrace their cultural roots such people must go back to their elders who may be found in urban areas. But they often live far away, some in remote regions. The modes of learning have been changed irrevocably for urbanized South Africans, for whom special learning environments may need to be developed. In Soweto, for example, when traditional weddings take place, many need tuition beforehand in order to be able to sing the required songs.

African music has become modified and adapted within the remarkable development of African popular genres. Popular music is, of course, a global phenomenon, but Africans have stamped their own experiences on this music. The common factor is described by Paul Gilroy as black peoples' 'sense of embeddedness in the modern world' (Gilroy, 1993, p. ix). This has been brought about in Africa by urbanization, but, as with the regional differences in tradition, each region has its own history of imported popular music and distinct styles. In South Africa, for example, adapting musically to situations of poverty and severe oppression in new meeting-places such as slumyards and shebeens, new genres emerged such as *marabi* and *mbaqanga*. For more information about regional styles see Manuel (1988), Ballantine (1993) and Coplan (1985).

Peter Manuel identifies two of the most notable shifts from tradition that urbanization brought about. First, in the cultural environment of the township, music was performed in different contexts and served very different social needs. Secondly, western musical characteristics were absorbed, adapted and simplified to suit the needs of an urbanized life situation: 'the modern city ... has little in common with the tribal village whence most Africans or their ancestors ultimately came. Urbanization entails a process of formidable adaptation and reorientation of cultural values, both on individual and group levels' (Manuel, 1988, p. 85). This has had a marked influence on the way in which the modern African approaches musical learning and development. Learning through socialization remains, but the societal situation of the learning is far removed from its roots.

These descriptions may be taken as typical across the entire, massive sub-Saharan continent. In Central, East and West Africa, Islamic influences are also strong, and African music in its turn had a profound influence on Islamic music, notably in Nigeria (see Graham, 1989). Naturally, each country has its own music education policies and informal music learning processes. Issues of upholding African and colonial traditions, while engaging the present global and technological cultures, are challenges common to all.

South Africa

Background

The racial divisions of apartheid into Black, White, Coloured and Asian were misleadingly simplistic. Post-apartheid South Africa now has eleven official languages: nine African – Isindebele, Isixhosa, Isizulu, Sepedi, Sesotho, Setswana, Siswati, Tshivenda, Xitsonga – plus English and Afrikaans (a daughter-language of Dutch, unique to Southern Africa). Indian, Chinese, German, Portuguese and Greek peoples, and the so-called coloured people of mixed race and/or Malay descent, all add further to the mix. South Africa's cultural diversity has emerged from the influx of European, Asian and Oriental settlers to the indigenous African populations over the past three centuries. After a turbulent history of wars over territorial rights and political power, white minority rule and apartheid policies, the world watched in 1994 as South Africa went to the polls to elect its first truly democratic government. There was an abrupt transfer of power to an African-oriented majority. Virtually overnight, dominant paradigms were challenged and scrutinized for their efficacy and relevance to the total population. Education inevitably fell under such scrutiny and a strong call went out for the transformation of the Eurocentric government educational system, including the prevailing western paradigm in music education. As a result, new education policies are now being implemented. Before considering the implications of these for music education, a broad scenario of some typical South African music learning situations, past and present, is outlined.

Routes to music learning

Independent schools typically include class music in their curriculum, and offer private instrumental tuition as an optional, extra fee-paying activity. Class music has been neglected badly in all South African government schools, in spite of some very good work by a few excellent teachers (see Hauptfleisch, 1993). Music education has focused more on individual instrumental tuition – through private teachers, subsidized music centres or, together with aural training and theoretical and historical studies, as an optional school matriculation subject. Until the dismantling of apartheid structures in education, this applied almost exclusively to white learners of western classical music. Government now has a policy to redeploy these resources, targeting previously under-privileged learners.

The main providers of music tuition for those disadvantaged by apartheid were the music schools established under the umbrella of non-governmental organizations (NGOs). Typically situated in large urban areas such as Johannesburg, Cape Town and Durban, they mainly supported the development of township jazz idioms. Some of these institutions nurtured musicians, including Miriam Makeba, Hugh Masekela, Abdullah Ebrahim and Jonas Gwangwa, who later won world renown through the African Music and Dance Association at the now legendary Dorkay House in Johannesburg. Opportunities for professional development and performance experience were opened up for many black musicians. However, NGOs later became impoverished and dependent upon foreign funding for their survival. 'With the worsening political climate and tighter segregation in the 1960s it became much more difficult for jazz bands to survive (there was less live work) or for young developing musicians to learn to read music' (Graham 1989, p. 260). In spite of this, unique South African musical styles continued to develop such as marabi, iscathamiya, kwela, mbube, and mbaqanga (for further information see Coplan, 1985). A subsequent generation grew up learning the music of liberation movements and these protest songs now have an established place in South African culture (see Gray, 1996). For the present generation, this is all now passé. They favour kwaito – an African version of rap – and other contemporary popular trends, such as Retro and Latino. '[R]adio, television, the press and computer, have been used to portray American and European cultures and values to such an extent that the majority of South Africa's black African youth have little interest in what is perceived as African' (Ndlovu and Akrofi, 1999, p. 14).

Experimenting with the voice or an instrument and imitating the style or sound of a favourite artist is a common path to musical learning for South African rock, jazz or pop musicians. This is a global phenomenon, and not unique to South Africa, but the African tradition of music learning is close to this way of working, hence the rich endowment of talented musicians. There has been virtually no scope for the development of these self-taught musicians within the formal education system. Nevertheless, many desire to be musically literate, and so they seek tuition elsewhere and enter for ABRSM or Trinity College theory examinations. In 1999, for example, an estimated 5 per cent of black candidates who entered for Trinity College theory examinations in the Johannesburg region also entered for practical examinations.

As with the rest of Africa, the European music training provided in various Christian educational institutions heavily influenced the development of African choral singing. The Lovedale Seminary in the Cape and the Marianhill Mission in Natal, among many others, produced music teachers, composers and choral conductors. For a list of these institutions and the musicians who emerged from them, see Malan (1979). Choral singing is thus another widely accessed means of informal music learning. The ability of choral singers to sing at sight from sol-fa notation is a remarkable phenomenon. It appears to be learned informally by osmosis and confined mostly to major keys. Minor keys, chromaticism and modulation are often negotiated with some difficulty. Very few choristers have been introduced to staff notation. Sadly, there are many talented South African musicians who have felt hampered by a lack of such music tuition. Professor Mzilikaze Khumalo, for example, rooted in Zulu and Christian traditions, never had formal music lessons. In spite of this, he is a revered choral conductor and one of South Africa's most renowned composers. (His cantata *Ushaka* was released on CD in 1998, and he is also retired Professor of African Languages at the University of the Witwatersrand.) The late Professor Khabi Mngoma was more fortunate, although his licentiates in teaching and performance were attained under difficult circumstances. He taught some of today's well-known African musicians, including his daughter, the renowned soprano Sibongile Khumalo, and inspired a culture of string playing in Soweto. At the same time he was a staunch champion of African traditional music and choral music.

Music and new school education policies

It will be noted that music learning in South Africa has developed mostly through informal or private tuition rather than as a result of school music education. However, new education policies have now been introduced (see Republic of South Africa, 1995 and 1996) and curriculum structures are being rolled into the school system aimed at implementation by 2005. The goal is to foster improved learning and to contribute to the transformation of South African society in line with the new constitution. The new curriculum

> emphasises the need for major changes in education and training in South Africa in order to normalise and transform teaching and learning. Emphasis is placed on the necessity for a shift from the traditional aims-and-objectives approach to outcomes-based education. This paradigm shift is a necessary prerequisite for the achievement of the following vision for South Africa: 'a prosperous, truly united, democratic and internationally competitive country with literate, creative and critical citizens leading productive, self-fulfilled lives in a country free of violence, discrimination and prejudice'. (Departments of Education Policy Document, Senior Phase, October 1997, p. 1)

Music has been included in the curriculum for the first ten years of schooling, to be integrated with dance, drama and visual arts in an Arts and Culture Learning Area. This is one of eight such Learning Areas which make up Curriculum 2005. The General Education and Training Band includes: Foundation Phase (Grades 1–3); Intermediate Phase (Grades 4–6); Senior Phase (Grades 7–9). The Further Education and Training Band includes Grades 10–12. Integration is seen as 'desirable', but 'particular knowledge, skills and techniques of the various art forms ... could however be experienced in their own right' (p. AC-9). Currently, schools are given freedom to design their own lesson plans which, nevertheless, have to dovetail with common learning programmes or themes, taught simultaneously across all learning areas.

Musical learning and development in this scenario must be geared to specific outcomes. Those for Grades 7–9 (ages 12–14) are:

1. Apply knowledge, techniques and skills to create and be critically involved in arts and culture processes and products.
2. Use the creative processes of arts and culture to develop and apply social and interactive skills.
3. Reflect on and engage critically with arts experience and work.
4. Demonstrate an understanding of the origins, functions and dynamic nature of culture.
5. Experience and analyse the use of multiple forms of communication and expression.
6. Use art skills and cultural expressions to make an economic contribution to self and society.
7. Demonstrate an ability to access creative arts and cultural processes to develop self-esteem and promote healing.
8. Acknowledge, understand and promote historically marginalized arts and cultural forms and practices.

These outcomes reach beyond the acquisition of performance skills, music literacy and 'music for music's sake', typical of the western classical music paradigm. They call for openness to differing paths to music learning and a willingness to shift entrenched attitudes and thought patterns. Grades 10–12 will constitute the Further Education and Training Band with music as an optional specialized subject area. This is still in the planning stage, but it will also require a major paradigm shift to move from the former Matriculation Examination syllabus in music, which was firmly rooted in western classical music, to a Further Education and Training Certificate which is expected to have a broader cultural base. But 'broader' here does not mean building upon the existing paradigm to 'include' the music of other cultures. It will call for a hard, critical review of taken-for-granted western assumptions concerning 'tradition' and ways of presenting African music in the classroom.

Problems of learning 'tradition'

Tradition involves something being handed down over successive generations, but the manner in which it is handed down can irrevocably change that tradition. For example, the teaching of national folk songs in British schools, using arrangements by Cecil Sharp and Vaughan Williams, created a tradition of its own but certainly did not preserve the tradition itself. The 'tradition' was learned with piano accompaniments and a harmonic language unknown to the folk who originally sang those melodies. Nevertheless, a generation of learners became culturally conditioned by this repertoire of national songs.

The yen for preservation of traditions has been extended to African traditional music. There is a large body of recordings preserving music performances for posterity (see Shelemay, 1991) and notated versions are increasingly being made available (see Kruger, 1998). In order to teach African music, teachers trained in the Euro-American teaching methods have called for such 'materials' to be supplied, but teaching an African song from a score has its pitfalls. A South African university student did not recognize a well-known song from his own Tswana culture when it was taught to him in such a classroom situation, saying that the 'feeling was all wrong'. Anticipating that my students would need to develop transcription skills to collect songs of their African culture, I used a taped example from a book of South African songs as a dictation exercise and gave them copies of the transcriptions from the book to compare with their own. This was met with a storm of protest: 'This is not correct. It's stupid. It should not be in 4/4 time.' These two examples highlight the dangers of notating orally transmitted music. This is not to say that the score has no use, but, in the absence of live models, sound and video recordings present closer ways of engaging the oral process as a primary learning tool.

Nzewi (1997) points out that the concept of rhythm 'is loaded with Western musical thought, sense and meaning. There is no universal order about musical intellection that constrains the African to conceive of rhythm as an isolatable, disembodied element of musical sound' (p. 32). 'It is an integral of a poetic perception of motion, not a statistical calculation'(p. 33). Tried and tested methods of teaching aligned with western assumptions can confuse or disturb African learners. Western methods that start with 'feeling the beat', for example – tapping, clapping or marching to it – are fundamentally different from the traditional African experience of rhythm.

Teaching African music

Musical development for the African child runs parallel with learning to talk. It is assumed that such skills are acquired by an early age. The idea of formally learning music in a school or tertiary institution is often met with resistance or disbelief from parents (see Primos, 1992). Formal music training in a school environment and assessment of achievement levels are also incompatible with African music practice since everyone's contribution is acceptable if the music carries the right spirit. Because of their context specificity, singing certain African songs in a formal classroom situation might also be considered incongruous or even absurd.

When Africans teach their songs to other Africans, the music is inseparable from the body movements, and so songs are usually sung standing. The leader starts singing and, almost instantaneously, people join in and sing, following the guidance of the leader. They sing to each other as if in conversation, sharing their music and reacting to the contributions of the others around them. Each participant in the song 'knows what they have to do' and songs are learned very quickly in this informal manner.

Dave Dargie (1998) relates how it took him 'some eight months to teach a group of Xhosa boys to perform a complete marimba mass of about twelve songs', attempting to adapt Western music teaching methods to teaching marimbas: trying to give theoretical explanations and so on. On one occasion the 14-year-old leader of the learning group simply told him 'You are teaching us all wrong'. So he had to 'shake up his ideas and note how the youngsters learned from him by observation'(p. 117). Later he sent those boys to another place to teach others. Using their preferred observation method, they successfully accomplished the task over only two weekends.

Music in African and Afro-American traditions depends largely on improvisation, re-creation and variation rather than duplication and reproduction of sound from the printed page. African traditional music transcribed in European staff notation 'misleads Western musicians who, in their characteristic ethnocentric manner, tend to interpret any music in their own terms, without reference to the tradition it is intended to represent' (Kebede, 1982, p. 122). Sensitivity to differing learning processes is clearly desirable. For example, the incorporation of African music into South African school classrooms is often done by 'adding' an African song or two to the repertoire, or 'incorporating' African tunes into western-designed recorder tutors. This 'tacking on' of African 'materials' on to the dominant culture of music learning may be well-meaning, but smacks of tokenism.

The contemporary challenge

Curriculum 2005 presents South African music educators with a golden opportunity to establish music as an important vehicle for reciprocal cross-cultural interaction. A review and shift of existing teaching paradigms should ensure that the Tswana student would recognize his song in the classroom as readily as he would in his community and that African rhythms would not be forced into western frames of reference. The policy of honouring all musics would assure a place for western classical modes of music learning. However, solving the tussle between western and African music traditions is no longer the core challenge for music educators and learners in Africa.

Paul Tiyambe Zeleza (1997), commenting on the role of philosophers in African contexts, states:

> while they may derive conceptual and methodological inspiration from ethnophilosophy and western philosophy, to be meaningful their texts and discourses have to critically engage Africa's contemporary conditions and challenges, an intellectual task that neither ethnophilosophy nor western philosophy is equipped to undertake. (p. 506)

This is precisely the task that music educators in Africa need to take upon themselves, turning to traditions for inspiration but developing methods and processes which will enable music learners to meet their own 'contemporary conditions and challenges'. African, western, global and any other ways of music learning and development will all have something to contribute to this process.

References

Agak, H. O. (1998) 'Gender in school music in the Kenyan history of music education', in *Proceedings of the 23rd International Society for Music Education World Conference*. ISME, Pretoria, 1–21.

Amoaku, W. K. (1998) 'My world, your world, our world: the sounds that bind us all: developing the child musician in African societies', in *Proceedings of the 23rd International Society for Music Education World Conference*. ISME, Pretoria, 22–5.

Ballantine, C. (1993) *Marabi Nights*. Johannesburg: Raven.

Coplan, D. (1985) *In Township Tonight*. Johannesburg: Raven.

Dargie, D. (1998) 'The teaching of African music using techniques based on traditional teaching/learning methods', in *Proceedings of the 23rd International Society for Music Education World Conference*. ISME, Pretoria, 116–30.

Flolu, J. (1996) 'Music education in Ghana: the way forward', in M. Floyd (ed.) *World Musics in Education*. Aldershot: Ashgate.

Flolu, J. (1998) 'In search of an African and relevance oriented music education system for Ghanaian schools', in *Proceedings of the 23rd International Society for Music Education World Conference*. ISME, Pretoria, 183–90.

Gilroy, P. (1993) *The Black Atlantic: Modernity and Double Consciousness*. London: Verso.

Graham, R. (1989) *Stern's Guide to Contemporary African Music*. London: Pluto.

Gray, A.-M. (1996) 'The liberation song, with special reference to those used by the African National Congress, the Inkatha Freedom Party and the Pan Africanist Congress'. Unpublished MMus thesis. University of the Orange Free State.

Hauptfleisch, S. (1993) *Effective Music Education in South Africa: Main Report*. Pretoria: Human Sciences Research Council.

Kebede, A. (1982) *Roots of Black Music: The Vocal, Instrumental, and Dance Heritage of Africa and Black America*. Englewood Cliffs, NJ: Prentice-Hall.

Kruger, J. (1998) 'Ideas for the classroom: four Venda songs', in E. Oehrle (ed.) *The Talking Drum*. Newsletter Issue No. 10, 2–6 December.

Malan, J. P. (ed.) (1979) *South African Music Encyclopaedia, Vol. 1*. Cape Town: Oxford University Press.

Manuel, P. (1988) 'Africa', in *Popular Musics of the Non-Western World*. Oxford: Oxford University Press.

Mngoma, K. (1998) 'Music and Ubuntu', in *Proceedings of the 23rd International Society for Music Education World Conference*. Pretoria, ISME, 427–33.

Mokwunyei, J. N. (1998) 'The role of women in African music education', in *Proceedings of the 23rd International Society for Music Education World Conference*. ISME, Pretoria, 434–42.

Ndlovu, C. and Akrofi, E. (1999) 'The state of research in the performing arts of South Africa'. *Bulletin: Issues in the Human Sciences*, **6** (1) 14–15.

Nettl, B. (1983) *The Study of Ethnomusicology: Twenty-nine Issues and Concepts*. Urbana, IL: University of Illinois Press.

Nzewi, M. (1997) *African Music: Theoretical Content and Creative Continuum*. Olderhausen: Institut fur Didaktik populärer Musik.

Primos, K. (1992) 'The cultural identity crisis: a challenge for South African music education in the 1990s', in *Proceedings of the Fourth National Music Educators' Conference*. SAMES, Cape Town, 129–41.

Republic of South Africa (1995) White paper on education and training. *Government Gazette*. **357** (16312).

Republic of South Africa (1996) National Education Policy Act 1996. *Government Gazette* **370** (17118).

Shelamay, K. K. (1991) 'Recording technology, the record industry, and ethnomusicological scholarship', in B. Nettl and P. V. Bohlman *Comparative Musicology and Anthropology of Music*. Chicago: University of Chicago Press.

Zeleza, P. T. (1997) *Manufacturing African Studies and Crises*. Dakar: CODESRIA.

Australia

Gary McPherson and Peter Dunbar-Hall

Background

The past four decades have seen significant changes at all levels of Australian schooling. During the 1960s and 1970s, funds for education increased markedly and this, in conjunction with a left-wing political climate, resulted in an expanded curriculum which attempted to respond to the diverse backgrounds, abilities and aspirations of all students (Livermore and McPherson, 1998). However, once Australia's economy began to falter, from the early 1980s, and budgetary constraints became a reality, federal and state politicians began the process of rationalizing education. This resulted in a concerted effort to develop a national framework for curriculum development according to eight broad areas of learning, one of which involved music joining dance, drama, media and visual arts (art, craft, design) in a Key Learning Area that became known as The Arts (Curriculum Corporation, 1994a, 1994b; McPherson, 1995).

One of the main recommendations within this area was a holistic view of arts education as serving the core goals of education. This is powerfully expressed in a federal government senate report which emphasized that

> The prime purpose of arts education for most students is to enrich their educational experience generally: to foster confident self expression – the desire to *have a go*; to foster creative and innovative thinking that may have the benefit of carrying through into other school disciplines and other areas of life, both in and out of paid employment; to foster the habits of being self-directed and being *involved* – habits which will be ever more important to the self-esteem

of many in a future of insecure job prospects and periods of unemployment, as the traditional place of work in people's identity and self-esteem breaks down. For some who have the desire, the talent and the opportunity to make careers in the arts, the prime purpose of arts education may be vocational; but it must be recognised that these are a small minority. (Arts Education, 1995, p. 22)

Within this context, our intention in this chapter is to highlight some of the issues that have shaped the way music is taught and learned in Australian schools. This is a complex task, since the separate state and territory political systems which administer education mean that there are distinct differences in music teaching across the country despite more than a decade of continuing efforts to standardize pedagogical practices around Australia. We begin with a brief overview of the main aims and objectives of Australian music education and use this as a springboard for discussing how an emphasis on creativity and a holistic musical training has led to a broadening of the content of school music programmes. This includes paying special attention to the music of Aboriginal and Torres Strait Islanders, as well as adopting a more eclectic approach that recognizes Australia's multicultural diversity, seen through the study of a wide variety of musics, past and present.

Australian music education: aims and objectives

Australian music education is characterized by its high levels of choice. Syllabuses allow teachers and students various levels of freedom in topic selection, repertoires for study, methods of teaching and learning and combinations of types of assessment. There is also an expectation that all children will have access to music across the thirteen years of schooling. Consequently, all children are exposed to *general* music until school years 7 or 8, after which *elective* classes are available for students who wish to pursue more specialized training to year 12.

Australian music education is principally classroom-based. In infant and primary grades (K–6) music is often taught by a generalist teacher, although some states and many non-government independent schools employ specialist music teachers. In secondary schools specialist music teachers are the norm. To become a specialist music teacher, trainees complete either a postgraduate teaching qualification or a four-year undergraduate degree in music education which equips them to teach general courses for all students up to year 8 and also elective classes which are offered from year 8 or 9. In addition, they are able to teach at least one area of co- or extra-curricular activity (e.g. band, orchestra, choir, popular ensembles or musical productions).

The move toward a more holistic approach to learning has led primary (elementary) teachers to explore ways in which the arts can be taught as an integrated activity in a common time slot: they are also encouraged to explore ways in which music and the other arts can enhance and complement learning in other disciplines. As an example, 'Bunyip in the Bathroom' is a typical Australian song that is taught to children in year 3 of primary school (NSW Department of School Education, 1997). Using the song, teachers encourage children to experiment with and explore the language used in the song (e.g. mother's line: 'Go and have your bath, son') and represent this in various ways (high, low, fast, slow, angry, sad). They might also create their own graphic notation to represent a bath-sound score. But the song can also serve an important function in linking musical learning to other areas of the curriculum. After learning the song, children might go on to dramatize the storyline (related to English), learn to measure the volume of water it would take to fill a bathtub (mathematics), research the various Australian landforms mentioned in the song (science and technology) or design a safe bathtub (related to personal development, health and physical education).

At the secondary-school level such cross-curricular practices are generally resisted by specialist music teachers, who prefer instead to focus their attention on a concept-based approach to music education involving four key aspects of music study: applications of creativity, aural skills, musicological understanding and performance. This emphasis appeared in Australian syllabuses in the early 1970s and has grown in prominence ever since. For example, the New South Wales syllabuses state that students are to study 'the **concepts** of music **through learning experiences** of performance, composition, musicology and aural within the **context** of a range of styles, periods and genres' (NSW Board of Studies, 1999, p. 12, original emphasis).

Even though Australian music education is classroom-based, a highly developed system of band, choir and orchestral programmes exists in many regions at both primary and secondary levels. However, in contrast to some other countries, these are often co- or extra-curricular in nature. As co-curricular activities they provide opportunities for students to perform works under study in classrooms, in this way providing a means of integrating performance with other learning activities, such as analysis or investigation of a style of music. As extra-curricular activities they provide opportunities for students to perform in a wide range of styles and repertoires, often at public venues.

The integrated nature of classroom music best characterizes Australian music education. *Performance* refers to activities in which practical experiences of aspects of a piece of music form the main means of understanding it, rather than merely the production of a complete score for public performance. Performance of harmonic, melodic, rhythmic, and textural features of a score, often utilizing tuned and non-tuned percussion, vocal sounds, movement or body percussion, forms the basis of the majority of classroom music lessons. In many cases, standard notation is learned through these means, while the development of students' own notation systems is used both to reinforce practical work and to emphasize the concept of notation as a means of representing sound, thus relating performance to aural skills.

The identification of musical concepts as separate features of a piece of music is also a basis of the *musicological* approach fostered in Australia. This involves promoting comprehension of the ways in which music is constructed in terms of pitch, duration etc., and the ways in which cultures differ in these respects. Relatively complex levels of analysis (especially at senior secondary levels of music study) and notation are required, and the use of secondary sources is discouraged. Thus students are actively encouraged to interview musicians and culture-bearers when investigating the role and importance of music in various cultural and historical settings.

In the area of *aural skills*, there is a distinct move away from dictation exercises of melodies, rhythms and chord patterns, to aural analysis and transcription of real and complete recordings of music. Typically, aural awareness is developed through a range of problem-solving activities, such as inventing new notation or altering existing notation when transcribing music from various sources. In states such as NSW, aural skills and musicological understanding are integrated by devising related activities from a single piece of music. For example, students in years 11 and 12 are expected to be able to analyse a piece of music aurally by recognizing, analysing, notating and commenting on the composer's use of duration, pitch, dynamics, tone colour, texture and structure, and also to make judgements about style, unity and contrast. The development of aural awareness is considered to be an integral part of activities involving performance, composition and musicological understanding.

Creativity

Australian music education is quite distinctive in its approach to creativity as a result of the ways in which composition activities are integrated with aural skills, musicological understanding and performance, and how creating music is perceived as an integral part of the process of music teaching and learning. Australian music syllabuses include arranging, composition, experimentation and improvisation (see Van Ernst, 1993; Hogg, 1994; Burnard, 1995; Barrett, 1997; McMillan, 1997). Although different terms are used, the expectation that forms of musical creativity are integrated into music teaching and learning is national.

Significant changes have occurred since 1968 when Bartle observed that 'creative music activities are tackled by relatively few teachers' (p. 238). The current emphasis on creativity in Australian music education is a result of three distinct evolutionary stages (Comte, 1988). The first involved appreciation (listening to set works), the second was a period of performance-based teaching and learning (often based around the ideas of Orff and Kodály which were introduced into Australia around 1970) and the third (dating from the 1980s) had a strong emphasis on creativity as part of teaching and learning. Along with these changes has gone the perception that student composing is an important method through which music learning occurs.

The most important change in this respect is a move away from the view of composition as the product of students' musical training (the formalized outcome of activities such as experimenting, arranging and improvising) to one in which creativity is seen in terms of a more holistic understanding of music. In this the focus of composition is on the processes of learning rather than on its final product. This is a reflection of postmodern philosophies which favour chance; process and dispersal, in place of fixedness; finished work and centralization (Harvey, 1989). In music education, this involves a move towards teaching in which the student is the source of knowledge rather than the teacher; it also involves a questioning of traditional canons and, coincidentally, works in tandem with increased use of information technology. As with creativity, which places each student at the centre of an individual musical world, IT fosters individual learning; it is a creative tool in music education; it allows student composers access to sounds formerly unavailable to them as well as to computer-driven technologies for the manipulation, storage, notation, performance and dissemination of music.

An activity labelled 'composition' has appeared in Australian music syllabuses for some decades. From the late 1950s to the early 1990s the term was used, erroneously, to refer either to theoretical exercises in harmony, melody writing and word setting (Bartle, 1968), or as an activity related specifically to extending gifted pupils who were to be encouraged to produce original compositions or to arrange (NSW Department of School Education, 1956). The term 'composition' was thus used to refer to two dissimilar aspects of music education: rule-driven exercises and original creative effort. The idea of (original) composition as a suitable activity for only some students continued through various syllabuses until the 1990s when, in NSW for example, it became mandatory for all music students in some final, senior-secondary examination-level courses to produce original compositions.

The teaching of composition differs from state to state, implying a range of different understandings of its role in Australian music education. For example, in South Australia, a student's composition is perceived as an outcome of study: it is intended to demonstrate comprehension of the practices of a musical style through the ability to model them. In NSW, composition is regarded as a learning process. It involves the formulation of problems through attempts to identify, interpret and manipulate musical materials and processes. Mandatory compositions by NSW senior-secondary students must show an under-standing of musical practices 'of the last twenty-five years' (NSW Board of Studies, 1999, p. 44), thereby maintaining contemporaneity. The ready availability of resources on Australian composers, performers and music history from organizations like the Australian Music Centre, which houses recordings and scores by a wide range of Australian composers, ensures that Australian music education maintains a strong national focus.

Many different methods for teaching composition are employed. These include encouraging students to engage in numerous component tasks of music creation, such as providing drum-kit rhythms to accompany a rock song or structuring pre-existing material into a new piece; stylistic modelling, in which students demonstrate under-standing of a style by imitating its practices; and utilizing the vocal and instrumental forces available in schools to hear and refine their own work. The underlying premise is that composition is a process of continual rethinking and reworking, rather than the instantaneous writing of a finished product.

Students are increasingly involved in compiling work diaries, journals, recordings, folios of work and reflective comments as a means of monitoring and reflecting critically on their own and others' works. For example, in NSW students are expected to compile a folio of the composition process for their Year 12 Higher School Certificate examinations (NSW Board of Studies, 1999). This should include materials which demonstrate background listening, musicological observa-tions, performance considerations, self-evaluations, the decision-making processes involved in composing, the development of compositional skills, reflective statements, evidence of technology used and appraisal of each composition submitted. In this way students are increasingly exploring music in ways that are both reflective and individual, so that they are actively engaged in 'doing' music and are encouraged at all stages of the learning process to act and think as musicians.

Music of Aboriginal and Torres Strait Islanders

Australian school systems consider all music worthy of study, and former boundaries governing content and topic choice have been removed. Thus, the study of popular music under various headings (e.g. contemporary, pop, popular, rock, rock 'n' roll) has become firmly established in Australian secondary music education and there is an increasing emphasis on the music of Australia's indigenous peoples and on that which reflects Australia's multicultural nature and origins. This policy is a reflection of political movements within Australia and of general trends in Australian education, and is an outcome of the interaction between music education, musicology and cultural studies. High levels of immigration after World War II resulted in a broadening of the cultural content of the general curriculum, with the result that European 'high art' is no longer regarded as the sole focus of attention. Moves toward recognition of, and reconciliation with, Australia's indigenous communities have resulted in a concerted effort by educational planners to provide for the cultural and spiritual needs of Aboriginal students as well as those whose background reaches outside the Anglo-European tradition (see Broughton, 1991; McPherson, 1995).

The study of Aboriginal and Torres Strait Islander (ATSI) music occurs across Australian state systems at different levels. For example, in Queensland Aboriginal music is listed as a topic area within Music in Australia (Queensland Board of Senior Secondary School Studies, 1995), while in Victoria, although not listed specifically, ATSI music could be taught through the topic of Diversity of Music in Australia (Victorian Curriculum and Assessment Board, 1991). In NSW, the study of Australian music is a mandatory topic in years 7 to 10 (junior secondary compulsory classes) with 'traditional and contemporary music of Aborigines and Torres Strait Islanders' listed as a possible application (NSW Board of Studies, 1994a).

Dunbar-Hall (1997) found that 89 per cent of NSW secondary music teachers surveyed taught ATSI music as a discrete topic and as an exemplification of concept-based teaching. The results of the survey also highlight problems in teacher training, poor student attitudes to

Australian indigenous peoples, difficulty of access to resources and ethical concerns in the teaching of music of unfamiliar cultural provenance. Many teachers with limited training in, or resources for, teaching traditional ATSI music indicated that they introduced Aboriginal music to students through popular-music repertoires, as this provides a viable means of implementing the topic. It is not uncommon for teachers to use the music of Australia's better-known Aboriginal popular-music groups such as No Fixed Address, Tiddas, Warumpi Band and Yothu Yindi to introduce traditional Aboriginal instruments such as the didjeridu. Issues of ATSI social and political comment can also be introduced to students through songs by these groups, in this way acknowledging the significance of music in ATSI cultures.

The presence of this topic in Australian music education acknowledges a musical system outside the western tonal tradition. It also reflects increasing acceptance of ethnomusicological thinking as a basis for music education, and national guidelines which encourage the study of ATSI peoples and their cultures (Curriculum Corporation, 1995). Through this study, cultural links between music and its owners and users are made more explicit, and teaching and learning methods which differ from those of the past are encouraged. At the same time, consultation with indigenous groups reveals discrepancies in their expectations and in government-imposed music-education systems (see York, 1995).

Increased acknowledgment of Australia's indigenous background and of the viability of contemporary Aboriginal and Torres Strait Islander cultures as topics of study are recent developments in Australian education (see, for example, Cook, 1995). Such post-colonial (at times anti-colonial) perspectives contribute to the movement in Australian critical thinking referred to as 'the new Australianism,' through which a newly defined post-Anglo-Celtic Australia is envisaged. The study of ATSI musics is an acknowledgment of the contribution of indigenous Australians to the national polity and a contradiction of two centuries of educational rejection of Aboriginal Australia. This new-found educational acceptance of ATSI cultures is greatly assisted by improved access to recordings, literature, personnel and knowledge about indigenous cultures.

Multiculturalism

The strong multicultural nature of Australian music education can be viewed as part of a worldwide phenomenon (Anderson and Campbell, 1989; Lees, 1992; Lundquist and Szego, 1998). In common with the teaching of ATSI music, it is a means of implementing the concept-based approach to music education, in that the diverse cultures which make up Australia provide a rich source of illustrations of the materials and processes of music. It also provides a means of tailoring education to reflect students' backgrounds, needs and interests, and is indicative of the general political and educational situation in Australia (Allan and Hill, 1995; Welch, 1996).

There are, typically, three ways in which multiculturalism can be applied in Australian music classrooms. The first of these is the presence in syllabuses of topics about music from non-western sources. Music syllabuses in NSW, for example, list 'Music of a culture' and 'Australian music from diverse cultural backgrounds' as areas of study. These topics have taken over from studies of Oriental Music and Music of Another Culture, which previously appeared in Australian music syllabuses as far back as the late 1950s. Suggestions for areas of teaching content for these topics include 'stylistic features, notation, dance and its music [and] cultural context' (NSW Board of Studies, 1999, p. 26).

The second application is in the selection of content to exemplify musical concepts. In common with most syllabuses in other Australian states, those in NSW are conceptual in approach, in the sense that students are expected to gain understanding of music through experience of 'pitch, dynamics, duration, tone colour and structure [in] a variety of learning activities involving listening, singing, playing, moving and organising sound' (NSW Department of School Education, 1984, p. 10).

The third means of encouraging multiculturalism in music education is evident in the teaching/learning strategies that accompany current music syllabuses in NSW. These strategies can be divided into two groups: the first involve practical activities which teachers might use in classrooms, such as 'performing music of a particular culture on traditional instruments; performing dances of different cultures; interpreting different forms of musical notation; singing/playing a wide range of music from Australia's diverse cultural backgrounds' (NSW Board of Studies, 1994b, p. 14); the second group of strategies includes those through which students can develop conceptualizations about culture; what culture is, how cultures change and develop and how culture is inherent to all people. In this form of meta-culturalism the aim is not to identify specific musical characteristics which can be used to define a discrete music (e.g. Andean music, Japanese gagaku, Balinese gamelan); it is rather to lead students to skills of analysis and critical thinking through which realizations about culture and its nature can be developed.

These aims move from the level of practical applications of multicultural musical content in classroom activities such as singing, performing on instruments and dancing, to a more complex level on which culture itself, rather than individual cultures, is the object of study. Some of the strategies through which this can be achieved are

> discussing the role of music in a particular society in its Australian context; gaining an understanding of music in its historical and cultural contexts; listening to music which has been influenced by music of another culture; studying changes in music when it is transported between cultural settings; discussing how music functions in the lives of people, societies and cultures; and describing the different processes used to share and preserve musical expressions. (NSW Board of Studies, 1994a, pp. 14–15)

Music education based on multicultural content and teaching strategies fulfils a number of aims including the promotion of knowledge of music in specific geographical and cultural settings; the exemplification of musical concepts and processes; the demonstration of the role(s) of music in defining, maintaining and brokering culture; and the analysis of the concept of culture as a force in peoples' lives.

Conclusions

Australian music education is distinctive from that in other countries in a number of ways. Its key strengths include the recognition that music should be available to all children throughout their schooling. Music – along with dance, drama, visual arts and media – is identified as a separate and important Key Learning Area within the curriculum and this has led to school music educators being in a stronger theoretical and professional position to justify the value of their work in the general education of all Australian children than at any time in the past. The emphasis on a classroom approach means that infant and primary-school children are exposed to a rich variety of activities that are increasingly cross-curricular rather than discipline-based. This contrasts with high-school music, in which a concept-based approach involving the integration of aural skills, creativity and musicology, and performance continues to be the norm. Australian music curricula are increasingly eclectic and student-centred, such that a strict adherence to a particular methodology occurs less than in previous times (Stowasser, 1993).

A core element of music teaching at all levels is an emphasis on music from various past and present contexts, which extends far beyond the western art-music tradition. As a result, the musics of Aboriginal and Torres Strait Islanders, styles of popular music, music from other cultures and that of contemporary Australian composers are recognized and valued within the repertoire chosen for study in schools around the country. To cater for this diversity there is a healthy and steadily increasing repertoire of texts and resources written by Australian music educators which serve to enliven and enrich music teaching around the country.

Music in Australian schools also involves much more than singing, playing, and learning to become musically literate. Australian music educators are aware of the need for a balance between the various components of the music curriculum and they recognize the need for reflection and individual expression in every aspect of musical learning. They also recognize the value of a broadly based approach to the teaching of music, and question the notion of music as a specialized craft in which performance is seen as important above all else. As a result, Australian students are required to think and act in ways that are quite different from the approaches of the past.

Outside Australian schools, music education flourishes. Many hundreds of thousands of children take instrumental or vocal lessons from their local studio teacher or community music programme, and over 150,000 candidates complete Australian Music Examinations Board (AMEB) and other similar external-graded performance examinations each year. These experiences are enhanced by special programmes for preschoolers which offer a wide variety of specialist or broadly based approaches, through such international organizations as the Suzuki Talent Education programme, the Yamaha Music Education System and the Roland Corporation. Through the formal years of schooling and beyond, Australian children have access to a wide variety of choirs, bands, orchestras and other ensembles, and these complement and extend opportunities for less formal engagement through the many social and recreational uses of music in smaller ensembles, particularly those encompassing popular forms of entertainment and performance.

In summary, the achievements of Australian music educators can be gauged not only by the number of students who graduate from high schools to undertake more specialized training in Australian universities and conservatoriums, but also by the high level of general participation in various forms of music-making within the wider community. Although financial constraints sometimes hamper what can be achieved in various school systems, music continues to be one of the most visible and imaginative subjects in the school curriculum. This high profile is due not only to the freedom teachers exercise in developing programmes and methods they believe to be relevant to their students' needs, but also to the nature of Australian education itself. Australians have always resisted a top-down approach by governments and education systems that prescribes a central curriculum. Instead, Australian music educators are, essentially, free to 'get on with the job' of devising programmes of study they believe cater for their own particular students, whether they be in metropolitan centres, rural towns or remote communities.

References

Allan, R. and Hill, P. (1995) 'Multicultural education in Australia: historical development and current status', in J. Banks and C. Banks (eds) *Handbook of Research on Multicultural Education*. New York: Macmillan.

Anderson, W. and Shehan Campbell, P. (eds) (1989) *Multicultural Perspectives in Music Education*. Reston, VA: MENC.

Arts Education (1995) *Report by the Senate Environment, Recreation, Communications and the Arts References Committee*. October. Canberra: Parliament of Australia. (ISBN 0 642 22923 6)

Barrett, M. (1997) 'Invented notations: a view of young children's musical thinking'. *Research Studies in Music Education*, **8**, 2–14.

Bartle, G. (1968) *Music in Australian Schools*. Hawthorn, Victoria: Australian Council for Educational Research.

Broughton, D. (1991) 'Shaping the national curriculum: issues for Australian arts educators', in E. P. Errington (ed.) *Arts Education: Beliefs, Practices and Possibilities*. Geelong: Deakin University Press.

Burnard, P. (1995) 'Task design and experience in composition'. *Research Studies in Music Education*, **5**, 32–46.

Comte, M. (1988) 'The arts in Australian schools: the past fifty years'. *Australian Journal of Music Education*, **1**, 102–21.

Cook, T. (1995) *Black on White: Policy and Curriculum Development in Aboriginal Education*. Sydney: Human Factors Press.

Curriculum Corporation (1994a) *The Arts: A Curriculum Profile for Australian Schools*. Melbourne: Curriculum Corporation.

Curriculum Corporation (1994b) *A Statement on the Arts for Australian Schools*. Melbourne: Curriculum Corporation.

Curriculum Corporation (1995) *National Principles and Guidelines for Aboriginal and Torres Strait Islander Studies*, K–12. Melbourne.

Dunbar-Hall, P. (1997) ' Problems and solutions in the teaching of Aboriginal and Torres Strait Islander music, in E. Gifford, A. Brown and A. Thomas (eds) *New Sounds for a New Century: Australian Society for Music Education 30th Anniversary National Conference* (ASME XI). University of Queensland, Brisbane, July 4–8.

Harvey, D. (1989) *The Condition of Postmodernity: An Enquiry into the Origins of Cultural Change*. Oxford: Basil Blackwell.

Hogg, N. (1994) 'Strategies to facilitate student composing'. *Research Studies in Music Education*, **2**, 15–24.

Lees, H. (ed.) (1992) *Sharing Musics of the World*. Proceedings of the 20th World Conference of the International Society for Music Education held in Seoul, Korea.

Livermore, J. and McPherson, G. E. (1998) 'Expanding the role of the arts in the curriculum: some Australian initiatives'. *Arts Education Policy Review*, **99**, (3) 10–15.

Lundquist, B. and Szego, C. (eds) (1998). *Music of the World's Cultures: A Source Book for Music Educators*. Perth: Callaway International Resource Centre for Music Education.

McLeod, J. (1991) *The Arts and the Year 2000*. Melbourne: Curriculum Corporation.

McMillan, R. (1997) 'Finding a personal musical "voice": the place of improvisation in music'. *Research Studies in Music Education*, **9**, 20–28.

McPherson, G. E. (1995) 'Integrating the arts into the general curriculum: an Australian perspective'. *Arts Education Policy Review*, **97**, (1) 25–31.

NSW Board of Studies (1994a) *Music Years 7–10*. Sydney: NSW Board of Studies.

NSW Board of Studies (1994b) *Music Support Document 7–12*. Sydney: NSW Board of Studies.

NSW Board of Studies (1999) *Music 2 and Music Extension: Stage 6 Syllabus*. Sydney: NSW Board of Studies.

NSW Department of School Education (1956) *Syllabus in Music*. Sydney.

NSW Department of School Education (1984) *Music K–6 Syllabus and Support Document*. Sydney.

NSW Department of School Education (1997) *Sync or Swing: A Teaching Resource for Teaching Music*. Sydney. (ISBN 0 7310 8315 6)

Queensland Board of Secondary Senior School Studies (1995) *Music: Senior Syllabus*. Brisbane: Queensland Board of Secondary School Studies.

Stowasser, H. (1993) 'Some personal observations of music education in Australia, North America and Great Britain'. *International Journal of Music Education*, **22**, 14–28.

Van Ernst, B. (1993) 'A study of the learning and teaching processes of non-native music students engaged in composition'. *Research Studies in Music Education*, **1**, 22–39.

Victorian Curriculum and Assessment Board (1991) *Music Study Design*. Melbourne: Victorian Curriculum and Assessment Board.

Welch, A. (1996) *Australian Education: Reform or Crisis?* Sydney: Allen and Unwin.

York, F. (1995) 'Island song and musical growth: toward culturally based school music in the Torres Strait Islands'. *Research Studies in Music Education*, **4**, 28–38.

China

Cheung-shing Yeh

In recent decades, broadening the curriculum through the inclusion of world musics has been a prominent issue in western educational systems. The need to include a wide variety of musics in the curriculum is particularly important in China because of its cultural diversity. China is a country comprising 56 nationalities, with 91 per cent of the population being of the Han nationality. China is therefore very rich in terms of minority cultures, languages and religions. Most of the national minorities speak their own language and 29 of them also have written forms. Since the formation of the People's Republic of China in 1949, pupils from all nationalities are required to master the official Chinese language, Putonghua. These minorities were therefore able to speak Putonghua fluently and to keep their identity by speaking also their own languages.

The art and cultures of these nationalities have diversified in accordance with their unique history and the place and way in which they live. These different cultures co-exist harmoniously in such a large country: despite some differences, they all share some common philosophy in their way of living. Traditional art, dance and music are intrinsic aspects of daily life within these groups, representing a natural and spontaneous means of expression and communication.

Aims and objectives of music education

Unlike most western countries, music education in China cannot be divorced from political influence. The purpose of music education in medieval and Renaissance Europe was mainly religious. Boys were trained intensively to perform religious functions and rituals, with music used as a means of spreading the theology of the Church. However, in the twentieth century, the focus has shifted from music as a functional tool in religion to a concern with music to be developed in everyone, as one of Gardner's 'multiple intelligences' (Gardner, 1983). For the Chinese, music is regarded as a means of education, so that it is functional to a very large extent.

This can be seen in the words of Yue Ji in the *Record of Music*, which is the earliest comprehensive treatise on Chinese music, written around 200–100 BC:

'Music (*yue*) is seen to join the various strata of society and family together in harmonious relationship. Thus if ruler and minister, and those in higher and lower positions listen to it together in the ancestral temple, they will all join harmoniously in respect; if father and son, and older and younger brothers listen to it together in the chambers, then they will all join harmoniously in mutual closeness, etc ... This, too, was the prescription of the former kinds in establishing Music (yue)'. (Cook, 1995, p. 68)

The notion of music education for its own sake is thus linked with morality, beauty and good throughout the history of China. 'Arise through poetry/songs, become established through rituals, and achieve completion through Music' (Liu, 1990, pp. 298–9) is the fundamental philosophy of Confucius that has dominated the learning of music for at least 2000 years. Musical learning is seen as a tool to encourage Chinese people to conform to virtuous living, to reinforce self-control and to improve one's own behaviour. Confucius embraced the cultivation of honesty, love and filial piety through the six arts: Music, Rituals, Archery, Charioteering, Writing and Numbers (Dawson, 1981, p. 20).

Music education in twentieth-century China continues to fulfil its functional role, but is also a political and social tool. The 1985 Communist Party document on the reform of educational structure set out the relationship between education, politics and economic development as follows: 'Education must serve the purpose of socialist construction and socialist construction must rely on education' (Teng, 1991, p. 750). Education in moral, intellectual, physical and aesthetic issues is geared toward the modernization of socialism and the building of a socialist country with uniquely Chinese characteristics.

The current rationale for music education in China therefore places a strong emphasis on its use as a political tool, and this has shaped music teaching and learning in primary and secondary schools. The aims of music education, as laid down by the Chinese government in the early

1990s, reveal that the socialist and utilitarian functions of music education are clearly given priority within this ideology:

1. To nourish pupils' love of country, people, work, science, socialism and unity through music education, and let them be the ideal, moral, educated and disciplined successor and builder of socialism.
2. To cultivate pupils' wisdom and aesthetic sense, so as to grow with physical and mental health.
3. To nourish pupils' interest in music, and to develop their basic knowledge, skill and reading ability in music.
4. To nourish pupils' national pride and self-confidence through the teaching of representative Chinese folklore, and widen their musical experiences with foreign musical compositions so as to enable them to feel and express through music.

(State Education Commission, 1994a, p. 131)

Contents and methods

Stages of development of Chinese music education

Music education in China has developed in three stages: (a) East meets West (e.g. giving rise to singing lessons), 1903–48; (b) the new China, 1949–76; and (c) modern China, 1976 onwards. Musicians trained in Japan (headed by Shen Xin-gong) introduced singing lessons to China in the early twentieth century, which were recognized by the late Qing government in 1903. In 1912, the primary- and secondary-school curricula of the new Republic of China officially incorporated singing lessons, which also included elements of music theory. Lyrics were added to tunes from Europe, Japan, North America and China in a singing curriculum known as *xuetangyuege* (singing music lessons). The content of these lyrics concerned building a wealthy nation and a strong army to expel foreign invaders. A number of song albums were compiled and published for use in primary-school singing lessons. Although these might seem like fairly mundane details to western readers, this period marked an important stage in the development of music education in which western music theory, singing style, five-line-staff notation, violin and piano playing were first introduced to China.

Following the introduction of western musical ideas in education, subsequent intellectual movements in the following years (e.g. the May Fourth Movement of 1919) reinforced and strengthened the discipline. Chinese intellectuals gained more freedom to experiment with new educational ideas emanating from the West. Musicians trained in Europe (such as Xiao You-mei, Huang Dzi, Cai Yuanpei and Zhao Yuanren) and other intellectuals realized the backwardness of China and advocated the reform of the country's music education along the lines of western systems. They composed a large quantity of solo songs and choral works in western musical style which aimed to motivate the people's love of China. Similarly, textbooks were written on harmony, piano, organ and violin playing.

China had close political and social ties with Soviet Russia after 1949, and a large number of people were sent north for music training. The Russian system of elite music education was implemented in China, and there were no music lessons for the general public during the 1950s. Nine music institutes were founded during this period, based on the model of the Russian schools of music. Although general music education was neglected, these music institutes made great achievements.

In addition to the way in which it was taught, the content of music education also changed considerably after 1949. A number of recommended composers and songs had to be studied or learned. Nie Er (composer of the Chinese national anthem) and Xian Xinghai (composer of the *Yellow River Cantata*) were hailed by the Chinese government as the greatest composers during the 1950s and 1960s. However, other composers like Jiang Wenye were intentionally ignored, despite their great contribution to music education in China, because their works were regarded as counter-revolutionary. Pupils were also deprived of the opportunity to learn twentieth-century western music, which was regarded as 'spiritual pollution', and therefore hazardous to Chinese communism.

In return, the homogeneous style of revolutionary compositional techniques flourished. It was characterized by the group composition of large revolutionary operatic works such as *Bai Mao Nu*. The addition to, or deletion of, individuals from the approved list of composers did not make any substantial difference to the resulting style of the resulting music since it was subject to political censorship and approval. Composers were required strictly to observe prescribed 'do's and don't's when composing. Musical development and style in the first twenty years of the People's Republic was characterized by its closed and homogeneous revolutionary style.

The closing of the schools during the Cultural Revolution of 1966–76 inevitably disrupted the growth of music education. Musicians were driven out of their professions and sent off to factories, construction sites or farms to be re-educated. The Cultural Revolution was one of a series of events that effectively isolated China from the outside world, and contact with other cultures was minimal or non-existent during these turbulent years. Compositional activity was focused on propaganda songs and opera, which were used for disseminating and popularizing political ideology.

Following the Cultural Revolution, Chinese foreign policy advocated peaceful co-existence and increased exposure to other cultures. The teaching methodologies of Kodály, Orff and Dalcroze were introduced to China after 1983 and a large amount of the music-education literature was translated into Chinese. Music has been a compulsory school subject since the introduction of nine-year compulsory education. Since the 1980s, music lessons in primary and junior secondary levels have focused mainly on singing. Similar to the *xuetangyuege* in the late Qing Dynasty, students are still learning songs by rote, and singing is the main focus of music activities in music lessons.

The 1980s saw reform and fundamental changes in Chinese music education. The Proposal for Improving School Music Education was signed by 37 leading musicians, composers and music educators, including the presidents of the Musicians' Association of China, on 18 September 1985 (Lu *et al.*, 1985). The proposal emphasized the importance of music education for the well-being of the country and the people, and urged the State Education Commission to take measures to establish this firmly in the education system. Government officials, school heads, teachers and students took this on board, and schools were given the necessary financial assistance to provide music facilities such as keyboards and teaching materials.

Music-education research and evaluation were also encouraged. The proposal also had some less immediate implications for reform. The vice-president of the State Education Commission, He Dongchang, remarked in August 1986, that 'education is not perfect without aesthetic education'. In December 1986 the Arts Education Office was set up by the National Educational Committee to direct arts education policy. The First National Music Education Reform Symposium was held in the same month, and measures have been taken to foster the aims of music education since then.

In 1994, the State Education Commission incorporated music into the curriculum at senior-secondary level. However, it is still not unusual to find no provision for music in the school timetable, not just because of a shortage of music teachers but also so that more time be made available for other subjects. In 1998, the Seventh National Music Education Symposium was held to discuss means of improving the quality of music education in the new millennium. The Symposium called for some major reforms including:

1. A redefinition of the aims of music education: music lessons must do far more than provide the opportunity to learn a few songs or play one or two instruments. Music education should be for all, and not only the talented few. All children have the right to understand, appreciate, feel, perform and compose music.
2. A revision of the present school music syllabuses which were prepared in the 1980s. Primary- and secondary-school music teachers should be consulted widely during the process of revision. The new guidelines should specify clearly the aims of music education, time allocation for music, teaching content, methodologies and the methods of student assessment. Lessons should encourage musical creativity, rather than adopting the traditional goals of skill acquisition, modelling music teachers and learning music theory. Finally, students should be given ample opportunities to appreciate the rich cultural traditions in Chinese music.
3. A child-centred approach should be adopted in which the teacher is viewed as a facilitator rather than an instructor. Students should be encouraged to be active participants in education, so as to cultivate their musical knowledge, skills, imagination and experience. Appropriate teaching materials should help pupils to learn and explore in an open and free atmosphere, rather than engaging in directed and teacher-centred activities. Pupils should understand music rather than learn it passively by rote.
4. Positive measures to increase the qualifications and number of music teachers. Music teachers should be treated similarly to other teachers in terms of tenure and incentives.
5. An assurance of the accountability of music teaching and the development of a comprehensive and scientific music-teacher appraisal system.
6. The development of a system to co-ordinate the exchange of ideas and innovations between all stakeholders in music teaching and learning.

(Xu, 1998)

Given these arguments, it is perhaps worth noting that the State Education Commission allows the flexible implementation of the guidelines on music curriculum by the provinces, autonomous regions and the metropolitan municipalities. Adaptations can be made according to the local conditions and need of individual areas. This should facilitate the implementation of a student-centred system of music education.

Music in practice

The standard of performance on western instruments in China is uniformly high. The Chinese have won hundreds of prizes in important international music competitions since the 1980s. Furthermore, these musicians are highly desirable in the international music market, providing them with opportunities to work and live elsewhere in the world. It is therefore not uncommon to find a paradoxical combination of senior music professors teaching music industriously, but a shortage of talented pupils willing to join the professional music education institutes in which they are employed. The Central Conservatorium of Music (CCM) in Beijing and the Shanghai Conservatorium of Music (SCM) are two of the key music institutes in China. They have the privilege of better resources, better government funding and, perhaps as a consequence, they recruit higher-quality music students. Admission to these institutes is extremely competitive and thousands of applicants from all over the country compete for only a few dozen places.

The remarkable achievement and success of these institutes internationally is due, to a very large extent, to their educational structure. Some of the conservatoriums are attached to primary and secondary schools, *fuziao* and *fuzhong* respectively. Musically talented children are recruited, as early as five or six years of age, to receive intensive musical training during their childhood. Repertoire such as Chopin études are used as standard works in the *fuziao* entrance examinations. Children spend most of their time in the acquisition of musical skills and knowledge. Although this equips them with the high performance skills required by the music institutes on one hand, it also deprives them of all-round education from middle childhood onwards.

Some young children display very high levels of technical ability and proficiency in art, music, athletics and acrobatics in the Youth Palaces or music conservatories. Such children would be immediately identified and sent to receive specialized training in one of Beijing's or Shanghai's top music or art boarding schools. Some negative reactions are expressed about this kind of streaming taking place at the age of three or four, since pupils are deprived of learning other curricula.

However, it is important to realize that in China, with over one-fifth of the world's total population, the driving force for enduring these hardships and undertaking highly specialized musical training often comes from the bottom of Maslow's (1970) hierarchy of human needs, i.e. for survival. This contrasts with most of the music/art students in the West or other developed countries, where the pursuit of artistic excellence serves higher-level needs in the hierarchy, i.e. intellectual achievement and ultimate self-actualization. In China, many such pupils focus on sustaining a living by devoting their early childhood to music or other art forms rather than on securing a better life.

Music education departments have only recently been established in these institutes. The music education department of the SCM, for example, was founded only in 1998. Their music education curricula are primarily concerned with the professional training of intending musicians, including topics such as western and Chinese music history, advanced harmony, aural training, composition, and also Marxist, Leninist and Mao Zedong's political theories. Students are educated as professional musicians rather than music teachers. However, some mismatch exists between the content of music education training in these institutes and the issues that students face in their everyday music classrooms. In particular, such an elitist approach to music can inevitably affect some students' attitudes towards general and gifted music education.

Music learning in the classroom

Music lessons in schools across China have very similar contents, with an emphasis on singing- and listening-based music instruction. In particular, music appreciation, rather than active music-making, is the key ingredient of most music classes. Recent attempts have also been made to also incorporate elements of musical creativity into teaching. These recognize that the process of creating is perhaps as important, if not even more important, than the product of this process. The process aims to nurture pupils' creative spirit.

However, what children learn in music lessons is often determined by the ability of music teachers, thus resulting in a wide variation of quality in general music teaching. As in some western countries (e.g. the United Kingdom) during the 1960s, China currently faces a severe shortage of music teachers. In 1997 China had a total of 70,000 primary and secondary schools but only 24,000 music teachers. Assuming that each school should have its own music teacher, China still has a shortfall of 46,000. This serious shortage is exacerbated by the uneven distribution of music teachers between urban and rural areas. In accordance with their financial strength, major cities, such as Beijing and Shanghai, enjoy an average of 1.4 music teachers per secondary school, whereas the corresponding figure for rural areas is only 0.15.

Major efforts have been taken to ease the shortage of music teachers, especially in rural areas. For example, in rural areas several village primary schools may share the same music teacher. Some schools also engage in what is known as 'duplex teaching', in which pupils of two or more ability levels share one music teacher in the same classroom. Given their differential abilities, the two sets of pupils cannot have their music lessons at precisely the same time. Instead, while one group has its music lesson, special retraining allows the music teacher to simultaneously teach another, comparatively quiet, arts subject to the second set of pupils. After a while, the two groups of pupils swap over so that the second set of children then receives its music lesson.

Despite imaginative solutions such as these, however, polarization and disparity characterize current music teaching and learning in urban and rural China. Indeed, the gap between some schools is wide. In addition to differences in the quality of teacher available, some of the primary and secondary schools in Shanghai and Canton have extremely sophisticated facilities such as a great variety of musical instruments, computing and software facilities and well-qualified music staff. Students in rural areas do not enjoy the same opportunities.

Before concluding this section, it is also worth noting one other very specific aspect of Chinese music education which hampers development, and particularly the introduction into the curriculum of much twentieth-century western music. *Jianpu*, a cipher notation system based on the movable *doh*, is a convenient and effective system for notating simple tonal melodies. In particular, it is a useful means of notating the folk songs of China's many cultural minorities and it fits well with the improvisatory style of much traditional Chinese music. It is thus commonly used throughout the country in music textbooks as well as in Chinese instrumental ensembles. However, it is almost impossible to apply *jianpu* to atonal music or music with multiple voices since it does not possess the graphical function of the five-line staff (i.e. melodic contour is represented in the staff notation, as is voice crossing or overlapping). As a consequence, the widespread use of *jianpu* inevitably hinders the introduction and development of modern musical styles in China. A further difficulty posed by the popularity of *jianpu* is that, despite its widespread use in schools and Chinese instrumental music, it is estimated that less than 15 per cent of university graduates can read *jianpu*, not to mention the five-line staff. This discrepancy has the potential to cause a range of difficulties.

Student issues

Attitudes of music teachers, students and parents

Although a compulsory part of childrens' education, music (like art and physical education) is regarded by many as a marginal subject. It is one of those conventionally called *fuke* (minor and non-academic subjects) or *xiaosanmen* (the minority threes). This seriously affects the attitudes of both music teachers and students. Students tend to concentrate their efforts on languages, mathematics and science subjects as part of the competition for limited university places. Music teachers are also the neglected minority in the education system. Although the Chinese government recently adopted a series of positive and effective measures to improve the provision and quality of music education, music teachers receive unequal political, economic, and social treatment as compared with that afforded to teachers of major subjects (and particularly so in rural areas). For example, music teachers have a low priority in the promotion system, as well as getting no, or lower, additional cash allowances for extra-curricular work compared to other subjects. Qualified music teachers rarely miss the opportunity to switch their teaching to major subjects, and school principals often assign the most able music teachers to major subjects. Music teachers are often prepared to sacrifice their specialism in return for an improvement in their political, social and economic status.

On the other hand, elite music education flourishes in some otherwise average primary and secondary schools. Pupils sit an audition to test their musical aptitude. Talented children are selected on the basis of this, and grouped to form a special music class in which they receive special one-to-one musical training similar to that received by those attending the *fuxiao* or *fuzhong* (attached primary or secondary schools). However, pupils who are not selected are then entitled neither to this kind of special musical training nor to general music lessons.

There is a further disadvantage of such elitism. Inter-school music competitions and concerts certainly provide the opportunity for music teachers to gain approval and recognition from their principals, colleagues and parents. However, too often these extra-curricular activities are recognized and valued more for their public relations than for their educational value. They are often merely a form of window-dressing with which to publicize the school, attracting the attention of parents and the public. It is thus, perhaps, understandable why extra-curricular musical activities can often overshadow general music classes.

Music learning outside the classroom

In an attempt to limit the fast growth of an already large population, China advocated a one-family-one-child policy during the 1980s. Parents, especially in urban areas and major cities, are eager to focus their efforts and provide the best life possible for their only child. It is therefore not uncommon to find parents enthusiastically encouraging their child to learn a musical instrument such as violin or piano either in school or through private tuition. Traditional Chinese instruments are learnt to a very large extent by rote. Such learning is based on the system of apprenticeship in which the relationship between teacher and the apprentice is extremely close. Although the system is superficially similar to private instrumental teaching in the West, the apprentice pays great respect to his or her master as not just a model in music but also as a moral guide.

In some of the big cities, it is common to find cultural activity centres such as the Youth Palace, the Children's Centre, the Workers' Cultural Centre or the Mass Arts Centre, all of which were established to provide training in dance, art and music for young children. Affluent parents are eager to send their children to these centres at weekends so that they can learn musical instruments or sing in a choir. Although the Chinese government recognizes these centres as the propaganda and educational 'front lines' for communist ideology and Mao Zedong's thought, they also provide an opportunity for gifted children to receive musical training. However, the limited number of centres like these means that children have to compete for places.

China's open-door policy since the 1980s has resulted in a gradual increase in contact with the outside world in many respects, including music education. China has to determine which aspects of these cultures it can profitably adapt for its own purposes. For example, popular music has long been a controversial issue in music education. Western pop songs, Cantonese songs from Hong Kong and mandarin songs from Taiwan gained wide acceptance and penetration throughout China because of the powerful visual and audio stimulation they provide. The Chinese authorities have been rather more suspicious, fearing that pop music might have a negative effect on the mind and soul of younger generations. However, a recent survey conducted in Beijing showed that more than 60 per cent of music teachers, students and government officials believed that pop music should be part of the school music curriculum.

Concluding reflections

In conclusion, we must emphasize that music education in China is influenced by a deep-rooted belief that musical learning is a means of achieving morality, beauty, self-control and virtuous living, and this stems from the influence of the fundamental philosophies of Confucius. Musical learning and development thus exist for the well-being of the individual, the family, society and the state.

As far as methods of teaching and learning music are concerned, some important changes are taking place. Chinese education has, traditionally, clearly adopted what Jackson (1986) calls the *mimetic* approach, in which students are expected to memorize the information given by the infallible teacher, and the nurture of literacy and basic skills is a primary concern. Chinese music masters are traditionally skilled at breaking down complex psychomotor performing skills into the simplest parts, and letting students practice day after day and hour after hour until they reach perfection.

Unstructured exploration and independent discovery, which represent what Jackson correspondingly calls the *transformative* approach, occur rarely in the process of musical learning in China. Gardner (1989) contrasts Chinese teachers, who are 'fearful that if skills are not acquired early, they may never be acquired; there is ... no comparable hurry to inculcate creativity' with American educators, who 'fear that unless creativity has been acquired early, it may never emerge ... skills can be picked up at a later date' (p. 283). As this chapter has shown, however, recent developments in the teaching and learning of music show that the Chinese are moving from a skill-based approach to a more creative approach. Problem-solving skills and exploration are being valued in the process of musical learning, and so some important changes are taking place.

Musical learning and development seldom exists in a laboratory; it inevitably involves students' beliefs, cultural traditions and sets of values towards music and other artforms. Ideologies and methodologies of musical learning cannot be transplanted into other countries regardless of their own traditions and cultural contexts. Each approach has its own merits and weaknesses: one should keep an eye open to alternative paradigms in other countries without endangering one's own culture and tradition. We should accomplish our musical visions in a world that values diversity and different cultural traditions, rather than in a homogeneous world through the processes of globalization.

References

Cook, S. (1995) *Yue Ji*. Record of music: introduction, translation, notes, and commentary. *Asian Music*, **26**, (1) 1–90.

Dawson, R. (1981) *Confucius*. Oxford: Oxford University Press.

Gao, Liushui (1990) (ed.) *Lunyu Zhengyi* by Liv, B. N. (1791–1855). (The corrected readings of the *Andlects* of Confucius). Beijing: Zhonghua.

Gardner, H. (1983) *Frames of Mind*. New York: Basic Books.

Gardner, H. (1989) *To Open Minds*. New York: Basic Books.

Jackson, P. (1986) *The Practice of Teaching*. New York: Teacher's College Press.

Lu, Ji, *et al.*, (1985) 'Proposal for improving music education in schools'. *The People's Music*. October, 44–5.

Maslow, A. (1970) *Motivation and Personality*. New York: Harper & Row. State Education Commission (1994a) *Nine Year Free Education Teaching Documents: Primary School*. Beijing Normal University.

Teng, Teng (1991) 'System of Education: People's Republic of China', in T. Husén and T. N. Postlethwaite (eds) *The International Encyclopedia of Education* Vol. 2 (2nd edn). New York: Pergamon Press.

Xu, Dong (1998) 'Reports on the seventh national music education symposium'. *The People's Music*. December, 2–6.

Federal Republic of Germany

Heiner Gembris

Music education and musical culture in the Federal Republic of Germany

The general and music education systems of a country and its cultural institutions and traditions are essential determinants of the musical development of its people. A central principle within the Federal Republic of Germany (FRG), as in other countries, is that a democratic government guarantees the freedom of the arts and sciences. This cannot be taken for granted everywhere and at all times, however. During the period of the Nazi government, between 1933 and 1945, for instance, certain kinds of music were censored in Germany. Jewish musicians could not practise their trade, and schools, institutions and the mass media used and abused music for their own purposes (see Gembris, 1997, 1998). Similarly, the freedom to produce music and to develop musical activities was constrained and regulated by the state in the former German Democratic Republic (GDR), as in other former Eastern Bloc countries.

The former GDR had a wide-ranging system of training opportunities for professional and amateur musicians, providing possibilities for their advancement and producing a richly developed concert and musical life (Noll, 1997). At the same time, the government imposed a strict control on the concert repertoire by censoring the performances of works that were perceived as incongruent with the ideological doctrine of the socialist regime. People who were considered politically unreliable because they held different beliefs were hindered in their musical training and excluded from music academies and universities. After the reunification in 1990, the entire educational and cultural system of the former GDR was completely reformed and aligned with the western parts of the country.

Organizational structure of the music education system

Due to the federal structure of the FRG, the sixteen *Bundesländer* (German states) run their educational systems autonomously. At the national level, the federal government provides general guidelines, the nature of which is determined by the *Kultusministerkonferenz* (KMK). This is the standing conference of the ministers of education and cultural affairs of the different *Bundesländer*. These guidelines contain recommendations for music education in the public school system, for the training of music teachers and for the development of those with special musical gifts.

The actual implementation of school music education and the professional training of musicians and music teachers are under the supervision of the individual *Bundesländer*, which therefore have varying provisions and curricula for music education. Their implementation is also influenced strongly by the community and local government, which is, of course, partly determined by financial resources. In all the *Bundesländer*, however, music education is a compulsory subject in public education and is considered an indispensable part of modern general education.

One of the most important organizations in German music culture is the *Deutscher Musikrat* (German Music Council). This body promotes the musical activities of a broad range of musical amateurs as well as the development of individuals with high abilities. It represents the interests of over eight million people who are professional or leisure-time musicians. The German Music Council comprises about 90 music organizations and the *Landesmusikräte* (state music councils) of the sixteen states. It co-ordinates the representation of educational, cultural, social and legal policy issues for its members.

The Council also provides information of national and international interest through its special Music Information Centre (*Deutsches Musikinformationszentrum*), which provides information and contacts regarding all aspects of German musical culture. Another of its primary functions is to promote younger musicians. Many activities are organized and sponsored to this end including: competitions; choral, orchestra and chamber music projects; instrumental and vocal master classes; and the production of CDs. These opportunities play an important role in the promotion of the musically gifted.

Music in the elementary education and public school system

Early support of musical activities for 3- to 5-year-olds takes place outside the family, in pre-school or nursery school, and the form that this takes depends on the training and personal inclination of the teachers involved. Children's basic musical activities are integrated with movement, dance, language and the visual arts. However, the musical training of pre-school teachers is considered to be generally in need of improvement or even lacking altogether (cf. Rohlfs, 1999a). This is a deplorable situation in view of the importance of encouragement in the early years of childhood for later musical development. Outside the pre-school system, early childhood music lessons can also be taken in the public music schools' basic programmes.

Music education is a part of all levels of general compulsory schooling, which extend over nine to ten years: students should receive 1 or 2 music lessons per week. However, this kind of provision is not always ensured because music education may be offered as an elective along with visual arts, drama or other creative subjects, or because there may be a shortage of staff who can teach music. Nevertheless, compulsory schooling is a very important influence on musical development in Germany because all children experience it. Whatever they encounter in these lessons will influence their interest in the arts and culture for the rest of their lives (Rohlfs, 1999a).

In the secondary schools, i.e. the *Gymnasium* (grammar school) and *Gesamtschule* (comprehensive school), there are basic music lessons for two to three hours per week, and more intensive optional classes, for specialists, for five to six hours per week. For those students who do opt to major in music, the subject becomes one of their four final high-school examinations. The number of schools that are able to offer these intensive classes in music is small, however. Only a small percentage of twelfth- and thirteenth-grade students elect a basic course in music (23.5 per cent in 1997/98), and even fewer opt for the intensive course (1.8 per cent) (Rohlfs, 1999a). The two main reasons for this are that music is considered to be a less important subject than most others, and that drama and visual arts can be elected as an alternative to the basic courses in music. A further problem is that expected musical achievements can often only be attained when students take additional instrumental classes outside school.

Furthermore, only about 250 general schools offer free instrumental music instruction in the context of an intensive music programme, and most of those which do are *Musikgymnasien* (special music grammar schools). These develop students with obvious musical talent, preparing them for entry to music academies. They also often collaborate with a local *Musikhochschule* (music academy) or *Konservatorium* (conservatory).

Although the level of take-up of music education and the availability of free instrumental lessons might seem disappointingly low, many students also take additional electives such as choir, orchestra, band, jazz or rock bands. The opportunity to take part in these is strongly dependent on the enthusiasm of the teacher and the interests and motivations of the students, however. Musical instruments are not generally taught in public schools because such provision for every pupil is considered to be neither necessary nor affordable. The instrumental skills required for participation in school orchestras and other ensembles are therefore most often acquired outside the school, privately or through music schools.

Music schools and freelance music instructors

Private music schools are among the most important institutions for music education outside compulsory schooling, and their programmes cater for people of all ages. There are approximately 980 in the FRG, most of which are public institutions run by cities and municipalities. Music lessons in these schools are generally paid for by students or their parents, although the schools do receive governmental support. Most public music schools are organized similarly, and are members of the association of *Verband Deutscher Musikschulen* (VdM). Although all of these schools adhere to common guidelines regarding educational goals and content, there is no binding curriculum. Their functions are to provide elementary music education, to promote amateur music making and to identify and develop musical talent. The private schools sometimes offer special classes to prepare students for music academy entrance exams.

Classes in private music schools are organized into four levels (elementary, lower intermediate, intermediate and advanced), which encompass between two and four years of instruction. The programmes range from early childhood music and elementary music education (starting at four years) to instrumental and vocal lessons, ensembles (classical music, jazz, rock and popular) and auxiliary courses in music theory and ear training. In 1998, the German census bureau stated that 35,000 music instructors at 979 schools were teaching 862,000 students. The schools promote more than 20,000 instrumental and vocal ensembles, with roughly 210,000 participants (Rohlfs, 1999a).

Freelance music instructors also offer instrumental and voice lessons. It is difficult to say exactly how many are working in Germany and how much teaching they do. Although 6000 of them are professionally organized, their actual number is almost certainly much higher. These teachers are especially important in smaller cities and communities without a music school.

nbris

kshochschule: institutes of continuing education, adult education and after-hour classes

lic educational institution specifically targeting adults, the *schule* (VHS) also offer music classes. In contrast with the music which offer only music instruction, the VHS offer a broad array of subjects in continuing education. These, typically, include theoretical classes such as general musicianship and music appreciation, or courses accompanying the local opera or concert season, rather than instrumental and voice lessons. However, they do also offer the opportunity to participate in performing ensembles, and this attracts over 100,000 members annually (Rohlfs, 1999a). These activities are important for the continuing development of adults who have interrupted or even given up active musicianship. Amateur groups provide an excellent opportunity to practise and improve musical skills.

Instrumental and vocal music performance by amateurs

Many amateur ensembles exist in Germany, and these often constitute an important influence on the future musical development of children and adolescents. Amateur choirs and ensembles may present the only opportunity for adults to be musically active. They thus form an important part of their social orientation and integration. In 1997, Germany had a total of about 61,000 choirs, with about 1,801,000 active singers (Allen, 1999). About 42,000 choirs are organized in associations: around 19,000 of these are secular (with 809,000 singers), while 22,500 choirs (with 614,000 members) are church-affiliated. On average, 17 per cent of the active singers are under 25 years of age. The representation of young people is somewhat lower in secular choirs (16 per cent) than it is in church choirs (20 per cent) (Rohlfs, 1999b). These figures indicate that amateur choirs present an important opportunity to engage in music, especially for adults.

The situation is somewhat different for amateur instrumental ensembles. In 1997 there were about 29,200 ensembles with 824,000 active participants. The majority of these were wind bands and marching bands (17,500) with an estimated 605,000 active instrumentalists. In addition to these, there were 3400 accordion orchestras with 60,000 members. The remaining ensembles consist of plucked instruments (mandolin, guitar) or zither music groups (around 700 ensembles with 14,000 musicians), along with orchestras (600 ensembles totalling 22,000 instrumentalists). In addition to these secular ensembles, there exist some 7000 church-affiliated trombone ensembles comprising

123,000 members. The proportion of children and young people is markedly higher than in the choirs (56 per cent), although this varies considerably with the type of ensemble. Involvement is highest (77 per cent) in the accordion orchestras, and lowest (32 per cent) in the symphonic and string orchestras (Rohlfs, 1999b).

Information about participation in rock and pop groups is virtually non-existent. These groups are often omitted from official statistics because the groups themselves have no interest in being included and often deliberately refuse to co-operate with institutions of public music management. The membership of these groups is also constantly changing, so that their exact numbers are difficult to assess.

In recent years, however, several *Bundesländer* as well as private sponsors have launched a series of initiatives to promote the development of young rock and pop musicians. These include competitions, workshops and career-counselling services regarding the music business. Sponsorship by individual enterprises or groups of companies is quite important, especially by companies from the music business. Some examples are the Volkswagen Sound Foundation, which has endorsed top stars as well as sponsoring a range of new bands since 1997, and the 'Let's Make Music' project, which includes touring schools with a 'music truck' which introduces students and teachers to modern rock- and pop-music equipment. Professional rock and pop musicians, and interested amateurs, with the help of federal grants, have also established projects and organizations to promote young musicians. Since 1994, the federally funded 'Rocksie!' project has supported the activities of girls and women through workshops, concerts, symposia and the European Music Network for Women. Current information concerning many aspects of the development of rock and pop music can be found in Gorny and Stark (1999).

Content and methods

Aims and objectives

Three arguments are used to justify the necessity for public music education in schools. The first of these is a pedagogical one. A report from the KMK (1998) states that

A practical encounter with music, alone or in a group, fulfils an existential human need for self-expression. It fosters perceptive and responsive abilities, creativity and tolerance. The approach to music, be it through reflection, re-creation or creation, develops equal emotional and cognitive competences. It promotes solidarity with and consideration of others ... and it educates toward a responsible usage of the media. With this, music education in schools lays the foundation for an independent concept of life. (p. 11)

The second argument is a cultural one. Music education should pass on the country's musical heritage to future generations, awakening pupils' understanding of varied musical phenomena. By doing so, music education contributes to the individual's own identity and enables and motivates 'tomorrow's audiences' to engage actively in cultural life. 'Cultural life' is explicitly described, in the same 1998 KMK report, as comprising the traditions of the region as well as the musical heritage of other peoples and cultures. It demands a broad concept of the term 'musical culture' which includes rock, popular and jazz music along with German and other folk musics. The third argument for music education is an institutional one. It emphasizes the many situations in which music education can provide schools with public visibility via musical events, and how these can create a sense of belonging among students, teachers and parents.

According to the type of school and grade level, these general ideas are being implemented in school syllabuses and curricula with varying emphases in different states. The following learning objectives, taken from the state of Hessen, are given as one example of the ways in which the general statements can be transformed into actual learning goals. Students are expected to achieve the following goals:

- the ability to appreciate familiar and unfamiliar music with knowledge and understanding;
- the ability to understand the importance and effects of music on human beings in the past and present;
- the ability to critically reflect on the different forms in which music is presented, especially those forms used by the mass media;
- the ability to handle music technology productively and independently, with an appropriate critical attitude;
- the ability to reproduce music using the voice and instruments;
- the ability to invent and form music, and to express oneself with music;
- the ability to read music.

It is difficult to assess the extent to which these goals are actually attained, and there are many practical problems that can prevent students from achieving them. In addition to difficulties concerning students and teachers (e.g. lack of motivation, frustration, burn-out of teachers) there are also various institutional constraints (e.g. poor scheduling of music education during the day; lack of musical instruments; suitability of classrooms for music teaching).

Learning tools and technical equipment

Teachers and students can choose from learning materials in various forms, such as songbooks, text and workbooks, musical examples and visual and audio-visual materials (see Helms, Schneider and Weber, 1997). Virtually all schools are equipped with technical media to play music back. Many schools also have keyboards at their disposal, although there are no specific data on this to date. In the state of Bavaria, Kraemer (1992) found that 57 per cent of the teachers surveyed had practical experience with keyboards, yet only 23 per cent actually used them in their classes. Only a few (8 per cent) of the schools in the survey had keyboard classrooms. Although 80 per cent of the teachers believed that keyboards had a motivating effect on students, their use in the classroom appeared constrained by problems of space and organization. Among other things, the large initial investment in time required for even the development of the simplest melodies, along with the divergent knowledge backgrounds of students and short practice phases during the lessons, seemed to hamper effective use of technology.

A later study found that around 13 per cent of the teachers surveyed had experience with MIDI technology in the classroom (Maas, 1995). When this is used, it is mainly with multimedia CD-ROMs to introduce instruments, for the analysis of musical works, for music history, and to promote the learning of basic music reading skills, ear training, composing and arranging.

Assessment and its role

Standardized performance and ability testing is not part of the assessment and evaluation of musical abilities and competencies in Germany. One reason is that, with the exceptions of the Seashore and Bentley inventories, no standardized tests have been produced or translated into German. Although there have been occasional attempts to develop inventories of musical competence, these tests have not gained wide acceptance. Indeed, there is general mistrust concerning the potential advantages of performance and talent assessment in the arts.

Opinions concerning the assessment and evaluation of performance differ widely in different types of public school. For example, opinions in elementary education range from a complete refusal to carry out performance assessments, to the view that assessment should be as much a part of elementary school as it is at other grade levels (Lohmann, 1997a). In the case of music education, the importance of assessment depends on the state guidelines covering the general functions of different types of schools (Lohmann, 1997b). For example, the secondary general school focuses on the process of individual students' learning relative to their potential. In contrast, competitive aspects of performance play a more pronounced role in the *Realschule* (intermediate school) and the *Gymnasium* (grammar school). This applies particularly to upper-level classes in the *Gymnasium* (grade 11 to 13), which stress scientific and scholarly thinking. Here, great importance is attached to performance and its assessment, and so the associated curricula for this type of school provide detailed suggestions for such assessments (Lohmann, 1997c).

Student issues

Use of mass media

The mass media play an important role in the listening habits and preferences of children and adolescents. Practically all German children grow up hearing music from the radio, TV or a walkman, and most children now own such equipment themselves. According to one recent study, 77 per cent of 14- to 17-year-olds own a Walkman, and 62 per cent own their own TV (*KidsVerbraucher Analyse 99*, 1999). The influence of the media begins before preschool and increases over time. In 1997, 3- to 5-year-olds watched an average of 81 minutes of television per day, 6- to 9-year-olds watched for 91 minutes, 10- to 13-year-olds watched for 113 minutes and those over thirteen years watched for 196 minutes (Feierabend and Klingler, 1998).

The same study shows that 93 per cent of 6- to 9-year-olds listen to music in their spare time, while the corresponding figures for 10- to 13-year-olds and 14- to 17-year-olds were around 98 per cent respectively (*KidsVerbraucher Analyse 99*, 1999). Another survey showed that 14- to 19-year-olds listen to the radio for, on average, 128 minutes per day (Media Perspektiven Basisdaten, 1998). This shows that the influence of the mass media on musical socialization begins before school age, and that the pupils are exposed to this influence for several hours every day. In comparison, the influence of only two hours of music education per week is presumably rather meagre.

Talent competitions

National competitions called *Jugend musiziert* are one of the most successful ways of developing the abilities of musically gifted children and adolescents. The competitions include instrumental performance, vocal performance and ensemble performance and have taken place since 1963 with the support of federal funding. These competitions serve both to promote musical activities among young people in the general population and to allow musically gifted individuals to be identified and fostered. The competitions are organized on three levels. District competitions take place every year at 140 different locations in Germany; those who earn first prize at this level move on to the competitions at state level, and those winning first prize and special recommendations at this level go on to participate in the national competitions.

The winners gain access to different kinds of support, such as special counselling from jury members, participation in state and national youth orchestras, participation in master classes, loan of valuable instruments, radio and CD recording sessions and monetary awards. The competitions are open to children, adolescents and young people who have not yet entered or prepared for a musical career. The number of participants in these competitions has increased continuously. Approximately 12,000 young instrumentalists and singers currently enter the district competitions, 4,000 take part at state level and 1200 at national level. Several empirical studies have been undertaken in conjunction with the *Jugend musiziert* competitions. These concern the personality and development of the winners (Bastian, 1989, 1991), and other aspects of the competition (Linzenkirchner and Eger-Harsch, 1995).

More competitions have been created in recent years, including *jugend komponiert* (composition), *Jugend jazzt* (jazz) and *Jugend singt* (vocal), and these serve to differentiate and widen the spectrum of youth musical activities. There are many others sponsored by foundations, initiatives and associations which also aim to promote gifted youngsters (see Eckhardt *et al.*, 1999/2000). However, these competitions do not have anything like the scope of the *Jugend musiziert* events.

In addition to *Jugend musiziert*, the *Institut für Begabungsforschung und Begabtenförderung in der Musik* (IBFF – Institute for the Research and Advancement of the Musically Gifted) was founded, in 1992, at the University of Paderborn (Bastian, 1994). The IBFF has two goals: the first is to identify and promote gifted musicians by offering advice and master classes for which young musicians can apply. The second is to undertake empirical research concerning musical giftedness. So far, these studies have concentrated on biographical and developmental research concerning musically gifted individuals, and on the transfer effects of enhanced music education in the public school system (Bastian, 1995, 2000). Every other year, an interdisciplinary symposium is organized which covers a broad range of topics (e.g. music and medicine, preparation of competitions, stress management).

Professional training in music

The training of professional musicians and music educators usually takes place at national, or nationally accredited, institutions. Professional instrumentalists and singers receive their artistic training mainly in *Musikhochschulen* (music academies) and *Konservatorien* (conservatories). Many schools of music maintain degree programmes not only in western classical music but also in the areas of jazz and popular music. Music educators receive their training at universities, music academies and conservatories. Special church-music academies and schools of music are responsible for the preparation of church musicians.

Training at one of these institutions is contingent upon successful auditioning. The nature of this audition depends on the degree programme, such that instrumental/vocal performance, ear training and music theory are of varying importance. The entrance requirements for performance degree programmes at music academies are particularly strict. Professional music training is currently available at 23 music academies, 11 conservatories, 65 universities and teacher training colleges, and 13 church-music academies. As of 1999, the total current enrolment of music students stands at approximately 30,000. In the academic year 1996/97, females constituted 53 per cent of the students in music degree programmes, but only 43 per cent of the students at music academies (cf. Rohlfs, 1999a).

Careers in classical music

Toward the end of their professional training, instrumentalists and singers audition with agents, orchestras, opera and radio choirs, or other ensembles. Recent graduates generally find it difficult to start their musical career, even though Germany has a varied and rich cultural scene (including 130 musical theatre stages, around 50 established professional orchestras and 30 festivals).

The two main reasons for this difficulty are an increase in the number of trained singers and instrumentalists, and a decrease in job opportunities with choirs, orchestras and opera ensembles. The latter is a result of the shortage of funding, which has resulted in the merging or disappearance of several orchestras. Rinderspacher (1999) has provided some disturbing data on this. For example, between 1993/94 and 1996/97, the number of artistic personnel working in musical theatres dropped by 1392 (i.e. 8 per cent of the total) to 16,031. Theatre orchestras, opera choirs and vocal soloists were among the worst affected. Similarly, between 1991 and 1998, a total of 1136 (or 9.3 per cent of the total) of orchestral positions were lost through the merging and dissolution of orchestras.

These developments have had an obvious negative impact on the employment opportunities of the 4000 instrumental musicians currently being trained in German music academies and conservatories. While, on average, only sixteen musicians applied for one orchestral position in 1980, in 1988 there were 52 applicants. Recent data (Rinderspacher, 1999) suggests that the current number of applicants per place is 57 on average, but the real number of applicants may be much higher because not all orchestras provide data for statistical surveys. Music agents' insight and experience suggests that there may be on average 200 to 300 applicants per position. Singers experience a similar problem: very few female singers can currently receive a permanent contract for the stage (Gembris, forthcoming). In contrast, very few male singers even enter professional training, leading to shortages in many theatres: their career opportunities are better than those of females.

These circumstances pose difficult and unresolved problems. Although unemployment exists in other professions, musicians have invested considerable amounts of time and money in instruments, lessons and practice. Furthermore, their sense of individuality and of being in some way 'special' is strengthened during their training, and this can make the burden of unemployment particularly heavy: their identities, personalities and long-term life goals are closely tied to their musical activities.

Singers face an additional problem in that the professional life of a soloist is no longer lifelong. Singers who have been working at one theatre for about thirteen years tend not to receive a new two-year contract: current German labour laws mean that fifteen years' consecutive appointment results in the right to a tenured position, and theatres are reluctant to grant these. Female solo vocalists, aged 40 to 45, often find it difficult to obtain new employment because of the competition from younger vocalists, and this can result in the interruption or even termination of a career. The limited temporary contracts for singers are supposed to ensure the flexibility of the solo ensemble, which can be adapted to the vocal demands of particular opera productions at any time. In contrast, positions in orchestras and opera choirs are mostly tenured due to historical traditions.

Careers in jazz and popular music

Very little information is available regarding the musical careers of jazz and popular musicians. In the academic year 1996/97, 425 students were enrolled in jazz and popular-music degree programmes at German music academies (Rohlfs, 1999a). Many amateur and professional rock and popular-music bands perform regularly, but we have no idea how many. It is estimated that there are around 650 to 700 bands in Cologne alone, a city with roughly one million inhabitants (Plaschke and Großmaas, 1995). Furthermore, only 6 per cent of the rock and popular-music bands surveyed by Niketta and Volke (1994) viewed themselves as professional.

With the exception of these findings, however, German researchers have largely neglected the factors that influence the careers of jazz, rock and popular musicians, and those that lead to this choice in the first place. In contrast with those working in classical music, the professional success of pop and jazz musicians seems to depend largely on their own initiative and entrepreneurial skills (Westerhoff, 1997).

Conclusion

In summary, we can suggest that the societal and socio-cultural conditions for the promotion of musical talent and musical learning are favourable in the FRG. There is good public and private support for the musically gifted, and even children from lower socioeconomic backgrounds have the opportunity, at least in principle, to receive musical training by way of mandatory music education in the schools and through stipends and other funding opportunities. There are also numerous opportunities for the public to participate in amateur choirs and ensembles.

However, this is not to suggest that no improvements are needed. For example, although two lessons of music education a week are scheduled through the tenth grade, in practice these classes are much less frequent, or even absent altogether, such that pupils choose other arts classes such as drama or the visual arts instead. There are strong current pressures to cut resources for music and arts education at public schools. The fact that music education in public schools is generally considered to be less important than languages or science subjects, therefore has negative consequences both at the political and at the local level. I believe that the implementation of more practical musical activities in the public schools, and better musical training for preschool teachers, would greatly improve the institutional framework for the musical enrichment and development of children and adolescents.

Acknowledgement

The author is grateful to Dr Andreas C. Lehmann for his helpful comments and support with the translation of this article.

References

Allen, H. (1999) 'Vokales Laienmusizieren', in A. Eckhardt, R. Jakoby and E. Rohlfs (eds) *Musik-Almanach 1999/2000. Daten und Fakten zum Musikleben in Deutschland*. Kassel: Bärenreiter/Bosse, 22–34.

Bastian, H. G. (1989) *Leben für Musik: Eine Biographie-Studie über musikalische (Hoch-)Begabungen*. Mainz: Schott.

Bastian, H. G. (1991) *Jugend am Instrument. Eine Repräsentativstudie*. Mainz: Schott.

Bastian, H.G. (ed.) (1993) *Begabungsforschung und Begabtenförderung in der Musik*. Mainz: Schott.

Bastian, H. G. (1994) '"Institutionalisierte" Begabungsforschung und Begabtenförderung in der Musik: Europaweit erstes Fachinstitut an der Universität-GH Paderborn gegründet', in H. Gembris, R.-D. Kraemer and G. Maas (eds) *Musikpädagogische Forschungsberichte 1993*. Augsburg: Wissner, 467–79.

Bastian, H. G. (1995) 'Musikalität, Intelligenz und andere Merkmale: Über Abhängigkeiten und Zusammenhänge bei Sechs-bis Siebenjährigen: Teilergebnisse einer Langzeitstudie'. *Üben & Musizieren*, **5**, 11–16.

Bastian, H. G. (2000) *Musik(erziehung) und ihre Wirkung. Eine Langzeitstudie an Berliner Grundschulen*. Mainz: Schott.

Eckhardt, A., Jakoby, R. and Rohlfs, E. (eds) *Musik-Almanach 1999/2000: Daten und Fakten zum Musikleben in Deutschland*. Kassel: Bärenreiter/Bosse.

Feierabend, S. and Klingler, W. (1998) 'Was Kinder sehen: Eine Analyse der Fernsehnutzung 1997 von Drei-bis 13jährigen'. *Media Perspektiven*, **4**, (98) 167–78.

Gembris, H. (1997) 'Time-specific factors influencing the life-long learning of non-musicians and musicians'. *Polish Quarterly of Developmental Psychology*, **3**, (1) 77–89.

Gembris, H. (1998) *Grundlagen musikalischer Begabung und Entwicklung*. Augsburg: Wissner.

Gembris, H. (forthcoming) 'The professional development of recent graduates from music academies'. Paper for the first European conference on research relevant to the work of music academies and conservatoires, Lucerne, Switzerland, September, 1999.

Gorny, D. and Stark, J. (1999) *Jahrbuch Pop & Kommunikation 1999/2000*. Düsseldorf: Econ.

Helms, S., Schneider, R. and Weber, R. (eds) (1997) *Handbuch des Musikunterrichts*, Band 1–3. Regensburg: Bosse.

Heukäufer, N. (1998) Musikunterricht mit digitalen Anteilen. Hinweise zur Ausstattung und Unterrichtsbeispiele. *Musik & Bildung*, **5**, 38–43.

KidsVerbraucherAnalyse 99 (1999) Bastei-Verlag, Axel Springer Verlag AG & Verlagsgruppe Bauer.

KMK Report (1998) See Sekretariat der Ständigen Konferenz der Kultusminister der Länder (below).

Kraemer, R.-D. (1992) 'Einstellung von Musiklehrern zum Einsatz elektronischer Tasteninstrumente im Musikunterricht', in H. Gembris, R.-D. Kraemer and G. Maas (eds) *Musikpädagogische Forschungsberichte 1991*. Augsburg: Wissner, 115–37.

Linzenkirchner, P. and Eger-Harsch, G. (1995) *Gute Noten mit kritischen Anmerkungen. Wirkungsanalyse der Wettbewerbe 'Jugend musiziert' 1984 bis 1993. Dokumentation und Kommentierung*. Bonn, München: Deutscher Musikrat.

Lohmann, W. (1997a, b, c) 'Leistungserfassung-Leistungsbeurteilung-Leistungsbewertung', in S. Helms, R. Schneider and R. Weber (eds) *Handbuch des Musikunterrichts*. Regensburg: Bosse. Vol. 1: Primarstufe, 63–9 (1997a); Vol. 2: Sekundarstufe I, 49–55 (1997b); Vol. 3: Sekundarstufe II, 43–9 (1997c).

Maas, G. (1995) 'Neue Technologien im Musikunterricht: Eine Erhebung zum Stand der Verbreitung und zur Innovationsbereitschaft von MusiklehrerInnen', in G. Maas (ed.) *Musiklernen und Neue (Unterrichts-) Technologien*. Essen: Die Blaue Eule, 96–123.

Media Perspektiven Basisdaten (1998) *Daten zur Mediensituation in Deutschland*. Frankfurt: Arbeitsgemeinschaft der ARD-Werbegesellschaften.

Niketta, R. and Volke, E. (1994) *Rock und Pop in Deutschland. Ein Handbuch für öffentliche Einrichtungen und andere Interessierte*. Essen: Klartext.

Noll, G. (1997) 'Musik und die staatliche Macht: Ausgewählte Beispiele aus der Geschichte der DDR zur Situation der Musiker, Musikpädagogik und Musikwissenschaft', in G. Maas and H. Reszel (eds) *Popularmusik und Musikpädagogik in der DDR*. Augsburg: Wißner, 9–51.

Plaschke, R. and Großmaas, U. (1995) 'Aspekte populärer Musik in Deutschland', in A. Eckhardt, R. Jacoby and E. Rohlfs (eds) *Musik-Almanach 1996/97*. Kassel: Bärenreiter/Bosse, 61–70.

Rinderspacher, A. (1999) 'Daten und Fakten zur Situation der Orchester und Musiktheater', in A. Eckhardt, R. Jakoby and E. Rohlfs (eds) *Musik-Almanach 1999/2000. Daten und Fakten zum Musikleben in Deutschland*, Kassel: Bärenreiter/Bosse, 47–55.

Rohlfs, E. (1999a) 'Musikalische Bildung und Ausbildung', in A. Eckhardt, R.

Jakoby and E. Rohlfs (eds) *Musik-Almanach 1999/2000: Daten und Fakten zum Musikleben in Deutschland*, Kassel: Bärenreiter/Bosse, 3–21.

Rohlfs, E. (1999b) 'Instrumentales Laienmusizieren', in A. Eckhardt, R. Jakoby and E. Rohlfs (eds) *Musik-Almanach 1999/2000: Daten und Fakten zum Musikleben in Deutschland*, Kassel: Bärenreiter/Bosse, 35–46.

Sekretariat der Ständigen Konferenz der Kultusminister der Länder (ed.) (1998) *Zur Situation des Unterrichts im Fach Musik an den allgemeinbildenden Schulen in der Bundesrepublik Deutschland.* Bericht der Kultusministerkonferenz vom 10 März, Bonn (cited as KMK Report 1998).

Westerhoff, S. (1997) 'Musikalische Werdegänge von Jazzmusikern: Eine Untersuchung anhand biographischer Interviews', in R.-D. Kraemer (ed.) *Musikpädagogische Biographieforschung: Fachgeschichte – Zeitgeschichte – Lebensgeschichte.* Essen: Die Blaue Eule, 201–17.

Appendix: websites of organizations cited in the chapter

Institut für Begabungsforschung und Begabtenförderung in der Musik (IBFF) (Institute for the Research and Advancement of the Musically Gifted, University of Paderborn) http://hrz.upb.de/fb4/ibff

Deutscher Musikrat (German Music Council) http://www.deutscher-musikrat.de

Deutsches Musikinformationszentrum (German Music Information Centre) http://www.miz.org

Verband Deutscher Musikschulen (VdM) (Association of German music schools) http://www.musikschulen.de

Volkswagen Sound Foundation http://www.volkswagen-soundfoundation.de

rocksie! http://www.rocksie.de

CHAPTER

5

India

Gerry Farrell

Introduction

Background

When approaching the vast subject of Indian music, it is essential to be as clear as possible about distinctions between different musical forms and genres. It is unrealistic, and hopelessly reductive, to speak of one Indian music – there are many. The musical traditions of the Indian sub-continent are a kaleidoscope of classical, popular, folk and religious traditions that interconnect and influence each other in numerous and complex ways. The manners in which music is taught and learnt are equally various.

Another point that requires clarification is what constitutes 'India' in the present discussion, for the term 'Indian music' has a wide range of cultural and geographical implications. Since 1947, 'India' has referred to a political and geographical entity, distinct from Pakistan, (and later Bangladesh) and Sri Lanka. The influence of Indian music and culture, however, is widespread across South Asia and certain facets of music education in India may be similar to those in Pakistan, Bangladesh, Sri Lanka, Afghanistan or Nepal (Wade, 1979; Baily, 1988; Grandin, 1989). I will make distinctions between regionally differing musical styles when this is appropriate, but when I speak of Hindustani classical music, for example, it refers to a system of music that has wide usage in Pakistan and Bangladesh as well as India.

For the purposes of this chapter I will focus on Indian classical music and attempt to show how certain aspects of the teaching and learning process in classical music have application across a wide range of Indian musical cultures. In Indian culture a conceptual divide has long existed between classical and folk music. This is expressed by the term *shastriya sangit* (classical) and *lok sangit* (folk). In the present chapter the term 'classical' refers to two systems of music: the north (Hindustani) system, and the south (Carnatic) system. Although these two systems share many similarities, there are also significant differences relating to melodic and metrical systems, methods of notation and conventions of learning and performance.

A central issue throughout this chapter will be the relationship between informal and formal methods of music education in Indian classical music; between systematized ways of learning music, and music learnt through less clearly definable processes of enculturation. By the latter I chiefly mean elements of the *guru-shishya* system which are often termed, erroneously perhaps, 'oral tradition', in contrast with the structures and curricula of school and university education.

Despite my central focus on classical music in this chapter, it is important to be aware of the massive influence of *filmi* song (songs from the films) on all levels of Indian society; an influence, in many respects, further reaching than that of classical music (Manuel, 1988). However, it is difficult to speak of *filmi* song in the context of formal music education; in relation to musical learning its influence is largely in the informal sphere. Specific research is lacking on the manner in which *filmi* song is learnt informally, or even within the professional milieu of the Bombay film industry. There has, consequently, been no large-scale research on the influence of *filmi* song on music education in India. There are, however, published books of film songs, with lyrics, musical notation and anecdotal evidence that film songs are used in schools in connection with festivals and religious events (*Filmi*, 1990a–g). On the contrary, the processes involved in learning classical music have been extensively documented in the form of didactic texts and in numerous ethnomusicological studies.

Systems of music teaching and learning

Even in relation to Indian classical music it is difficult to be precise about distinctions between formal and informal methods of teaching and learning. Further distinctions can be made between the northern and southern systems of classical music. The traditional method of teaching music is the *guru-shishya perampera* (master–disciple tradition, or *ustad-shagird* in Urdu) that has a history stretching back several centuries and has parallels in other forms of learning in Indian culture, such as dance and various types of religious instruction. The social organization of the *guru-shishya perampera* system is complex and operates on a number of formal and informal levels (Neuman, 1990). *Gharana*s (literally 'households') have developed, and these define specific musical and stylistic traits. Although these are based essentially on a familial lineage, anyone who has learnt in that style can be said to be of the *gharana* musically. To be a member of a *gharana*, confers great musical status. This system is considered to be the cornerstone of traditional teaching in Indian music, although as Neuman has shown it is a cultural form that is in a continual state of adaptation to suit changing social, economic and cultural circumstances.

Since the early decades of the twentieth century, classical music has been taught in formal learning environments such as colleges and universities with defined curricula and examination systems (Ghose, 1978; Kuppuswamy and Harihan, 1980; Sambamoorthy, 1985; Kippen, 1988; Alter, 1994; Chakravarti, 1994; Chaudhuri, 1999). The rise of the college system of musical training in India was influenced by a combination of western education models and the work of reforming musicians and educators, notably Sourindro Mohan Tagore (1840–1914), V. D. Paluskar and V. N. Bhatkhande (1860–1936). A large body of conflicting theory and practice was formalized by Bhatkhande for use in formal music education. He travelled throughout Northern India, collecting different versions of *rag*s from the musicians of the day. From this information he derived a system of ten *that*s (scale types) under which Hindustani *rag*s could be classified. The South Indian *mela* system of classification has 72 scale types and has different theoretical roots to the *that* system espoused by Bhatkhande (see Kaufmann 1976; Wade 1979). The *that* system, and a form of notation based on *sargam*, have been highly influential in music education. Bhatkhande's major work was *Kramik Pustak Malika*, a six-volume collection of musical exercises and compositions in over 70 *rag*s. This work is still widely used in schools, colleges and universities. It is a central text in Indian music education and has influenced the forms of curricula, teaching methodology and examination systems throughout the twentieth century. Bhatkhande's theories of *rag* classification are, however, also controversial. Aspects of it have been criticized or amended in a number of important studies (Kaufmann, 1968; Jairazbhoy, 1971; Widdess, 1995; Bor, 1999).

During the British Raj the question of how music should be taught in late-nineteenth- and early-twentieth-century India was an ideological and political issue as well as an educational one, linked closely to questions of national identity, modernization and westernization (Capwell, 1991; Farrell, 1997a). In present-day India, music education does not have a high profile in political or educational terms. Music is not a sought-after profession, and the purpose of much music education is to produce educated listeners and amateur performers. Although there are national standards set for education in the state sector across India, the musical curriculum is not defined in any great detail. Curriculas in universities tend to follow a set pattern, specifying a set numbers of *rags* (sometimes as many as 50) and *tals* to be completed in the course of a diploma or degree course. Chaudhuri (1999) gives a useful overview of these curriculas for a number of major Indian universities. Curricula are set by the institutions themselves. Chaudhuri also notes how a number of institutions have been set up in recent years in which attempts are made to replicate the *guru-shishya* system within the structure of a college system (*ibid.*).

The *guru-shishya* and college systems have continued to exist in parallel with some *gurus* also teaching within the college system. Although they ostensibly cover the same musical ground, the two systems are distinct in many ways, and the proponents of each do not always see eye to eye on matters of teaching methodology and learning outcomes. Much controversy surrounds the purpose of the college system, and traditionalists insist that it cannot produce teachers and performers of any calibre, but rather, at best, informed listeners. On the other hand, college music educators charge *gurus* with being the self-serving preservers of outdated musical hierarchies; secretive and sparing with their knowledge and unable to adapt to the needs of the modern music student. However, there is still a widespread cultural assumption that the *guru-shishya perampera* is still considered the only true way to produce good players, and it is often the case that someone who has been through the college system will go to a *guru* for intensive training afterwards if they have any ambitions to be a professional performer. Part of any musician's worth in India is a visible and public link to an acknowledged lineage of learning: cultural and musical status of this kind can only be conferred through training with a recognized *guru*. The whole question of teaching methodologies in a modern education system is of central concern to musicians and educators in contemporary India (Sharma, 1995).

One striking point in this discussion is that, despite the clear influence of western structures on certain aspects of the Indian education system and despite the history of colonialism in India, western classical music has had little or no impact either on the materials or performance practices of Indian classical music. This contrasts with, for example, the situation in China or Japan. However, the influence of the West in Indian popular music is widespread. This is a complex issue that cannot be dealt with in detail in the context of the present discussion.

Music psychology and Indian music

Although texts exploring the psychology of Indian music date back to 1916 (Rao, 1986) there has been little research in aptitude and musical acquisition from a broader psychological perspective, and methods that have been employed have been based on western models that are not always suitable for Indian music. This is particularly the case in musical tests where certain parameters such as pitch and harmony, as conceptualized in western terms, are inappropriate to Indian systems. For example, in their work, Kuppuswamy and Harihan refer to the Seashore Measures of Music Talent, Kwalwasser-Dykema Music Test, Aliferis-Stecklien Music Achievement Test, and others, advocating their use in Indian music education, with no critical comment about how appropriate any of these tests may be to the learning of Indian (or indeed any) music (1980). Other work has focused on music ability and criterion-referenced tests in music education (Sharma, 1995), but more recent strands of thought in music psychology, particularly cognitive and developmental aspects of musical learning, do not, as yet, appear to have had any significant impact in Indian music education. Similarly, little work has been done on music education in primary schools and its relation to the wider musical environment. The whole question of children's music education in India is a subject that requires sustained and in-depth research (see Sharma, 1995). Also, the manner in which Indian musicians and theorists have looked to western scientific models in general to explain their own music has a long and complex history which cannot be discussed in any great detail here, but see Farrell (1997a) for a discussion of this in relation to questions of tuning, intonation and notation.

Contents and methods

This section examines different ways of teaching Indian music, focusing on contents and methodologies. In particular, it focuses on musical materials of Indian classical music and how the methodologies employed in the *guru-shishya* system and the college systems approach these materials.

The guru-shishya way of teaching

Anyone observing a traditional Indian music lesson for the first time would be struck by a number of features that may differ from their previous experience of musical learning. In the *guru-shishya* way of learning it is likely that the lesson will be one to one, in the guru's home, and open-ended in duration. Striking features would be a stern, didactic atmosphere where strict adherence to the instructions of the guru is expected and demanded but where periods of intense instruction are interspersed with more relaxed moments when tea is taken and musical gossip exchanged. There would be a notable emphasis on the use of the voice, even in instrumental teaching, with a corresponding lack of written notation, but the extensive use of mnemonic systems for representing parameters of pitch and rhythm. The guru's teaching would demonstrate a complex balance between the demand for strict imitation and the encouragement of expressive originality. The accomplished Indian musician is expected to have both a firm grasp of traditional melodic and rhythmic structures and an original approach to creative improvisation. The achievement a fine balance between these parameters of musical knowledge and action is highly respected within the culture.

Traditional teaching takes the form of a long process of instruction in the nuances of *rag* and *tal*, the melodic and rhythmic bases of Indian music. Although the temperaments of gurus may vary, the methodology employed is relatively consistent. In both the northern and southern systems a central feature of music learning is the exhaustive practice of melodic scalar patterns and rhythmic formulae that are the building blocks for variation-making and improvisation. The famous sitarist Ravi Shankar vividly recalled his early years of training and the central part these exercises played in it:

> I was quite advanced in music. But my hands were far behind, because I had spent so little time practising the basics. I used to hate the scales and exercises; it was a spiritual torture to me, because my hands could never catch up to the idea of the music in my head. (Shankar, 1968, p. 73).

Practising melodic and rhythmic formulae as a basis for building improvisational skills is a common strategy in a number of musical cultures (Berliner, 1994; Nettl and Russell, 1998). However, it is fair to say that in this respect few musics have as systematized and rigorous a procedure as Indian classical music.

In north-Indian music these formulae are called *palta* or *alankar*. The term *alankara* is used in the south. Although these two terms are often interchangeable, in Indian music teaching they have rather different meanings. *Palta* means literally 'turning over, turning back, return', or 'change, transformation' (McGregor, 1997, p. 612). In musical terms this relates to the permutational manner in which *palta*s are structured. *Alankar*, on the other hand, is a more general term for exercises and sometimes, melodic ornamentation.

A clear distinction should be made at this point about exercises that are concerned with generic scale patterns and those that are specific to particular *rag*s. It is the former type of exercise that is by far the most common. These processes are best explained by a few simple examples using *sargam*, the system of naming notes in Indian music.

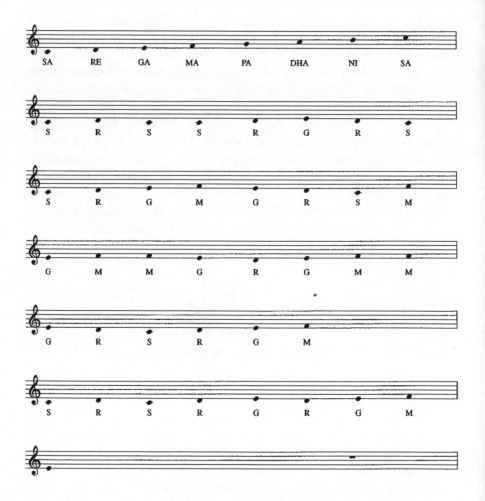

Figure 5.1 Music example 1
Source: Bhatkhande, *Kramik Pustak Malika* (1990, p. 16)

N.B. For ease of reading, 'SA' is given as 'C' in all music examples. However, in Indian music the pitch of SA does vary, depending on the tuning of instruments and the range of the singer's voice.

These *palta*s are in the scale of Bilaval. They are typical in that different sections of the scale are often chosen for permutational treatment, in this case the first four notes. Another feature is the repetition of the same patterns starting on successive degrees on the scale. These examples appear simple in structure but they serve a number of important functions in the process of learning Indian music, developing a sense of pitch and melodic contour, as well as permutational skills which later become explicitly rhythmic in emphasis.

Other *palta*s may take in a wider melodic range, with more complex rhythmic divisions. A *palta* may teach the learner to phrase in $3+3+3+3+4$, across a 16-beat *tal* (metrical cycle) which is subdivided $4+4+4+4$. Similar *palta*s would be structured with different subdivisions:

$$3+3+6+4$$
$$2+2+2+3+3+4$$
$$6+3+3+4$$
$$5+5+6$$

Extensive practice would also take place with the basic subdivision of $4+4+4+4$.

Such exercises would be practised with all permutations, in *all* scales. This adds up to literally thousands of melodic and rhythmic formulae which become the backbone of the learner's musical knowledge and the fund of material which allows extensive improvisation in performance. For seven notes alone there are 5040 permutations possible without repetition.

A striking feature of Indian music teaching is the amount of time devoted to the practice of *palta*s and *alankar*s, and how little time is given to fixed compositions in different *rag*s. In the *guru-shishya* way of teaching, the purpose is not to teach many different *rag*s but to teach only a few in detail, with the understanding that the melodic and rhythmic strategies learned can, in time, be applied to any other *rag*, although each may have specific melodic details. So the above *palta*s could be practised in other *rag*s that have different notes. The emphasis in the *guru-shishya* way is therefore much more on the process of becoming a musician, rather than the building of a large repertoire of complete pieces.

Similarly, in rhythmic training it is the manipulation and permutation of beat patterns that are important. Again, the voice and mnemonic systems play a central role. Figure 5.2 shows the basic *tabla* (set of two hand-drums) stroke pattern for *tintal* (16 beats):

theka of *tintal* (16 beats)

dha dhin dhin dha   dha dhin dhin dha   dha tin tin ta   ta dhin dhin dha

Figure 5.2 Music example 2

Each sound, 'dha, dhin, tin, ta', relates to a particular double- or single-handed stroke of the different parts of the heads of the *tabla*. These mnemonics are called *bol*s, from the Hindi verb *bolna* (to speak). *Bol*s are the essential building-blocks of the tabla player's skill and they serve a number of functions:

- memory aides for stroke patterns;
- device for coordinating hand movements;
- oral notation;
- written notation;
- compositional tool for creating variations.

Variations can be made by using simple permutations of *bol*s. These variations are also called *palta*s and are based on a particular *bol* pattern called a *qaida* (formula). Such permutational processes can become extremely complex (see Kippen, 1988). Each *tal* has a different number of beats and its own individual stroke pattern, and it is familiarity with and mastery of the thousands of *bol* permutations that are at the heart of the *tabla* player's art. Several important ethnomusicological studies of the *tabla* traditions of north India and *mrdanga* of south India have examined in detail the social, cultural, cognitive and musical complexities of these rhythmic systems (Brown 1965; Gottlieb 1977; Kippen 1988). These and other studies tend to focus on the training of performers, and there is little in the ethnomusicological literature on Indian music education in other contexts, for example children as learners (Farrell 1997b).

The acquisition and accumulation of such melodic and rhythmic skills is the process by which a learner becomes a performer in Indian music. This is the prime purpose of the *guru-shishya* system, a long and complex one. In traditional Indian music teaching, the discipline of *riaz* (practice) is, consequently, highly valued, and tales of the practise regimes of great musicians abound (Shankar, 1968, p. 51; Neuman, 1990, pp. 32–7). The *guru* will instil a sense of dedication and discipline into the *shishya* and will often tell tales of his or her own *guru's* dedication, to make a point or give musical (and sometimes moral) guidance. *Guru-shishya* training takes place over a number of years and although, in the past, a pupil would, ideally, stay with one teacher, in contemporary India this is no longer the norm. The economic and time restrictions of modern life mean that pupils move from *guru* to *guru* and may have several teachers within a short span of learning.

The college system of teaching

The question of whether traditional systems of teaching can be translated into institutionalized learning situations has been central to discussions of music education in India in the twentieth century. Due to the disintegration of older forms of patronage, such as the royal courts, music in India has become integrated into the wider educational system, not as a specialist subject designed only to produce performers in traditional styles, but as a central facet of a broader liberal education. As Sambamoorthy (1985, p. 7) puts it: 'Any education which ignores training in music and which does not provide adequate opportunities for development of musical talents is incomplete.' He further describes music education in India as being of two types: professional and cultural (*ibid.*, p. 9). It is the distinction between these that characterizes the *guru-shishya* and college systems.

As noted above, the roots of the college system in India can be traced to the early decades of the twentieth century. In particular, several issues which would have a long-term effect on the structure of college music teaching concerned educational reformers like Bhatkhande and Paluskar. A central issue was that of notation, and how to create a uniform system suitable for mass music education. Staff notation had been proposed as a solution in many quarters, but for a number of complex reasons it never caught on in Indian music education despite having many important and influential supporters (Mudaliyar, 1893). However, in order to produce teaching materials, and organize curricula and examinations, a standard notation was essential. Bhatkhande's system of notation, based on *sargam* rather than staff notation, was widely adopted and has become standard.

The following example shows type of notation, first in Hindi, then translated into roman script, and then staff notation:

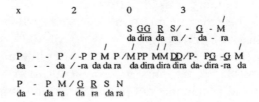

राग मुल्तानी गत रजाखानी – तीनताल

Source: after Chand (1969)

rag Multani razakhani gat - tintal

rag Multani, fast composition in 16 beats

Figure 5.3 Music example 3

This is a *gat* (composition) for the sitar. This type of notation has three elements:

- a representation of the *tal* division (in this case 16 beats);
- the tones represented as *sargam* syllables;
- the right stroke patterns for the *sitar*.

Staff notation is not designed to show these parameters in this manner. Bhatkhande's notation allowed large numbers of compositions and exercises to be published in a standardized way, and textbooks for college and university music teaching use collections of such notated material as the basis for instruction. Typically, each composition would be accompanied by a short pre-composed *alap* in the chosen *rag* and a number of *tan*s (melodic variations), which are based on the structure the *gat*.

Herein lies the basic difference between the *guru-shishya* way of teaching and the college system. It should be remembered that the composition shown above is, in itself, only an outline on which variations will be based. Learning compositions in a number of different *rag*s is not the main thrust of *guru-shishya* teaching but rather building familiarity with an improvisational style of which compositions are a part. Notation of this type is only used in the *guru-shishya* system as a method of shorthand for an essentially orally transmitted music; it is not a prescriptive representation of musical form or style.

The focus of college teaching is very different. As my own teacher once remarked, 'How can one learn 30 *rag*s in a year?' Yet in most cases this is what is expected in institutionalized music learning in India, and syllabuses define a certain amount of *rag*s and *tal*s to be learned in one year, and also the type of variations to be played, in order to pass on to the next stage. Thirty *rag*s may be an exaggeration, but ten a year is common. This has the effect of pre-composing and fixing the music in a different manner from traditional teaching. The institutionalization of Indian music represents it in a particular way, highlighting certain aspects as against others, and ultimately alters its form. Although the names of *rag*s and *tal*s may be the same, the Indian music learnt with a *guru*, or in a college, are, in effect, different musics.

Often the knowledge imparted in the college situation is more technical than practical. Kippen relates how the 1981–3 syllabus for *tabla* at the Bhatkhande Sangit Vidyapath in Lucknow, north India, shows that, by the end of the course (five years), a large number of *tal*s and compositions should have been learned. He comments:

> The *tal*s mentioned ... above are usually only heard in the repertoires of a limited number of *pakhawaj* players ... They are totally unrelated to the tabla repertoire and represent part of an attempt to root the instrument in a largely alien historical and musical context. (1988, p. 138)

This astute observation relates to the 'Hinduization' of Indian musical culture for the purposes of mass education, a trend that has its roots in nineteenth-century Hindu nationalism (Farrell, 1997a). The overall picture Kippen gives of the college system is not flattering and points to a lack of commitment on behalf of the students and teachers (1988, pp. 140–1). Kochak (1995) also paints a grim picture:

> These days practically all institutions of music, imparting higher education, are facing a great problem of the non-availability of proper teachers to teach higher classes in music and for guiding research. The universities are facing this problem to a greater extent. In a number of universities, the posts of Professors, Readers and Lecturers remain vacant due to the non-availability of the right type of teachers. Again and again, these posts are advertised, selection committees meet, and finally they discover that most of the candidates are not even able to tune their Tanpuras or Sitars properly. Most of the sitarists are not able to play a single Meend correctly. (p. 117)

Both Kippen and Kochak are commenting upon the north Indian system of college teaching. However, a college system also developed in the south at the same time, in the first two decades of the twentieth century (Sambamoorthy, 1965). An important point should be noted here about the differences between north and south Indian classical music. Although they share many similarities in terms of notation and metrical and modal organization, they are essentially different systems of music (Wade, 1979). In particular, the status of the composer is greater in the south and more comparable to the place of composer in the canon of western art music. Musicians such as Muttuswami Dikshitar (1775–1835) and Tyagaraja (1767–1847), wrote hundreds of compositions which still form the basis of the south Indian repertoire. Essentially, it is a written, text-based repertoire, unlike classical music in the north. Consequently, south Indian classical music is more through-composed on every level, although some sections of performance allow improvisation. The prior existence of a written repertoire in south Indian music has meant that it was immediately more amenable to institutionalization. In north India a written repertoire had to be created by musical theorists and educationalists which has distanced institutionalized music teaching from its source in an entirely different manner.

Who is learning Indian classical music?

As is the case in most societies, in India a profession in music is a risky business. Whereas most universities in India offer music as a main subject or a subsidiary subject in general arts degrees, the numbers of students taking music is small in comparison to other subjects (Association of Indian Universities, 1992). On the other hand, those studying music in small private colleges of music throughout India are numerous (Meer, 1980). In contrast, the numbers studying only with *gurus* in the traditional manner are declining. However, as Neuman has pointed out, what he calls the 'ecology' of Indian art music is highly adaptable and admits a continuum between different modes of learning music in contemporary India (1990, pp. 202–29). It is now common for anyone who has studied music at a college, and who wishes to continue their studies, to carry on with a *guru* afterwards, or maybe even have separate private lessons during their time at college.

In India there is an identifiable division of musical labour along the lines of gender. In the professional world, typically, women are singers and men are both singers and instrumentalists, although this is a situation that is changing rapidly in modern India. Now there are young, female professional performers (mainly the daughters of famous male musicians, such as Ravi Shankar and Ram Narayan) on *sitar, sarangi, tabla* and other instruments that were formerly the domain of men. Interestingly, this musical divison of labour has never been the case in the college system where large numbers of women study instruments as well as singing. The reasons for this appear to be social as much as musical:

I know people who ask if a girl knows singing or some other musical genre, when they meet to discuss marriage. And it's a great plus-point if the girl has been to Bhatkhande College and passed her exam. It speeds up the process and people agree to take such girls more readily. (Kapoor, quoted Kippen, 1988, p. 106)

There is little evidence to suggest, however, that the college system serves as a significant route for women to enter professional music, although it may be significant in teacher training.

Conclusion

In this chapter I have discussed some of the complex issues involved in contemporary Indian music education, particularly in the sphere of classical music. Specifically, I have looked at the manner in which methodologies and ways of approaching musical material vary between institutionalized forms of learning and more traditional methods. It is no exaggeration to say that Indian music education now stands at a crossroads, and the competing demands of mass education and training in specialist musical knowledge need to be reconciled. This concern has been a central theme in Indian music-education literature from the early decades of the twentieth century to the present. It remains to be seen how the conflicting positions of music as profession, music as entertainment, music as liberal education and music as social accomplishment may be resolved in the rapidly changing social and cultural environment of present day India.

Daniel Neuman's observation should be kept always in mind: 'The adage that "in order for things to remain the same they have to change" finds its mirror image in India. There we might say that "in order for things to change, they have to appear the same"' (1990, p. 234).

References

Alter, A. (1994) 'Gurus, shishyas and educators: adaptive strategies in post-colonial North Indian music institutions', in M.J. Kartomi and S. Blum (eds) *Music Cultures in Contact*. Basle: Gordon and Breach.

Association of Indian Universities (1992) *Universities Handbook*. New Delhi: Association of Indian Universities.

Baily, J. (1988) *Music of Afghanistan: Professional Musicians in the City of Herat*. Cambridge: Cambridge University Press.

Berliner, P. (1994) *Thinking in Jazz: The Infinite Art of Improvisation*. Chicago. Chicago University Press.

Bhatkhande, V.N. (1990) *Kramik pustak malika*, Vols 1–6 (in Hindi). Hathras: Sangeet Karyalaya.

Bor, J. (ed.) (1999) *The Raga Guide: A Survey of 74 Hindustani Ragas*. Nimbus Records and Rotterdam Conservatory of Music.

Brown, R. (1965) *The Mrdanga: A Study of Drumming in South India*. (2 vols). Ann Arbor: University Microfilms.

Capwell, C. (1991) 'Marginality and musicology in nineteenth century Calcutta: the case of Sourindro Mohun Tagore', in B. Nettl and P.V. Bohlman (eds) *Comparative Musicology and Anthropology of Music*. Chicago: Chicago University Press.

Chakravarti, I. (ed.) (1994) *Music: Its Methods and Techniques of Teaching in Higher Education*. New Delhi: Mittal.

Chand, P.S. (1969) *Sitar Vadan, Bhag Do* (in Hindi). Allahabad: Sahit Sadan Prakashan.

Chaudhuri, M. (1999) *Indian Music in Professional and Academic Institutions*. Delhi: Sanjay Prakashan.

Farrell, G. (1994) *South Asian Music Teaching in Change*. London: David Fulton.

Farrell, G. (1997a) *Indian Music and the West*. Oxford: Oxford University Press.

Farrell, G. (1997b) 'Thinking, playing, saying: children learning the tabla'. *Bulletin of the Council for Research in Music Education*, **133** (Summer), 14–19.

Filmi shastriya git ank (1990a) (in Hindi). Hathras: Sangeet Karyalaya.

Filmi ghazal ank (1990b) (in Hindi). Hathras: Sangeet Karyalaya.

Filmi prem git ank (1990c) (in Hindi). Hathras: Sangeet Karyalaya.

Filmi prayana git ank (1990d) (in Hindi). Hathras: Sangeet Karyalaya.

Filmi yugal gan ank (1990e) (in Hindi). Hathras: Sangeet Karyalaya.

Filmi bhajan git (1990f) (in Hindi). Hathras: Sangeet Karyalaya.

Filmi sanskrit git ank (1990g) (in Hindi). Hathras: Sangeet Karyalaya.

Ghose, S. (1978) *Music and Dance in Rabindranath Tagore's Educational Philosophy*. New Delhi: Natak Akademi.

Gottlieb, R. S. (1977) *The Major Traditions of North Indian Tabla Drumming* (2 vols). Munich: Emil Katzbichler.

Grandin, I. (1989) *Music and Media in Local Life: Music Practice in a Newar District of Nepal*. Linkoping: Linkoping University.

Jairazbhoy, N. A. (1971) *The Rags of North Indian Music: Their Structure and Evolution*. London: Faber and Faber.

Kaufmann, W. (1968) *The Ragas of North India*. Bloomington: Indiana University Press.

Kaufmann, W. (1976) *The Ragas of South India*. Bloomington: Indiana University Press.

Kippen, J. (1988) *The Tabla of Lucknow*. Cambridge: Cambridge University Press.

Kochak, U. S. (1995) 'Teacher's training and future prospects', in I. Chakravarti (ed.) *Music: Its Methods and Techniques of Teaching in Higher Education*. New Delhi: Mittal.

Kuppuswamy, G. and Harihan, M. (1980) *Teaching of Music*. Bangalore: Sterling.

McGregor, R. S. (1997) *The Oxford Hindi–English Dictionary*. Oxford: Oxford University Press.

Manuel, P. (1988) *Popular Musics of the Non-western World*. Oxford: Oxford University Press.

Meer, W. van der (1980) *Hindustani Music in the Twentieth Century*. New Delhi: Allied Publishers.

Mudaliyar, A. M. C. (1893) *Oriental Music in European Notation*. Madras: Ave Maria Press.

Nettl, B. and Russell, M. (1998) *In the Course of Performance*. Chicago: University of Chicago Press.

Neuman, D. (1990) *The Life of Music in North India*. Chicago: University of Chicago Press.

Rao, H. K. Krishna (1986) *Psychology of Music*. Delhi: Sh. Ganjendra Singh.

Sambamoorthy, P. (1985) *The Teaching of Music*. Madras: Indian Music Publishing House.

Shankar, R. (1968) *My Music, My Life*. New Delhi: Vikas.

Sharma, M. (1995) *Music Education: New Horizons*. Delhi: Nirmal.

Wade, B. (1979) *Music in India: The Classical Traditions*. New Jersey: Prentice-Hall.

Widdess, R. (1995) *The Ragas of Early Indian Music*. Oxford: Clarendon Press.

Italy

Johannella Tafuri

Aims and objectives

Models of music education

The great musical tradition which developed in Italy in composition
and performance after the Renaissance did not give rise to similar
developments in the field of music education. The conservatoire was
born in Italy in the fourteenth century with the aim of preserving
(*conservare*) orphans and poor children from poverty, and teaching them
arts and crafts, including music. However, it quickly became an
institution specializing in teaching music. From the beginning, the
conservatoire was an institution where people might learn the 'trade' of
musician. Acquiring more prestige in the seventeenth and eighteenth
centuries, by offering courses in singing, composition, string and wind
instruments, conservatoires became very famous throughout Europe
and they were imitated by other institutions that retained the same
name and the same function of training professional musicians.

Yet the idea of a general music education for all did not exist. People
listened to music typically through public performances, particularly in
churches and theatres. In the nineteenth century and the beginning of
the twentieth, Italian musical culture was based mainly on opera, which
was very popular and familiar to the people. As music was becoming
more complex, stylistically varied (with the diffusion of German
symphonic music) and was developing different tendencies, the novelty
of musical form and structure meant that the masses found it
increasingly difficult to understand the new repertoires.

The first introduction of some kind of musical activity in Italian school was in the reform of 1888, which saw the introduction of 'choral singing exercises'. In the first years of the twentieth century, two of the most famous Italian pedagogists considered musical and rhythmic activity, namely Rosa Agazzi (1908 and 1911, in Tamburini, 1993) and, mainly, Maria Montessori (1916), who suggested in the programmes of her famous 'children's houses', activities such as singing, ear training (given the importance of sensorial education in her method), rhythmic-motor activity and use of percussion instruments. Nevertheless, the governmental syllabus remained limited to singing for many years, sometimes in addition to theoretical elements (cf. the reform of 1923) where the concept of singing (called 'choral singing') hovered between an educational and recreational role (Tafuri, 1994). One of the reasons for this lay in the conviction that musical studies were necessary only for professional musicians and that they should be taught only in the conservatoire. Another reason concerned the position of philosophical and literary culture at the time: as opera was the predominant musical form, it was considered a 'popular' product and, therefore, on a lower level than other cultural forms.

In his 1923 educational reform, one of the most authoritative philosophers, Giovanni Gentile, attached great importance to literature, philosophy and the figurative arts, but not to music. This situation developed in the context of general and political indifference. The only intervention of the Fascist government was the imposition in schools of a national songbook containing religious and patriotic songs possessing 'educational power' and 'political value'. It was only with the big educational reform of 1962 that the development of the concept of 'music education for all' began, in conjunction with the increasing specialization of performers and a renewal in composition. Nowadays a broad provision of music education is available in Italy at all levels, in different situations and using various models of the teaching–learning process.

Each model derives from a different theoretical conception of the process. We know that learning has been defined in different ways according to the chosen theoretical point of view, e.g. behaviourism, Gestaltism, functionalism, cognitivism etc. (Hilgard and Bower, 1975), but there is general agreement that it constitutes an acquired and relatively stable modification of behaviour. Also, according to Italian pedagogy, it is, first of all, a spontaneous, natural process related both to biological/physiological and cultural factors; for example, learning how to avoid fire, to speak native language etc. (Laporta, 1993). It is also a process organized by a society in order to 'transmit' specific abilities (reading and writing) or, more generally, the transmission of a cultural heritage (Bertolini, 1990). After learning something, the person is not the same, since he/she changes his/her own behaviour (Ballanti, 1988). For this reason learning is normally considered an individual process. We can, of course, learn through different methods and in varying situations. Here we are interested in dealing with the educational situation, that is when teaching and learning interact reciprocally in order to produce behavioural modifications.

Efficacious education also depends on the interaction between other factors such as motivation, a system of values conducive to learning and an appropriate cultural context in which education can take place. The latest Italian pedagogical theories stress that the essence of the teaching–learning process is the relationship between people (normally two, e.g. teacher and pupil) with respect to a particular content (e.g. music) in a more or less planned situation (e.g. a classroom lesson). Teachers have realized over recent years that any methodology of the process should have four basic components: (a) the interaction between two types of behaviour – on the one hand, *teaching*, as the ensemble of the behavioural interventions of a person that provokes learning in others and, on the other hand, *learning*, as the ensemble of behavioural modifications produced by teaching (Ballanti, 1988); (b) the protagonists of this relationship – namely teachers and students – their identity, their needs and interests, their competence, their role in this process (Demetrio, 1994; Ferrari, 1994); the term 'competence' is used in the Italian debate to refer to knowing, knowing how to do, knowing how to communicate (Stefani, 1982); (c) the context in which the relationship develops, namely the educational community and the particular disciplinary field (Albarea 1994); and (d) the objectives, contents, methods and evaluative processes of the educational situation (Della Casa, 1985).

In order to have a better understanding of Italian musical learning and development, a brief specification of certain Italian terms could be useful. Three key words are used in Italian pedagogical discussions, namely *educazione*, *istruzione*, and *formazione*. The first and the second terms correspond substantially to the English word 'education'. *Educazione* refers to the transmission of cultural contents and value systems that occurs either during the teaching process or outside of it (e.g. in the family). It is oriented to the development of people as human and social beings. *Istruzione* refers to the aims and contents of teaching in the sense of concepts and skills, of attainment targets in a particular disciplinary field. *Formazione*, which is closer in meaning to the English word 'training', is a wider term that describes the process that leads to the acquisition of either professional skills or cultural models.

In the field of Italian music education, the first two terms are usually used to differentiate two aspects of musical learning: *istruzione musicale* is strictly oriented to the acquisition of the skills of reading and performing music with one instrument (or composing or conducting). *Educazione musicale* is more open to the development of various skills (performing, composing, singing etc.) but at a less demanding level. Within this division we can recognize the existence of two different models of the teaching–learning process. On the one hand we find models that stress objective goals, concerning technical and interpretative abilities, that must be reached irrespective of the actual ability of the individual student. On the other hand we find models that aim to develop students as unique individuals who acquire certain skills according to their individual needs and possibilities. In other words, we could say that these models are music-centred and student-centred respectively. We now examine where these models are found within the Italian system.

Musical learning and development can occur in the conservatoire, where students can start at eleven years old (or later) and finish at 18–20 years or older, according to their chosen career. It is considered a specialist education, oriented towards a particular musical profession (e.g. performer, composer, conductor). It is very demanding and competitive, and strongly oriented toward technical and interpretative goals. In a word, it is music-centred.

Alternatively, musical learning and development can occur in the general school system, where the general aims of music education are based more on the need to develop the student as a musical person enjoying music, who can express him/herself through music. Such an approach is more open and less demanding. It is a student-centred music education, and the expression *educazione musicale* in Italy is commonly taken to mean the type of music taught in general school. When music education started to take shape in Italy following the Second World War, the first learning objectives involved singing, theory and history. However, by 1962, and even more by the 1970s and 1980s, music education became an autonomous discipline aimed at giving all students the opportunity to develop their own musical potential (through exercising imagination, creativity and critical thinking) and the ability to express themselves through music (Decreto Ministeriale, 9/2/79). In other words, music education in general schools aims to produce students who can consciously use, and are critically aware of, musical products: this gives them the competence necessary to become an autonomous and critical 'enjoyer' of musical culture.

In summary, music-centred courses, such as those found in conservatoires, aim to maximize production abilities such as performance, composition and conducting. Student-centred courses, such as those found in general music education, are less demanding and place more emphasis on students' needs, interests and potential.

Learning objectives

Various Italian theories (e.g. Della Casa, 1985; Ferrari, 1991; Stefani, 1982; Tafuri, 1987, 1995) have produced a general consensus about the role of 'understanding' and 'producing' as the main objectives for music education in general schools. In order to have a better understanding of Italian classroom music education, a brief specification of the fields of activity is useful.

The objective of 'knowing how to understand' is considered as the ability to 'interpret' music. Unlike other countries, the importance of the interpretation of music as a means of developing the more general objective of 'understanding' has received considerable support in Italy since the 1970s (see, for example, Stefani, 1976; Baroni, 1978). In these studies 'interpretation' is the activity in which people grasp the meanings, functions, contexts and styles of a particular piece of music, and then discover, through analysis and semantic correlations (even at a very elementary level), the musical structures that gave rise to them. Interpretation is not viewed simply as a process of decoding structured data: rather it is intended as a creative act that can depend on the relationship between the identity, culture, values and ideology of the listener and those of the composer. In fact, to interpret a piece of music the listener needs to possess some background knowledge (even as little as that possessed by three-year-old children), which, of course, develops with age, familiarity and education.

'Knowing how to produce' (i.e. improvising, composing and performing) is the ability to organize sound material, to create sound objects by improvising, and to work out musical products for the realization of various goals (e.g. expression, communication etc.). Knowing how to produce also involves performance skills, such as mastering voice and instruments.

'Knowing how to perceive' helps understanding and producing. It means a sharpening of perceptive capacities in terms of discriminating, analysing, comparing, recognizing and memorizing the various elements which constitute music (e.g. pitch, duration, texture, structure, form etc.). This sort of musical competence is not only acquired at school but also during the course of everyday life (e.g. through music on TV), and even pre-birth (since the ear is known to function from the sixth month of prenatal life). Teachers have to take into account the competences already acquired by students through these experiences.

These three aims are not intended to be achieved progressively, one after the other, but in a circular manner: the first songs invented by children aged 1–2 years manifest and develop compositional and, at the same time, perceptual ability. In the same way, listening to some songs develops interpretative and perceptual abilities. When someone is producing a piece of music, he/she invents, is interpreting what he/she is producing, and is analysing the result in order to improve it. This means that the three abilities are related to and reinforce one other. In summary, the general objectives of Italian music education are essentially the ability to understand and to produce music. Underlying both of these, although not an educational objective in itself, is, of course, the ability to perceive music.

The Italian national curricula for different levels of schooling (i.e. kindergarten, primary, lower-secondary and upper-secondary) were prepared and approved in different periods. For kindergarten, the 1990 governmental guidelines (*Orientamenti delle attività educative per la scuola materna statale*, 1990) suggest that teachers should develop the musical sensitivity of children, promote listening to music and stimulate and support individual musical activity. The use of movement as the most important means of experiencing music is strongly recommended. The objectives of music education at this level are exploring, producing and listening to music.

The official 1985 guidelines for primary-school music education (Decreto Ministeriale 12/2/1985) consider music as a language which provides children with a means of communicating and expressing themselves. This resulted from the shift that occurred in the late 1960s away from the notion of music as an object for aesthetic contemplation and toward the notion of music as language instead. Consistent with this approach to music, the main objectives at primary level are to foster the ability to understand, produce and perceive different sound languages in terms of their own communicative and expressive components. The use of the voice and singing are particularly important at this level, as is a knowledge of the repertoires of different cultures and of different styles and their functions (e.g. music for theatre, for dance and for cinema). Composition also begins at this stage, with the first attempts to write music with invented signs and, later, some knowledge of musical notation. Performance is a little neglected.

The guidelines for lower-secondary-school music education are the oldest, dating from 1979 (Decreto Ministeriale, 9/2/79). As with primary education, there is an emphasis on music as language, such that the aim of music education at lower-secondary level is to promote the ability of pre-adolescents to communicate and to express themselves.

The objectives are: ear training to sharpen perceptive abilities (recognizing, memorizing rhythms, melodies, instruments etc.), listening, composing and performing. Traditional music notation is also included. There is also a lower-secondary school oriented to musical studies (*Scuola media a indirizzo musicale*) where learning to play a musical instrument, reading music and ensemble music are part of the curriculum.

Upon completion of compulsory schooling (at 14 years of age), there are many different upper-secondary schools with different names according to their orientation: scientific, humanistic, pedagogical, technical etc., with only a few institutions teaching musical subjects. Since 1991, the policy at this educational level has been to emphasize an understanding of music in its variety of forms – students' aesthetic experiences; active participation in musical experiences; and the connection between music and society. Understanding, composing and performing are the three objectives, with particular attention being paid to the relationship between music and other cultural manifestations, such as dance, theatre, poetry, painting, cinema and science. Unfortunately, this subject can be found only in 'pedagogical' secondary schools and, as an option, in 'humanistic' secondary schools.

As noted above, the principal organization for more specialist musical learning is the conservatoire, the guidelines for which date back to 1930 (Regio Decreto, 11/12/30). Students have to choose one instrument, composition or conducting as their principal subject, studied for a specified number of years (with violin lasting ten years, composing ten years, singing five years, flute seven years, etc.). Throughout this period, students must also take other subjects such as reading, orchestra, history of music etc. The main objective of conservatoire education is for students to perform the required repertoire to the highest possible level. The heavy emphasis on technical, performance-based issues leads, however, to the neglect of communicational aspects of music (such as the role of music as a cultural product which conveys moods, systems of values, views of the world etc.) and of other topics such as the psychology of music, analysis and theory.

There are also many private music schools in Italy, often run by local municipalities. Some of these schools, the *Istituto Musicale Pareggiato*, normally try to follow the model of the Conservatoire, but others are more flexible in their objectives, contents and methods. In December 1999 a reform of the conservatoire was approved that transformed all the conservatoires and the *Istituti Musicali Pareggiati* into *Istituti Superiori di Studi Musicali*. They are to be supervised by the ministry of the university, but are not actually considered to be university level. In these new *Istituti Superiori* only the last cycle of studies will take place. The new organization and the new programmes are not yet ready (2000), although course materials are expected to be issued shortly.

In the universities, musical studies are only theoretical, and do not include performance. Some Faculties of Humanities within Italian universities have begun to offer a course in musical studies that includes subjects such as history of music, ethnomusicology, music analysis, semiology of music, etc. On completion of this course a degree in Disciplines of Art, Music and Performing Arts (DAMS), music section, is awarded. One university also specializes in musical paleography and philological studies. According to the reform approved on 4 August 2000, in the Italian University students receive a degree after three years (instead of four, the present length of the majority of university courses) and a further degree of specialization after a further two years study. Another type of vocational course has also been born recently: in some faculties of *conservazione dei beni culturali*, and sometimes in faculties of humanities, there are now courses, oriented toward the *conservazione dei beni musicali*, that include subjects such as musical iconography, musical informatic archives, acoustics, etc. Furthermore, many university faculties of humanities offer history of music as an optional subject for non-musician students, and four universities offer a doctorate in music lasting three to four years.

This educational system highlights another characteristic of Italian culture and mentality: the importance attributed to *knowing*, in the sense of theoretical knowledge. The distinction between theory and practice, theoretical and practical studies (*knowing* and *knowing how to do*), has remote historical roots and has produced, after several centuries, the two different institutions that we have just considered: the university and the conservatoire. In summary, we can say that learning music at an Italian university means studying theoretical disciplines (history, philosophy, analysis, theory etc.), while in the conservatoire it means studying practical disciplines (e.g. playing, composing, conducting) together with a little history and theory.

The training of music teachers for general schools happens in different places, depending on the type of school at which they intend to practise. The training of teachers for primary schools takes place (since 1998) in the university on the *corso di laurea in scienze della formazione primaria*, which is taught within faculties of education. Training in the methodology of music education lasts one or two semesters, according to the decision of each university.

Teachers of music in secondary schools (lower and upper) need to have gained a diploma in a conservatoire or a university degree in music. Many conservatoires offer a course on *didattica della musica* that lasts four years and includes five subjects, namely pedagogy of music, history of music, choir conducting, composition and piano sight-reading. All the subjects are oriented toward music teaching, primarily in general schools and also in music schools and conservatoires. A recent law also dictates that teachers of all subjects in secondary school have to gain the *diploma di specializzazione* after completing university (or the conservatoire). In this new course students have to study sciences of education in general terms, and the disciplinary didactics of their own specialization: music is one of them. In 1999–2000, some universities are starting to organize this specialization school, which lasts two years.

Contents and methods

Music or musics?

Musical learning and development do not occur in a vacuum; rather, they occur in a specific cultural context that embodies particular social practices. For example, the development of tonal knowledge occurs through exposure to a culture of tonal music. The definition of and choice of content for music education raises many problems, including the definition of the concept of the subject (i.e. What is music?), and the amount of attention paid to students' needs, interests and competences. We have said that the main objectives of Italian music education are knowing how to understand and to produce. Now we need to specify further: understanding and producing what? Music, certainly, but in what sense? The symphonies of Beethoven or the eskimo play of *katajjaq*? The *Sequenze* by Berio or compositions made by children with stones and drums? Ethnomusicologists have been arguing for many years that the notion of what constitutes music varies according to eras, races, cultures and even the age of people. The position assumed by teachers towards the notion of what constitutes 'music' will influence their choice of contents. In the Italian conservatoire, 'music' is essentially the traditional classical heritage, even if nowadays there is increasing interest in jazz, electronic and contemporary music.

A wider perspective is adopted by general school music education, with Italian teachers being more open to the use of a wide variety of repertoires drawn from a range of cultures and historical periods. An ostinato can be discovered in a lied by Schubert (*Erlkönig*), in a song by Sting ('We work the black seam together') or in music from the Burundi; the relationship between certain emotions and particular structural patterns can be pointed out by listening to the Preludio from Verdi's *Macbeth*, to a song by the Beatles, to *Lux Aeterna* by Ligeti or to music from the Solomon Islands. Nevertheless, the resistance to repertoires, other than western classical music, persists in some Italian teachers as a consequence of having studied in the conservatoire.

We have, so far, considered the content of Italian music education in the sense of repertoires. but the content of learning also includes musical structures and theory. Italian music education considers structural aspects such as morphology, rhythm and melodic and harmonic syntax; semantic and pragmatic aspects; and historical and anthropological features. It is worth noting that the precise nature of these contents varies between different repertoires. For example, the key structures of western classical music are not the same as for popular or ethnic music. The concept and the shapes of melody can be learnt by listening to Beethoven or Schubert, but these might well be different from those learnt by listening to rock or rap. The use of different repertoires, therefore, enlarges the number of musical concepts in which Italian students can become competent.

Another criterion determining the choice of contents for music education is the amount of attention paid to the needs, interests and existing competences of students, even the little competence already possessed by children aged 3 to 4. It is easy to guess that the favoured repertoire of Italian students from the age of 9 or 10 years is popular music (Ferrini and Burzacchini, 1996). Pop music provides more complex experiences than the simple act of music listening because the musical medium conveys models of interpretation of the world, value systems, ideologies, knowledge and beliefs. It is therefore not surprising that an Italian study of the musical taste of young people aged 11–14 showed that adolescents have a symbolic investment in popular music and demonstrate disregard, and even contempt, towards classical music ('the music of adults'), in addition to ignorance of ethnic music (Baroni and Nanni, 1989). Findings and arguments such as these are difficult to ignore, given that learning is more effective when it occurs at a cognitive and emotional level, and, indeed, popular music has been given increasing prominence in Italian school-music education.

A different problem is represented by the ethnic repertoire. First, it is true that Italy possesses very rich and beautiful musical traditions. However, these are studied only by university academics: ethnomusicology does not exist in the conservatoire. Moreover, ethnic music concerts are not well publicized. Secondly, Italy is becoming a multi-ethnic society: almost all primary schools have pupils from outside the European Community. It is therefore clear that the amount of attention paid to non-western music is increasing. Teachers cannot limit their activity just to teaching a small number of songs from other cultures: some teachers have already started to realize specific projects through which students can share different musical cultures, and use these to discover different systems of values and views of the world (Facci, 1997). Music education can provide an ideal place for contact and cohabitation between different cultures.

Teaching strategies

In addition to the more policy-oriented issues discussed in the previous section, operational procedures and strategies are also required to put teaching/learning into action. These procedures and strategies can vary according to the concrete objectives and contents of each lesson. By analysing different methods used in teaching practice, we can identify three general courses of action. These are not teaching methods in the strict sense, but should instead be considered as three orientations in which certain types of behaviour can be more or less accentuated (Della Casa, 1985). They are:

1. the transmissive-training method: teachers transmit information and students learn by repetition; this is a unidirectional process;
2. the euristic-guided method: this is bi directional in that the teacher proposes, guides and provides learning tools while students acquire practical and conceptual abilities through discussion and problem-solving; and
3. the spontaneous activism method: the teacher observes or moderates while students act as they will.

The transmissive-training method accentuates the content of learning (e.g. this or that particular rhythm has to be learnt by students); the euristic-guided method emphasizes the role of students in the learning process (e.g. if students are interested in learning rhythms, how could they best learn this one or that?); the spontaneous activism method puts the emphasis more completely on the students alone (e.g. leave the students to learn what they wish about rhythm). If the content is a certain rhythm, the teacher applying the first method presents this rhythm by performing it (with voice or hands), writes it on the blackboard, explains the mathematical relationships (double and half) and asks children to repeat it several times. Teachers using the second method ask students to sing a familiar song incorporating this rhythm and, through performing (clapping hands or walking) and confrontation activities, ask students to analyse it in order to perceive the relationship between sounds. In this way the teacher guides students toward sensorimotor and conceptual awareness. Then children are requested to listen to different musics (either pop and classical) in order to identify and repeat that rhythm (e.g. by clapping their hands or walking in time). Teachers using the third method leave students to choose the precise nature of the activity they perform, and when this or that rhythm appears they ask students to focus on and analyse it.

It is clear that the choice between these three methods can also be made according to the particular learning objective in question. In particular, the transmissive and spontaneous activism methods are chosen for some specific types of learning: teachers use the former when they teach a song, for example, or the latter when they ask students to explore the soundscape. It is also clear, however, that the most efficacious approach is likely to be the euristic-guided method because it provides direction while still respecting the autonomy of students in the learning process. The transmissive-training method was most widely used in Italy until some years ago. After studies, debates and seminars, however, many teachers nowadays often try to use the euristic-guided approach, since they are more convinced of the importance of actively involving students in the learning process.

It is worth noting that during the 1970s, research as a method of learning was used extensively in Italian schools, mostly in areas such as science, history and geography, but not in music. The aim was not to produce junior researchers but, instead, to orientate students towards scientific ways of thinking, given the general cognitive benefits that accrue from carrying out research in any area (e.g. the ability to acquire new knowledge in a systematic manner, improved cognitive functioning etc.). Unfortunately, after some years, this practice declined, simply because of teachers' lack of competence in issues of research methodology.

Before concluding this section, a word about three famous methods: Dalcroze, Orff and Kodály. Here the term 'method' is used in the sense of a systematic and organic set of procedures and repertoires oriented to the acquisition of specific musical skills. Comprehension of these three methods requires knowledge of their historical, musical and pedagogical context. Italian teachers do not normally use one of these methods taken in isolation. Instead, they prefer to use some aspects of each of these methods according to students' needs, their own programme and local conditions (since, for example, not many schools have Orff instruments or big classrooms that allow work on music and movement or dance).

After discussing several issues in Italian music education, we could conclude that in the last twenty years the situation of music education in general schools has improved from the point of view of research and quality of publications, and also from a legislative standpoint. In particular, the semantic aspect of music (i.e. emotions, sensorimotor images etc.) and its relationship with musical structures (rhythms, melodies, forms) is more developed in Italy than in many other countries. The field of creativity (i.e. composing and improvising) also receives a good degree of attention. Teacher-training is improving: we can identify an advanced group of teachers who are more innovative and well-trained; a majority who stay in the middle, between innovation and a more conservative approach; and a third group which is extremely resistant to change and innovation.

This is different to the situation of music education in professional schools, however, where the importance given to technical aspects produces a lack of a deeper knowledge about, and understanding of, music, and where improvisation is not yet considered necessary for a professional performer. The very recent reforms, and the interest demonstrated by a small, advanced group of teachers, allow us to hope.

References

Albarea, R. (1994) 'Pedagogia della musica: individuazione del campo, problemi e prospettive', in M. Piatti (ed.) *Pedagogia della musica: un panorama*. Bologna: CLUEB.

Ballanti, G. (1988) *Modelli di apprendimento e schemi di insegnamento*. Teramo: Giunti e Lisciani Editori.

Baroni, M. (1978) *Suoni e significat* (2nd edn). Torino: EDT.

Baroni, M. and Nanni, F. (1989) *Crescere con il rock*. Bologna: CLUEB.

Bertolini, P. (1990) *L'esistere pedagogico*. Firenze: La Nuova Italia.

Decreto Ministeriale (9/2/79) 'Nuovi programmi d'insegnamento nella Scuola Media'.

Decreto Ministeriale (12/2/85) 'Programmi didattici per la scuola primaria'.

Della Casa, M. (1985) *Educazione musicale e curricolo*. Bologna: Zanichelli.

Demetrio, D. (1994) 'La pedagogia come campo del sapere logico e narrativo nelle molteplici vie dell'educazione', in M. Piatti (ed.) *Pedagogia della musica: un panorama*. Bologna: CLUEB, pp. 95–112.

Facci, S. (1997) *Capre, flauti e re*. Torino: EDT.

Ferrari, F. (1991) 'Ascoltando', in C. Delfrati and J. Tafuri (eds) *Scoprire la musica*. Milano: Ricordi, pp. 78–100.

Ferrari, F. (1994) 'Ripartire dall'identità musicale', in M. Piatti (ed.) *Pedagogia della musica: un panorama*. Bologna: CLUEB, pp. 131–45.

Ferrini, M. and Burzacchini, E. (1996) 'Nascita e sviluppo dei gusti musicali'. *Musica Domani*, **99**, 19–22.

Hilgard, E. R. and Bower, G. H. (1975) *Theories of Learning*. Englewood Cliffs, NJ: Prentice-Hall.

Laporta, R. (1993) 'Natura e finalità dell'educazione', in A. Canevaro, G. Cives, F. Frabboni, E. Frauenfelder, R. Laporta, F. Pinto Minerva *Fondamenti di pedagogia e di didattica*. Roma-Bari: Laterza, pp. 5–41.

Montessori, M. (1916) *L'autoeducazione*. Milano: Garzanti (Loescher-Maglione and Strini, 1992).

'Orientamenti delle attività educative per la scuola materna statale' (1990).

Regio Decreto (11/12/30) Norme per l'Ordinamento dell'istruzione musicale ed approvazione dei nuovi programmi d'esame.

Stefani, G. (1976) *Introduzione alla semiotica della musica*. Palermo: Sellerio.

Stefani, G. (1982) *La competenza musicale*. Bologna: CLUEB.

Tafuri, J. (1987) 'L'ascolto musicale: problematiche e progetti', in C. Delfrati (ed.) *Esperienze d'ascolto nella scuola dell'obbligo*. Milano: Ricordi, pp. 9–32.

Tafuri, J. (1994) 'L'educazione musicale nei programmi della scuola italiana', in G. Grazioso (ed.) *L'educazione musicale tra passato presente e futuro*. Milano: Ricordi, pp. 10–35.

Tafuri, J. (1995) *L'educazione musicale: Teorie, metodi, pratiche*. Torino: EDT.

Tamburini, F. (1993) 'L'educazione musicale nell'esperienza agazziana'. *Cultura e Educazione*, 33–6.

CHAPTER

7

Japan

Tadahiro Murao and Bernadette Wilkins

Introduction

Japan is an island country in the Far East, surrounded by the Sea of Japan to the west and the Pacific Ocean to the east. This geographical position meant that science, arts and religions imported from the Asian mainland in the early centuries did not pass beyond Japan, but were cultivated to create an indigenous Japanese culture with a distinct identity. Japan has had few experiences of invasion by other countries, such that various aspects of Asian culture have been absorbed over the centuries without outside force. Japan has developed into a country of uniformity in which sameness, equality and interdependence are more important virtues than uniqueness, independence and individualization. The well-known 'group-oriented' behaviour of the Japanese originates from these virtues, and is evident in the education system. It dominates teachers as well as parents, even though the education system is based on European and American models.

In this chapter we will outline the present situation of music education in Japan. To put this into context, the history of the Course of Study (national curriculum) for music will be outlined and its philosophy, aims and objectives will be discussed. The chapter will also consider the role of traditional Japanese music and forms of music learning outside the classroom, such as karaoke, culture schools, the influence of the NHK (Japanese national broadcasting company) and private music schools.

The Course of Study (National Curriculum Standard)

After World War II, educational reforms took place which brought major changes to Japan's education system. A Course of Study was introduced into Japan from the USA and developed into a controlled national curriculum. In the monocultural society of Japan this was easily adopted and adapted. The Ministry of Education regulated the details of teaching content, materials and methods so that every Japanese student was required to learn the same subject knowledge, with a similar timetable and to an equal level. As a result, a high minimum standard of education developed in Japan.

The first provisional Course of Study, introduced in 1947, was a framework for school curricula with flexible guidelines, and was not strictly controlled. In 1958, however, the third Course of Study became the first official mandatory and standardized National Curriculum Standard. Within this 1958 version, one of the stated objectives was 'to cultivate the fertile mind in children's daily life through musical experiences': the aim of music education was seen in terms of the importance of the arts for human development, rather than only for the arts in their own right. Since the fifth version of the National Curriculum in 1977, which became the third official Course of Study, the Ministry of Education has continued to liberalize its contents. In the latest version (1998) there is less regulation of teaching materials, contents and evaluation.

Philosophy of education in Japan after World War II

After World War II, Japanese music educators needed to re-evaluate their fundamental philosophy. It was clear that the ultra-nationalistic view of prewar music education, which was primarily a means of promoting patriotism, morality or allegiance, needed to be changed. The dilemma for school music educators was whether they should 'teach music to students' or rather 'educate students through music'. This has been a fundamental question since the days of the ancient Greeks, and it fell to Saburo Moroi, a distinguished Japanese composer, to suggest a way forward with respect to the role of music in the first Course of Study in 1947. His conclusion, which is stated in this first Course, was that the aim of music education is: 'to understand and appreciate the beauty of music as an art so that children might elevate '*joso*' (aesthetic and moral sentiments) and cultivate a fertile mind'.

The idea that music education should be 'joso' education is unchanged to this day, although this does not mean that music is only taught in order to elevate one's aesthetic and moral sentiments. Music is an art, and as such should not only be a means to an end but also an aim in itself. That music education should be 'joso' education means, therefore, that teaching music for its own sake also results in the elevation of one's aesthetic and moral sentiments.

This view of music education is close to the view of aesthetic education that was developed by Reimer, in his book *A Philosophy of Music Education* (1970, p. 25):

> The nature and value of the art of music education are determined by the nature and value of the art of music. One can share the insights of art not by going outside of art to non-artistic references, *but by going deeper into the aesthetic qualities the art work contains*. The most important role of music education as aesthetic education is to help children become progressively more sensitive to the elements of music which contain the conditions which can yield insights into human feeling.

This philosophy lays emphasis on the significance of music understanding and appreciation rather than on performance and composition. Moroi, on the other hand, hardly mentions the significance of appreciation. His concern was to change a curriculum based on singing to a broader music education that covered aspects such as instruments, composition, appreciation and theory, as well as singing. In this respect, Moroi and Reimer diverge: however, both regard the nature and value of music education as the nature and the value of music as an art. In other words, they dispute the view of music education as serving the practical value of human life. It is worth pointing out that Moroi's statement in the Course of Study appeared over 20 years before the publication of Reimer's book, during which time Japanese music education had been based on this principle.

Aims and objectives in the present version of the Course of Study

In December 1998, the Japanese Ministry of Education, Science, Sports and Culture published the new National Curriculum Standard which is to start in 2002. The revised general objective of music education reads as follows (direct translation from Japanese to English): 'To cultivate the children's inclination for music, elevate their musical sensitivity and develop their musicality and fertile aesthetic sentiments through performing and appreciation.' These objectives are explained more clearly in English on the Ministry's internet home page, as follows:

MUSIC, ARTS (MUSIC)

a. Music classes will emphasise that children enjoy music, find pleasure in musical activities and have a mind to appreciate music throughout their lives.

b. Activities of self-expression and music appreciation will be improved in order for students to deepen their interests and understanding of the music culture in Japan as well as those in foreign countries. Additionally, the instruction of the national anthem '*Kimigayo*' will be enhanced.

These objectives are clearly different from the statement, 'An art should not be a means but an aim in itself', from the first Course of Study. The latest objectives are closer to the recent philosophy of 'praxial music education', which has been elaborated by Elliott (1995) and Regelski (1997), than to the philosophy of aesthetic education. However, Moroi's basic spirit still remains in these objectives in the sense that music education is not seen as a means of communicating political or ideological doctrines.

Music teaching in the classroom

After the School Education Law of 1947, a new school system was established which reflected the orientation of the USA both in teaching methods and curriculum. Six years of elementary and three years of lower-secondary (junior-high) school became mandatory for every child from age 6 to 15, with school textbooks given free to every child during these nine years. Music in the elementary and lower-secondary school in Japan is known as 'general music' and includes various activities such as appreciation, composing, performing and theoretical study in various styles. General music is compulsory but band, orchestra and chorus are extra-curricular club activities.

In the elementary curriculum, pupils are currently required to study 68 standard school units of music per year in grade 1 and 70 in grades 2–6. Each unit represents two 45-minute music classes a week, and this requirement has not changed since the first Course of Study started in 1947. As from 2002, however, pupils will spend less time in music lessons at all levels. The elementary school grades 1–6 will study 68, 70, 60, 60, 50 and 50 units respectively, and the lower-secondary school grades will study 45, 35 and 35 units in grades 7, 8 and 9 respectively. By 2002, all Saturday classes will also have stopped, and music in the high school will become an elective subject which is more likely to be part of an integrated arts programme.

The National Curriculum Standard prescribes teaching content and materials in every grade: every music textbook authorized by the Ministry of Education, Science, Sports and Culture must follow this content and materials as standard. Figure 7.1 shows, as an example, the detailed contents and materials that are specified for the fifth grade by the current National Curriculum Standard, which was proposed in 1989 and implemented in 1992.

Teaching contents and materials in the fifth grade

A. Self-expression (singing, instruments, composing/improvising):
1. Singing and playing instruments by model performance and sight-reading:
   (a) singing and playing the instruments by model performance.
   (b) singing and playing the instruments by sight-reading of the melody noted in F major.
2. Expressive performance:
   (a) devising the expressive performance through understanding the musical structure and the meaning of the song words.
   (b) musical performance and body expression responding to the change of tempo and dynamics through feeling and the ongoing beat and phrase structure.
   (c) chorus and instrumental ensemble relishing the texture and harmony.
3. Performance skill:
   (a) singing with head voice carefully controlled by good breath and pronunciation.
   (b) playing percussion and melody instruments based on the characteristic timbre of these instruments.
4. Composing pieces and playing (improvising upon) these:
   (a) devising the texture and structure, and composing.
   (b) composing pieces with freedom from stylistic constraints and improvising upon them.
5. Understanding the following music symbols in music notation:

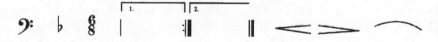

6. Teaching materials:
   (a) singing materials must be around 11 pieces that include unison, canon, two-part and three-part choruses.
   (b) Instrumental ensemble materials must be around three pieces that have main melody with harmony and rhythmic percussion.
   (c) singing materials must include the following pieces as 'common singing materials'. 'Koinobori' (a carp streamer), 'Lullaby' (a Japanese traditional song), 'A Song of Skiing, Fuyugeshiki' (winter scenery).

B. Appreciation (listening):
    Appreciation materials must be around six pieces including three 'common appreciation materials'.
    (a) variety of styles of music, which includes local traditional music and artistic lieder.
    (b) variety of performance styles of music which includes vocal solo and chorus.
    (c) characteristic pieces in timbre and sound so that children might deepen the joy of listening.
    (d) appreciation materials must include the following pieces as 'common listening materials':
         Kobiki Uta for Orchestra, by Kiyosige Koyama; one of three songs by Rentaro Taki – 'Kojo no Tuki', 'Hakone Hachiri' or 'Hana'; Piano Quintet ('Trout') by F. Schubert (fourth movement).

Figure 7.1

We can see from this that every detail, including the number of teaching materials, the names of the songs to be learnt and even the names of musical symbols which children must learn in a given year are all regulated. The contents, in general, are conservative and oriented towards western music. However, one relatively recent innovation is the introduction of what might be called 'free composition', 'creative music making' or 'sound composition'. Although Paynter and Aston's (1970) book *Sound and Silence* was translated into Japanese in 1982, music educators were not very concerned with it at that time.

Since the National Curriculum Standard reforms in 1989, in-service workshops sponsored by the government, city offices and private organizations have been carried out all over Japan. In addition to these workshops, many introductory books on 'creative music making' or 'sound composition' have been published. As a result, music education practice has changed drastically in the 1990s, especially in elementary schools. The heavy emphasis on class choral singing has meant that the change is not so extreme in the elementary schools, so that the most rapid changes have been in lower- and upper-secondary schools.

According to the new National Curriculum Standard Reform, due to start in 2002, all teaching contents have been liberalized, except for the specification of common singing materials in elementary school. The Ministry of Education, Science, Sports and Culture's website explains this liberalization, in English, as follows:

Plenty of time will be allocated to the flexible instruction suitable to the actual situations of individual community, school and children.

For example, children will be allowed to choose the contents they wish to learn and the teaching contents for two school years will be shown together.

In principle, common teaching materials for appreciation will not be shown in order for individual elementary and lower-secondary schools to develop various music activities suitable to the actual situation of individual community and school, and only advice on choosing materials will be given. Elementary school's teaching materials for singing will be chosen among the songs recommended by the Ministry of Education since people have loved them for many years. At lower-secondary school, advice on choosing materials will be given but specific pieces will not be shown.

The significance of this latest reform lies not only in its liberalization of the curriculum content, but also in that all lower-secondary students will be required to learn Japanese traditional instruments. In the new National Curriculum Standard, music educators are required to teach various vocalizations, not only use of the 'head voice', and also instrumental techniques from traditional Japanese and other non-western music. In previous National Curriculum Standards, these were included as appreciation materials, which could be taught by teachers who could not sing or play non-western instruments. The new requirement for playing and teaching traditional instruments will have a strong impact on music educators, especially at lower-secondary school.

Another significant feature of the new National Curriculum Standard Reform is that a 'period of integrated study' has been newly established. Although the teaching content is not prescribed, examples are given, and each school can select the teaching content according to their situation. Music educators are expected to teach 'integrated study' through traditional Japanese music, computer music and multimedia arts, soundscape, design and so forth. In fact, music is not seen as an independent art form but as deeply rooted in literature (story), dance, *Kabuki* and *Noh* drama, religious ceremonies, as well as in the daily life of society. Traditional music itself is therefore a subject of 'integrated study'. This extension of the curriculum means that lower-secondary school music teachers can no longer confine themselves to the role of classroom chorus (choir) director.

Teaching traditional Japanese music in the classroom

In the first Course of Study there was little room for traditional Japanese music: it was not until the third Course of Study, in 1958, that this was included on the list of 'common teaching materials' issued to teachers. Although a major leap forward, the appreciation materials included only five compositions of traditional Japanese music in the whole nine-year curriculum. The fourth National Curriculum Standard, in 1968, put more emphasis on the teaching of traditional Japanese music in lower-secondary schools. Children's folk songs (traditional game songs) became compulsory, and more traditional Japanese compositions were added to the listening appreciation list.

At this time the Kodály and Orff systems were introduced into Japan. Both systems use principles of systematic learning based on the music of the mother tongue. This development brought about the so-called *warabeuta* (Japanese children's folk song) boom in Japan (Murao, 1985). Amongst other parties, teachers' unions showed enthusiasm for creating teaching materials based on Japanese traditional nursery rhymes and folk songs. In 1977, however, a policy change designed to increase flexibility saw the number of Japanese pieces reduce in the fifth National Curriculum Standard. Music teachers showed little interest in traditional music and, instead, concentrated on classroom chorus singing. The present Standard states that Japanese music should be studied as much as the situation allows: the new National Curriculum Standard Reform (1998) deregulates appreciation materials but states that, from 2002, all junior high school students must learn to play a traditional Japanese instrument.

Japanese music education has been oriented towards western music ever since the National Institution of Music Research was established in 1879. Although its main purpose was 'to compose and compile children's songs suitable for school use which were to fuse Western and Eastern musical elements' (Izawa, 1884), the problem was how best to fuse western and eastern music. Comparative musicology (ethnomusicology) was very undeveloped in Japan at that time, and any attempts at such a fusion were unsuccessful. It was Japanese children themselves who found the most natural way of mixing western tonal melodies and Japanese children's game song melodies.

Traditional Japanese children's melody is considered to be based on 'hypo-re penta mode', which can be explained in terms of Koizumi's revised 'tetrachord theory' (see Tokawa, 1992). 'Chatumi' is one of the common teaching materials in elementary schools which music educators regard as representing western tonal music. However, when Japanese children use this in traditional play songs (clapping-hand games), it takes on a Japanese rather than western character. Figure 7.2 shows a song of 'Chatumi' based on a two-bar melody.

Figure 7.3 shows a melody, 'Hide-and-Seek', which was written by

Figure 7.2

Figure 7.3

the distinguished Japanese composer Yoshinao Nakata. He composed it using the same principles of fusion that Japanese children discovered for themselves. Note that the tonic (ending tone) fluctuates between re (A) and do (G), which is quite natural for the Japanese, who are familiar with both Japanese and western tonal schemata.

Though 'Hide-and-Seek' is a particularly successful example of fused music, most singing materials composed by Japanese musicians are recognizably Japanese. Murao (1987) analysed singing materials composed by Japanese musicians using information theory and found that the descending pattern re-do-la or la-so-mi has the highest probability of occurrence within these melodies: this coincides with the frequency of melodic patterns found in traditional children's music. Japanese children seem to develop both western and Japanese tonal schemes simultaneously and without confusing the two.

Music and learning outside the classroom

Suzuki and Yamaha music schools

Suzuki schools are not a part of the state system in Japan. The Suzuki 'whole-child' approach was originally devised for very young children, and had an emphasis on thorough learning, memory training, repetition, good posture and movement patterns. Suzuki (1969) believed that 'musicality is a human aptitude which can be nurtured from birth'. His method is rooted in Japanese culture in that it emphasizes teaching traditions, family structure and rote learning.

The Yamaha Corporation established a Music Foundation in Japan, in 1966, in order to promote music education and to teach customers how to use the products they had bought. The Yamaha Music Education system has developed into various courses for children aged 4 and upwards, and for adults, and emphasizes the importance of pitch and singing. These courses require a parent to be an 'at home learning partner' and the idea is to create happy and rewarding early musical experiences. Children learn keyboard skills, music reading, musical sensibility, self-expression, performance skills, improvisation, singing and ensemble skills in classes taught once a week in groups. They learn not only how to play instruments but also how to study music and to achieve expression through music. The keyboard course offers ensemble playing, 'fingerobics' (special exercises that develop finger dexterity) and piano playing in many different styles. The Yamaha philosophy promotes the concept that 'music knows no national boundaries' and has spread worldwide.

The number of elementary and junior high school students receiving private music lessons out of school is increasing, especially in urban areas. In addition to private teachers and music schools, such as Yamaha and Suzuki, the Japanese national broadcasting company, NHK, provides an education channel for television and radio that exerts a strong influence on children's music. One example is the song 'Three Dango Brothers'. Broadcast for a nursery programme, this song's use of repetition, rhymes and a tango rhythm was so appealing that the CD single sold over three million copies.

Karaoke, traditional singing and gender in Japanese society

Karaoke – singing along to pre-recorded music – began in Japan and can today can be found in homes, schools, workplaces and many public spaces. The roots of karaoke can be traced back to the NHK's *Nodojiman* programme, an amateur singing contest with a history of 54 years of live public broadcasts involving 60,000 singers. Every Sunday, for 45 minutes, about twenty singers take part in each contest alongside two professional pop singers. The participants can be young or old, male or female, soloists, duets or groups. A winner is selected at every local contest, and 16 of the 47 local winners are invited to participate in the annual National Championship at the NHK Hall.

The most popular music programme in Japan, and now a national custom, is *Kouhaku Utagassen*, which translates as 'The Red and White Song Contest', but is given an English title, 'New Year's Eve Grand Song Festival'. It takes place every New Year's Eve and is a live national song festival lasting for three-and-a-half hours, featuring two teams of popular Japanese singers with 25 individuals or groups in each. The singers are chosen according to their level of musical activity in the past year, their popularity and their suitability for the theme of the current year's contest. They compete on performing skills and various other elements. To ensure a fair selection, the NHK Broadcasting Culture Research Institute conducts an annual, nationwide survey of the singers and songs that the general public wish to hear. The programme has been running for 45 years and, with a viewing rate of 50.7 per cent, is the most popular of all TV programmes. Many pop singers dream of appearing in this contest as it would establish their careers and reputations.

Since the late 1980s it has been noticeable in these contests that young Japanese women have been inclined to sing men's pop-song repertoire an octave lower than notated. This is because recent male vocal pop songs are pitched too low to be sung within the normal vocal range of young women. Young men have sung women's repertoire at the original pitch, although this is not so common (Murao, 1998; Kitayama *et al.*, 1999). This indicates that the difference between the singing range of men and women is getting smaller, almost to the point that they might sing at an identical pitch.

A similar phenomenon can be found in the singing style of Japanese traditional music: the men's singing range is close to the women's range. For example, the difference between the tuning of the *shamisen* (three-string banjo) accompaniment for men and women is around a major second or third. Accordingly, it is common for men and women to sing in the same key in teaching and learning sessions. The gender changes in pop singing may, therefore, be neither extraordinary nor abnormal, but may derive from the Japanese tradition, as Hirai (1995) suggests. The vocal range of the songs in Japanese music textbooks is within the limit of B♭3–E♭5 (Ogawa *et al.*, 1995), because young men's vocal range, typically, falls by one octave after their voice change. The relationship between these phenomena in pop, traditional and school music needs to be reconsidered.

Although we can see why the singing keys of young men and women are converging, it is more difficult to explain why this convergence is still increasing. One possible explanation is that the trait of 'masculinity' has virtually disappeared. Young men tend to wear colourful clothes and use the same cosmetics and perfume as women, such that we may be seeing the beginnings of a 'unisex society'. The closeness of the singing range in pop songs for men and women might reflect this shift of socio-cultural values.

Learning traditional music in 'culture schools'

Japanese traditional music is taught under the *iemoto* system, an extended apprenticeship system in which the head of the institution controls advancement and graduation. Each genre of traditional music, such as *nagauta* (lyrical songs with *shamisen* accompaniment), *kiyomoto* (the high, light singing of *kabuki*), *sokyoku* (koto music), *shakuhachi* (bamboo flute music) and *noh* (the oldest Japanese theatre music) is taught in many schools. The head family of each school has an apprentice school and uses its own teaching methods, although this traditional system is undergoing change as a result of current educational reforms.

A very popular new institution is the 'culture school' or 'culture centre', which is managed by major newspaper companies, TV companies, gas companies, city offices, churches and so on. These culture schools can be found in a variety of places where people congregate, such as department stores or other large city buildings. In residential districts, public houses, churches and temples provide similar community schools. Though some of the schools provide courses for small children, students are mostly adults – housewives, retired people and office workers. Courses are not popular among businessmen. Culture schools can be regarded as one of the providers of lifelong education.

It is interesting that Japanese traditional music classes are far more popular than western music classes in the culture schools. The Asahi Culture School, managed by the Asahi Newspaper Company, for example, provides most styles of Japanese traditional music such as *shakuhachi*, *noh* dance and singing, folklore *shamisen* and singing, *nagauta*, *kiyomoto*, *gidayu*, *shinnai* and so on. The tuition fees are relatively low and instructors of Japanese music teach students in groups rather than adopting the apprenticeship style. Most of the students learn Japanese music as a hobby, and so some of the instructors try to introduce staff notation into their teaching. Although the future success of these developments remains to be seen, there can be no doubt that the new school reforms are changing traditional teaching systems.

Conclusion

The new National Curriculum Standard, which was introduced in December 1998, included some important points of reform such as the liberalization of teaching contents, the new requirement to learn traditional Japanese instruments and the establishment of a period of integrated study. Music educators are likely to be reluctant to accept these for three reasons: first, because even the traditional Japanese music in the 'common appreciation materials' of the current National Curriculum Standard tends to be ignored by teachers; secondly, music teachers do not have the time to learn nor the skill to teach traditional Japanese instruments; and thirdly, music teachers are required to teach computer-assisted MIDI instruments, Asian and African music, popular music, creative music-making using contemporary compositional techniques, as well as traditional Japanese instruments, which is impossible in the decreasing amount of time allocated to music classes. There is little room for optimism about the positive impact of the new National Curriculum Standard Reform.

There are some grounds for optimism about the future of traditional Japanese music, however. Music educators who are poor at playing Japanese instruments often seek help from local volunteer teachers who are specialists in traditional music. In each school district there live quite a number of older people who, although not professional, are good at playing Japanese instruments and are willing to help children learn their local traditional music. School music teachers often learn Japanese instruments together with the children. Because Japanese schools are becoming more open to volunteer teachers, this approach to traditional music may grow in the near future.

Another significant development is that music industries are launching 'educational traditional Japanese instruments', which are inexpensive and accessible to the learner. Various computer-assisted instruments and sound sources have already been developed, which enable music teachers to become more involved in traditional Japanese music, Asian music, computer-assisted music and sound design, free composition/improvisation and integrated study, rather than being restricted to classroom chorus and recorder ensemble work.

Japanese music education is currently in the process of change. The pace of change has been slow so far, especially in lower-secondary schools, and may therefore not clearly be seen from outside. Over the next decade or so, however, Japanese music education may change beyond recognition.

References

Elliott, D. (1995) *Music Matters: A New Philosophy in Music Education*. Oxford: Oxford University Press.

Hirai, S. (1995) 'Singing voice of my mother, 90 years old' (in Japanese). *The Journal of Japanese Traditional Music*, **97**, 29–30.

Izawa, S. (1884) *Official Report of National Institution of Music*. Ongaku: Torshirabegakari.

Kitayama, A., Ogawa, Y. and Murao, T. (1999) 'On the unisex phenomenon of young people's singing voice'. *International Music Education Symposium on Children and Music: Developmental Perspectives*, University of Tasmania, pp. 160–2.

Murao, T. (1985) 'Two-stem system based on the tonal organisation of children's folk songs' (in Japanese). *Japanese Journal of Music Education Research*, **16**, 76–83.

Murao, T. (1987) 'Music analysis and cognition', in G. Hatano (ed.) *Music and Cognition*. Tokyo: Tokyo University Press, pp. 1–40.

Murao, T. (1998) 'Why is the singing voice of the Japanese young getting so high?' (in Japanese). *Aofuchi*, 40–3.

NHK (1999) *The Three Dango Brothers*. NHK website.

Ogawa, Y., Kitayama, A. and Murao, T. (1995) 'A comparative study of the range of children's textbook songs and children's vocal range' (in Japanese). *The Journal of Music Perception and Cognition*, **1**, 53–60.

Paynter, J. and Aston, P. (1970) *Sound and Silence: Classroom Projects in Creative Music*. Cambridge: Cambridge University Press.

Regelski, T. (1997) 'From modernism to post-modernism: music as praxis'. Paper presented at the third Symposium on Philosophy of Music Education, Los Angeles, CA.

Reimer, B. (1970) *A Philosophy of Music Education*. Englewood Cliffs, NJ: Prentice-Hall.

Suzuki, S. (1969) *Nurtured by Love: A New Approach to Education*. New York: Exposition Press.

Tokawa, S. (1992) *Re-examination of the Theory of Scale in Traditional Japanese Music* (in Japanese). Tokyo: Ongakunotomo Press.

Korea

Myung-sook Auh and Robert Walker

Korea was established in 2333 BC by Dan-koon, the legendary first great king, with descendents of the Mongolian race. Koreans comprise one people and use one language which is completely different from Chinese and Japanese, although the three countries share many cultural aspects. Korea has a unified culture, which is a blend of Buddhism, Confucianism, Shamanism and, since the eighteenth century, western influences. Until 1910, when Japan annexed Korea, Koreans lived independently with their own governmental, social and cultural systems. When Japan surrendered at the end of World War II, Korea was occupied by the USA and the Soviet Union and was divided into North and South Korea. South Korea followed the path of western democratic countries, and currently plays a major role in economic, political, cultural and educational issues internationally, as well as regionally. North Korea followed the path of communism and is one of the most closed societies in the world.

This chapter describes music education in South Korea and includes the traditional influences of Korean culture as well as some more recent empirical studies of music education based on western models of psychological and educational enquiry. The term Korea is used to designate the Republic of Korea throughout, and does not include North Korea (which is known as the Democratic People's Republic of Korea).

Korean traditional views on child development in music

Korean views of development and learning are embedded in powerful family traditions, and those which relate to music are best described in

S.-k. Kim's (1993) *Korean Traditional Play Songs*, the main aspects of which are summarized below.

Korean traditional use of music for prenatal babies

Neonates are regarded as one year old so as to account for the nine months spent inside the mother's womb, since Koreans believe that a baby's cognitive, emotional and physical development begins from conception. The *Analects* of Confucius emphasize the use of music for organizing and controlling the mind, and these suggest that a pregnant woman should not see, talk about or listen to unpleasant or aversive experiences. Similarly, the Korean king, Moon-wang (Choson Dynasty), emphasized in *Ye-ahk* (i.e., good manners and music) that pregnant women should maintain a 'gentle mind' by listening to good music. These traditional Korean views have clear parallels with more recent western research on the effects of hearing music in the womb (e.g. Lecanuet, 1996).

Korean traditional child developmental stages

Koreans traditionally divided child development into four stages, namely a) the newborn (birth–1 month); b) the infant (1 month–12 months); c) 'sweet' – 3 years; and d) 'naughty' – 7 years old. The origins of the terms for three- and seven-year-olds are not difficult to determine, although it is interesting that these stages have given rise to many old Korean sayings which still influence parents and educators (e.g. 'The habits of the three-year-old continue until they reach the age of 80').

Mothers' experiences of musical development in children

Koreans traditionally did not conduct empirical research on children's musical development in the same way as westerners, but they nevertheless gained understanding of it by carefully observing children and by sharing mothers' experiences in child-rearing and music. For example, they observed that amniotic fluid disappears from babies' ears about one month after birth, and thus they start responding more effectively to sounds in their environment. Similarly, at seven years, children's play and singing show clear distinctions in terms of gender identity, and so girls' play and songs are separated from those of boys.

Dan-koon's commandments for educating the baby

Dan-koon's *Ten Commandments for Educating the Baby* made recommendations for the first year of life. During the course of everyday play activities, the mother recites short phrases from Dan-koon's commandments to simple tunes, hoping that the baby will grow up as a good person by assimilating the ideas represented. For example, in one such activity, the mother gently taps as she breast-feeds the baby, and recites the phrase 'Si-sang Si-sang Dal-goong' (which means 'you should respect parents, teachers, kings and ancestors, which is the way to becoming an important leader of the country'). These practices have continued for 4000 years until the present day, and form the basis of traditional Korean educational thinking and practice.

The role of the lullaby in Korean traditional society

The lullaby is an important part of child-rearing in Korean society. In the past, Korean mothers believed that lullabies were essential for the baby, demonstrating the mother's love through her singing voice and physical contact. Lullabies have also reflected typical female concerns in the past. For example, in some lullabies the mother begs the baby not to cry because she has so many household chores to complete (see, for example, S.-k. Kim, 1993). Indeed, the lullaby in Korean culture contains many background stories and contexts which make lullabies not just songs for babies but also passionate expressions of parent–infant relationships.

With these old traditions as the foundation for their practices, contemporary Korean music teachers implement various government statements about what should be taught in their classrooms (Department of Education, 1997; Music Curriculum Revising Committee, 1997), and these are summarized in the next section. These curriculum guidelines have resulted in a great deal of uniformity in the content and style of music teaching throughout Korea.

The Korean National Music Curriculum

The current primary and subordinate aims of music education in Korea are as follows (Music Curriculum Revising Committee, Korea, 1997):

Primary Aim
Students should develop musical ability, musical creativity, and

musical sensitivity through experiencing various musical styles and musical activities.

Subordinate Aims
1. Students should understand the basic concepts of music;
2. Students should develop musical creativity through experiences in various musical activities; and
3. Students should be encouraged to incorporate music into their daily lives through an understanding of music's functions and values.

These aims change slightly every five years according to curriculum revision. For example, during the 1990s the emphasis was on 'aesthetic experiences of music', whereas the seventh music curriculum, to be implemented in 2000, emphasizes 'learning the basic concepts of music'. Notation and music reading are not regarded as separate parts of music learning, but are incorporated into students' composing and performing activities.

The Korean National Educational Committee, consisting of government administrators, educators, and music educators determines the National Music Curriculum for all grade levels. Textbooks are written and published on the basis of this curriculum. There is only one music textbook for elementary-level education, and thus the contents of elementary music classes are almost identical throughout Korea, although teaching practice does vary somewhat. There were nine versions of music textbooks available at high-school level as of 1999. Most teachers find that they need only these prescribed textbooks, and so the importance of the National Music Curriculum and music textbooks in Korea cannot be over-emphasized. Indeed, several analyses of these music textbooks and their relationship to the changing music curriculum have been conducted (Sung and Kwon, 1992; Sung and Baek, 1994).

Despite this prescriptive framework there remain some gaps between curriculum aims and teaching practice. Although textbooks constitute the principal material for music classes, teachers are allowed to develop their own special interests in terms of the amount of time allocated to different topics and the musical content of lessons. The gaps between the curriculum and actual practice depend on factors such as teacher competencies or beliefs concerning what students should learn. In general, however, the aims and objectives of the curriculum are pursued in the majority of the schools in Korea and achieved in many of them.

A dramatic change in the curriculum was the introduction to the grade one and two curriculum of a subject called 'Joyful Life', in 1995. In this, music is combined with other subjects (e.g. visual arts, mathematics, social studies, literature) in an attempt to emphasize its role in daily life (Department of Education–Korea, 1995). Examples of tasks in the Joyful Life textbooks include asking students to make a daily schedule which includes piano-practice times; and teaching students about the rules of traffic lights through a song called 'Crossing Roads'. Although the integration of music with other subjects has been suggested in some countries (e.g. Reimer, 1989) and implemented in others (e.g. Australia), confusion exists among Korean teachers over how to teach 'Joyful Life'. Furthermore, some of the curriculum aims and objectives, such as demanding notation skills from first- and second-graders, seem unrealistic, and some revision is clearly required.

How Korean students produce and perceive music

Only a few studies have investigated how Korean students compose, perform, listen to and read music. Most studies in the major music education research journal *Korea–Research in Music Education* concern theories and teaching methods, and many of these tend to deal with the application of western ideas in Korea.

Composing

How do Korean students compose music? In what musical styles do they compose? Auh (1999b) proposed a distinction between 'Musically creative' and 'Musically-correct-but-not-original' products. The latter were those which were likely to receive high marks from music teachers because they conformed to well-known theoretical concepts about musical structure, but were also derivative, with few original ideas from the student. Interestingly, Auh (1996) found that Korean students' compositions differed from those of their American contemporaries – they were more song-oriented, for example – and this may be because, unlike American music textbooks, Korean books are song- rather than concept-oriented.

Auh (1999a) found that the criteria Korean students use to evaluate their own compositions can be categorized into five types. These are: a) musical-analytical criteria (e.g. Is the structure of the composition good?); b) the sounds (e.g. Does the music sound peaceful?); c) achievement of expressive intent (e.g. Does the composition express my thoughts?); d) I did my best; and e) comparison with peers (e.g. I did not do well in comparison to my peers' compositions). Auh also found that the aesthetic criteria students adopt for liking certain parts of their compositions fell into four categories, namely: a) musical-analytical (e.g. the arrangement of pitches); b) interesting sounds; c) achieving expressive intentions; and d) working hard for the result.

Performing

There are two aspects to performing, namely singing and instrumental playing. Cho *et al.* (1997) found that about half of all fourth-grade Korean students played the piano, indicating that this is the most popular instrument. However, singing is a major component of students' music learning in Korean schools, particularly prior to the dramatic curriculum reform which took place in the late 1980s. It involves reading solfège and singing the melody using the solfège names; song lyrics are then added as students sing along with the music teacher's piano accompaniment. It is essential for music teachers to be able to play the piano so that they can accompany their students.

Although there are few studies of singing in Korean schools, Lim's (1989) study is of particular interest. In this study, 228 tenth-grade students attending a girls' senior high school were tested to see if systematic instructions in sight-singing could improve their sight-singing ability. One group received systematic instruction in sight-singing and ear training, while a control group received traditional instruction in singing (mainly from a music textbook, with students copying their teacher's demonstrations). The control group were found to have poorer sight-singing ability, which indicates that adopting systematic teaching methods can offer great opportunities to improve the singing abilities of Korean high-school students.

Music listening

Cho *et al.* (1997) asked fourth-grade Korean students from urban and rural areas to state what media they used to listen to music. The results, which are shown in Table 8.1, indicate that TV was the most common medium for listening to music, that school was found to be an unpopular place for music listening and that none of the rural students attended concerts. The results reflect several aspects of rural and urban life in Korea. First, music listening classes in schools focus on masterpieces of western classical music and Korean traditional music, which may not easily attract many students. Second, lifestyles in urban and rural areas are very different: rural areas are comparatively disadvantaged in terms of

Table 8.1 Cho *et al.*'s (1997) study of music listening

Medium	Total	Urban	Rural
Radio	14%	15%	13%
CD, record player	13%	16%	11%
TV	41%	23%	52%
Cassette tape player	19%	19%	19%
Concert	1%	4%	0%
School	3%	2%	4%

cultural benefits; not many concerts are held in places other than Seoul and a few other major cities in Korea. Finally, while equipment such as the Walkman, CD and cassette-tape players are easily accessible to high-school students, they are not as accessible for children of primary-school age. The major source of hearing music for these younger children seems to be TV.

Notation and music reading

Notation and music reading are major components of Korean students' music learning. This is partly because music reading and theory occupy about 50 per cent of the assessment of music in schools, and standard notation is taught from the third grade. Korean students' notation ability can be inferred to a limited extent from Auh and Walker's (1999) study in which seventh-grade Korean students were asked to notate their compositions: only seven of the twenty participants were able to utilize standard notations for their compositions. The other boys and girls notated their compositions using solfège names (e.g., do-mi-sol-mi, sol-ti-do-la, sol-mi-re-mi-re, etc.), pitch-only notations, Kodály rhythm signs with different lengths and thicknesses, and self-invented symbols.

Although about half of the students could not notate their composi-tions, they could, nevertheless, perform their compositions from memory. An interesting comment was made by the music teacher of the students studied, when one girl gave a brilliant performance of her composition on the piano and handed in her notation to the teacher. The notation was far from correct standard notation, comprising instead a mixture of round dots for pitches, Kodály rhythm signs, solfège names written between staff lines and a big, thick circle to emphasize the ending. The teacher asked incredulously: 'Is this what you played?' and was unable to see much connection between the notation and the sounds produced.

These results suggest that traditional notation ability and creative ability in music are likely to be unrelated. Music teachers in Korea should, thus, probably not assess students' compositional ability through staff notation, which is currently standard practice, but by listening to the actual musical sounds of the composition. The small proportion of students who were able to use correct notation, despite the best efforts of their teachers, is an obvious cause for concern.

How Korean teachers teach music

General music education

Music is a compulsory subject at both primary and secondary levels in Korea. In general, primary schools have two music classes per week throughout the semester, while secondary schools have one music class per week. Grade 12 is excused from music classes due to their intensive preparation for university entrance examinations.

Music classes in primary schools are taught mostly by general classroom teachers, who typically did not major in music but in primary education; music classes in secondary schools are taught by music teachers who majored in music at a university. Recently, some private schools have recruited specialist music teachers to teach exclusively music. In June 1999, the government selected 200 specialist music teachers to serve public primary schools. This was a good move both for public primary schools and university graduates with music-teaching qualifications, since for the past five years or so there has been a large surplus of prospective music teachers waiting for school-teaching positions.

Specialist music

The most popular performance activity in schools is the choir. One possible reason for this is that singing is a major source of pleasure for Korean people (Hahn, 1994) as well as a way to release stress, as observed in the 'Singing Room' (Korean-style Karaoke) boom in Korea. Other special music-education activities in schools are instrumental ensembles (which play mostly western classical music) and school orchestras. School bands or jazz ensembles are rare in Korean schools. In addition to the choir, the most likely musical activities for Korean students are the school orchestra, church choir, private music lessons and private piano tutoring.

Assessment

Most music assessment involves teachers' evaluations of students' performances and multiple-choice examinations of students attainment in music reading and music history. Some innovative schools have recently been conducting profile assessments of students' musical progress. These involve written descriptions of how well students are doing in singing, instrumental playing, music reading and music history, and how much progress students are making throughout a semester or a year. Profile assessments are not yet prevalent in Korean schools, but their importance has been recognized by several educators and music educators (Seog, 1998). Other researchers have investigated assessment systems in music for all grade levels in schools and some have suggested a model for music assessment (Sung and Kwon, 1992a and 1992b). Sung and Kwon's conceptual model for music assessment was developed to evaluate the goals, content, teaching materials and methods of music learning, and the suggested assessment methods employ Bloom's (1956) taxonomy of cognitive, affective and psychomotor domains.

Computers and music

A significant proportion of Korean children (especially boys) play computer games at home. However, although the computer is familiar, its use for music learning is not yet common in Korea. Music educators with expertise in computers have given lectures and demonstrations to school teachers to show what computers can do for music theory, music history, composing music and other topics (e.g. Choi, 1998). However, only a few private schools can afford to have a computer laboratory available for music learning. Moreover, music teachers tend to feel more comfortable with musical instruments and singing than with computers, probably because that is how they were themselves taught music. It is also worth noting that, in addition to the software that has now been developed using the timbres of traditional Korean instruments (such as the Kayakeum, the Daekeum, and the Korean drum), children are encouraged to explore different acoustic sounds (Moon, 1996).

The Korean music education literature

Several music-teaching method books have been published which introduce systematic approaches to music teaching in Korea (Sung, 1988; Lee, 1990, 1992; Ahn, 1996; Ghil and Lim, 1996; Kim, 1996; Seog,

1996). Many western books on music education have also been translated into Korean (Mursell and Glenn, 1987; Ahn, 1984, 1992; Jo, 1994). Many of these authors have suggested teaching strategies specifically involving twentieth-century musical styles (e.g. Lee, 1995) and traditional Korean music (Youn, 1995), and these publications have been important for enhancing music educators' knowledge and practices.

This literature has established the theoretical foundations of music education in Korea, which was previously lacking. The introduction of western knowledge (e.g. Piaget's theory), pedagogies (e.g., Kodály, Orff, Dalcroze, Suzuki) and concepts (individual instruction, concept-oriented music teaching) have resulted in a gradual westernization of the theoretical basis of Korean music education. The main problem lies in adapting such theories to Korean ways of thinking: music educators have felt an urgent need to develop the theoretical foundations of music education in Korea not simply by imitating western theories, but by adapting them to the Korean educational system.

Psychological and sociological issues

Those Korean music educators who had gained doctorates in music education in the USA, England and Germany started conducting research utilizing western traditions (i.e. collecting data and analysing them empirically) from the late 1980s onwards. They concentrated mainly on studies of how students learn in music, looking at topics such as musical self-esteem, musical aptitude, musical preferences, gender differences, multicultural issues and popular music. These areas are illustrated briefly below.

Musical self-esteem

Jong (1997) investigated the relationships among popular music preferences, musical self-esteem and the musical experiences of Korean high-school students. Responses to Schmitt's (1979) Musical Self-Esteem Questionnaire indicated that their mean musical self-esteem score was 97 (maximum = 172, minimum = 43). Girls exhibited significantly higher musical self-esteem than did boys, and students' musical self-esteem correlated positively with their musical experiences as measured by Auh's (1996) Musical Experiences Questionnaire. Responses to the latter also indicated that girls indicated having significantly more musical experiences than did boys. Finally, responses to an Attitudes Towards Popular Music Questionnaire showed that girls showed more positive attitudes than did boys.

It is interesting to compare these results with those obtained by Laycock (1992) and Auh (1996), who employed American students as participants, also using Schmitt's (1979) questionnaire. First, both American studies gave rise to higher musical self-esteem scores among Americans than those found for Korean students. This may be due to a real difference between students from the two countries or to the Korean students demonstrating a Confucian tendency towards humility: presenting oneself in a humble way is greatly valued in Confucian societies. Secondly, Laycock also found a positive correlation between musical self-esteem and the number of musical experiences that students have. Caution should be exercised when making comparisons between Korean and western students, since Korean students tend to speak modestly of their musical ability when compared to American students. However, for both Korean and American students, high musical experience was found to be an indicator of high musical self-esteem. Musical self-esteem is one of the most neglected research areas in Korea, and should therefore receive more attention from Korean music educators.

Musical aptitude

The first study to develop a musical aptitude test appropriate for Korean students was conducted by Ryu (1982). His test draws on western musical aptitude tests such as the Seashore test, consisting of sub-tests of rhythm, timbre, tonal-pitch matching, time, loudness, tonal-pitches, tonal memory and notation imagery. It was piloted with a sample of 4567 Korean students in elementary, junior high, and secondary high schools. The final version of Ryu's musical aptitude test showed reliabilities of 0.80 for elementary level, 0.81 for junior high school level, and 0.80 for senior high school level. Its validity was left for future studies to determine.

In the mid-1990s, several researchers investigated the possibility of using Gordon's musical aptitude tests with Korean students. Cho *et al.* (1996) conducted a study with 950 Korean primary-school students, using Gordon's Intermediate Measures of Music Audiation. The results showed that students' tonal aptitude was higher than their rhythmic aptitude and that Korean students showed a higher general level of musical aptitude than US children. Hyun and Seog (1997) developed the Hyun-Seog Music Aptitude Test (HSMAT–1) on the basis of Gordon's musical aptitude tests, with 1711 students between the fifth and ninth grades. This test showed a reliability of 0.51 for tonal aptitude and 0.77 for rhythmic aptitude.

Similarly, Y.-h. Kim (1997) administered Gordon's Advanced Measures of Music Audiation to 261 Korean high-school students majoring in Korean traditional music and western classical music in the National Korean Arts Institute. The Korean students scored 15–19 points higher than the American students overall, and Korean traditional music majors outperformed western classical music majors. Y.-h. Kim suspected that Korean traditional music majors learn music mostly by ear; their high levels of ear training might have contributed to their higher scores in Gordon's test, which could be viewed as an auditory test. The higher levels of tonal rather than rhythmic aptitude in Korean students might be related to the fact that Korean people love songs, especially those with fluent melodies.

Musical preferences

A cross-cultural study of musical preferences in Korean, American and Greek 8–18-year-olds was conducted by LeBlanc *et al.* (1999). They found that older Korean students showed low mean overall musical preferences, while older American students showed high mean overall musical preferences. Both Korean and American students showed no significant differences in musical preferences by gender. Auh *et al.* (1999) found that Korean university students' ratings of Korean popular music were significantly higher than their ratings of western popular music, which is consistent with Cho *et al.*'s (1997) results.

Although Korean musical culture is said to have become westernized, this result indicates that Korean popular music still has a special status for Korean people, and it is readily distinguished from western popular music. This is partly because English is a second language to Korean students, and thus not easy for them. It is also partly because the emotions expressed in Korean popular music are different from those in western popular music: their lyrics involve more nostalgic and less violent themes, as well as less explicit sexual content.

Gender differences

Gender differences among Korean students emerge in several domains. As we have already seen, high-school girls scored significantly higher than boys in tests of musical experiences, musical self-esteem and attitudes towards popular music (Jong, 1997). Cho *et al.*'s (1997) study of 422 fourth-grade Korean students considered gender in relation to urban v. rural location.

Table 8.2 Results of Cho *et al.*'s (1997) study of attitudes towards music

Questions	Urban	Rural	Total
1. Do you have private music lessons?	80% (M = 74%; F = 85%)	53% (M = 43%; F = 73%)	63%
2. Do you have a family member with high musical ability?	50% ('Sister' was the most common response)	43%	45%
3. Do you like music? (% responding 'Yes')	58% (M = 42%; F = 72%)	45% (M = 26%; F = 79%)	50%
4. Attitudes towards music classes? (% responding 'Like it very much')	63% (M = 50%; F = 76%)	42% (M = 25%; F = 76%)	50%

The results, shown in Table 8.2, indicate that more urban than rural students enjoyed music lessons and concerts and that there were higher numbers of females in each category. Sisters were more likely than other family members to be reported as having high musical ability. Higher numbers of urban than rural students liked music and music lessons and, of these, female students outnumbered males by almost three to one. It appears from these data that music is an activity more common in urban areas and more likely among females than males.

Korean traditional music and multicultural issues

Non-Korean ethnic groups constitute less than 1 per cent of the total population, and so educators and music educators do not pay much attention to multicultural issues in schools. However, being aware of the importance of multiculturalism in other countries, Korean music educators have included world music sections in their textbooks. These include representative songs from various countries such as Iran, India, China, Japan and others.

Korea's most important task, however, lies in promoting Korean traditional music. The strong political and historical influences on Korea of Japan and the USA have shaped the country's educational system, which is effectively a combination of the Japanese and American systems. From the beginning of the Japanese colonization of Korea (1910–45) until the 1988 Olympics in Korea, only a small number of

Korean musicians worked to revive Korean traditional music. This often had little effect, and the majority of Koreans accepted foreign influences with little criticism. However, the Olympic Games forced Koreans to ask themselves just what 'Korean identity' actually involved, and people realized the extent to which they had neglected their own traditions.

Since 1988, dramatic changes have therefore been made by increasing the amount of space given to Korean traditional music in textbooks, initiating a Korean traditional music-major course at universities and acknowledging Korean traditional music performers to a much greater extent. Another manifestation of this has involved making Korean traditional music more accessible to young children, so that they now grow up listening to this music. Y.-y. Kim (1998), for example, collected traditional Korean children's songs from elderly Koreans and produced recommendations for their use in teaching music for preschool children.

Popular music

Cho *et al.* (1997) investigated the musical preferences of fourth-grade Korean students using a survey questionnaire. Their results are shown in Table 8.3, which indicates that Korean popular music was the most liked of the five musical genres investigated. However, this preference stems largely from the preferences of rural students. Urban students like this style a lot less: even their preference for western classical music was higher than that for Korean popular music. Secondly, very few of the sample expressed a liking for Korean traditional music, and this was particularly true of rural students. Thirdly, preference for western popular music was not as high as might have been expected, particularly among students from rural areas, who liked western classical music more than western pop music. Finally, the moderate level of liking for children's songs may be unique to Korea, probably resulting from its musical traditions.

Overall, the findings indicate that students in urban areas, where rich musical culture is available, showed varied musical preferences ranging from western classical to Korean traditional. Students in rural areas, which are musically disadvantaged, showed a predominant preference for Korean popular music.

Table 8.3 Results of Cho *et al.*'s (1997) study

Musical genre	Total	Urban	U–M	U–F	Rural	R–M	R–F
Korean traditional	3%	8%	5%	9%	1%	1%	0%
Western classical	20%	27%	24%	29%	16%	14%	19%
Children's songs	16%	18%	9%	24%	14%	13%	19%
Korean popular	45%	19%	26%	14%	61%	63%	57%
Western popular	8%	13%	14%	12%	5%	5%	4%

Key: U = Urban; R = Rural; M = Male; F = Female

Epilogue

This account of music education in Korea reflects something of the development and evolution of the Korean nation prior to Japanese occupation during the first half of the twentieth century, and the gradual adaptation of the Republic of Korea to the postwar world. Korean music education currently struggles to retain important links with its more ancient traditions while simultaneously employing contemporary western models of enquiry and educational delivery. The language barrier lessens the impact of some of the worst excesses of the lyrics of some western popular music, and Korean popular music is preferred to its western counterpart. Korean music education, nevertheless, relies on traditional discipline and love for songs, and this dual identity will no doubt develop and evolve further in the new millennium.

References

Note: All the publications produced in Korea are written in the Korean language and were translated into English by M.-S. Auh.

Ahn, Jae-sin (1996) *Early Childhood Music Education*. Seoul, Korea: Educational Science Publishers.
Auh, M. (1996) 'Prediction of musical creativity in composition among selected variables for upper elementary students'. Doctoral dissertation, Case Western Reserve University, 1995. *Dissertation Abstracts International*, **56**, 3875A.
Auh, M. (1997) 'Prediction of musical creativity in composition among selected variables for upper elementary students'. *Bulletin of the Council for Research in Music Education*, **133**, 1–8.
Auh, M. (1999a) 'Enactive and reflective thinking during the compositional process by seventh-grade Korean students'. Proceedings of the International Music Education Research Symposium, 'Children and Music: Develop-

mental Perspectives'. Tasmania, Launceston: University of Tasmania Press, 57–66.

Auh, M. (1999b) 'Identifying creativity in compositions through a musical analysis: musically creative vs musically correct'. *Proceedings of the XII Australian Society for Music Education (ASME) National Conference.* Sydney, Australia: ASME Inc., 7–14.

Auh, M. and Walker, R. (1999) 'Compositional strategies and musical creativity when composing with staff notations versus graphic notations among Korean students'. *Bulletin of the Council for Research in Music Education* (Special Issue).

Auh, M., Walker, R., Jong, J.-H., and Kim, S.-W. (1999) 'A cross-cultural investigation of the effects of informal and formal musical experiences on musical tastes of university students in Korea, the USA, and Australia'. Paper submitted to the 18th International Research Seminar of the 2000 ISME.

Bloom, B. S. (ed.) (1956) *Taxonomy of Educational Objectives. Handbook I: Cognitive Domain.* New York: McKay.

Cho, Hyo-im, Choi, Eun-shik and Jung, Jin-won (1996) 'Research on Korean primary school students' music aptitude using Gordon's intermediate measures of music audiation'. *Korea–Research in Music Education*, **15**, 437–71.

Cho, Hyo-im, Choi, Eun-shik, and Jung, Jin-won (1997) 'A comparative study on music aptitudes and musical backgrounds with Korean primary school children'. *Korea–Research in Music Education*, **16**, 147–71.

Choi, Eun-shik (1998) 'The development and implementation of interative multimedia instrumental discrimination skills training courseware for beginning clarinet students', in E. Choi (ed.) *Searching for a New Paradigm of Music Education Research.* Seoul: Hawoo Publishers, pp. 103–13.

Department of Education–Korea (1995) *Joyful Life 1–1.* Choong-nam: The National Textbook Publishers.

Department of Education in Korea (1997) *Korean Seventh Music Curriculum Revision–Research.* In-chon National University of Education, Music Curriculum Revision Committee (Kye-hyu Shin, Moon-joo Seog and Byung-hoon Hwang).

Ghil, Ae-kyung and Lim, Mi-kyung (eds) (1996) *Elementary Music Teaching Methods.* Seoul: Soomoon-dang.

Hahn, Yong-hee (1994) *Korean Children Song: 70-Years History of Children Song.* Seoul: Se-kwang Music Publishers.

Hoffer, C. (trans. Ahn, Mi-ja) (1984) *Foundations of Music Education.* Seoul: Ewha Woman's University.

Hyun, Kyung-sil and Seog, Moon-joo (1997) 'Development of music aptitude test for Korean students of fifth through ninth grades'. *Korean–Research in Music Education*, **16**, 119–45.

Jo, Hong-ghi (trans.) (1994) *Kodály's Principles in Practice.* Seoul: Da-ra Publishers.

Jong, Jin-hee (1997) 'Relationships between popular-music preference and musical self-esteem for high school students. Unpublished master's thesis, Ewha Woman's University, Seoul.

Kim, Sook-kyung (1993) *Korean Traditional Play Songs*. Seoul: Chung-maek.

Kim, Young-yun (1996) *Early Childhood Music Education*. Seoul: Hahk-ji sa.

Kim, Young-yun (1998) *Traditional Korean Children's Songs: Collection, Analysis, and Application*. Unpublished doctoral dissertation, University of Washington, USA.

Kim, Yun-hee (1997) 'An investigation of the possibility of measuring music aptitudes of Korean students using a western music aptitude test – Gordon's advanced measures of music audiation. *Korea–Research in Music Education*, **16**, 329–60.

Laycock, R. R. (1992) 'The relationship of musical experience, musical aptitude, self-concept, age, and academic achievement to the musical problem solving abilities of high school students'. Doctoral dissertation, Case Western Reserve University. *Dissertation Abstracts International*, **53**, 2728A.

LeBlanc, A., Jin, Y. and Stamou, L. (1999) 'Effect of age, country, and gender on music listening preferences'. *Bulletin of the Council for Research in Music Education* (Special Issue).

Lecanuet, J. P. (1996) 'Prenatal auditory experience', in I. Deliege and J. Sloboda (eds) *Musical Beginnings*. Oxford: Oxford University Press, 3–34.

Lee, Hong-soo (1990) *Contemporary Approaches to Music Education*. Seoul: Se-kwang Music Publishers.

Lee, Hong-soo (1992) *Music Education Through Feelings and Insights*. Seoul: Se-kwang Music Publishers.

Lee, Youn-kyung (1995) 'Creative musical activities for understanding twentieth-century music for primary school children'. *Korea–Research in Music Education*, **14**, 1–40.

Leonhard, D. and House, R. (trans. Ahn, Mi-ja) (1992) *Foundations and Principles of Music Education*. Seoul: Ewha Woman's University.

Lim, Kye-soon (1989) 'An experimental study on improvement of sight singing ability of senior high school students'. *Korea–Research in Music Education*, **8**, 147–75.

Moon, Dae-dong (1996) 'Development of computer software for sound exploration'. *Korea–Research in Music Education*, **15**, 349–401.

Mursell, J. L. and Glenn, M. (trans.) (1997) *Psychology of Music Education*. Korean Music Eductional Texts Committee. Seoul: Se-kwang Music Publishers.

Music Curriculum Revising Committee, Korea (1997) *A Study on the Seventh National Music Curriculum Revising*. Seoul: In-chon National University of Education.

Reimer, B. (1989) *A Philosophy of Music Education* (2nd edn). Englewood Cliffs, NJ: Prentice-Hall.

Ryu, Duck-hee (1982) 'An experimental study of implementing a music aptitude test'. *Korea–Research in Music Education*, **1**, 19–34.

Schimitt, M. (1979) 'Development and validation of a measure of self-esteem of musical ability'. *Dissertation Abstracts International*, **40**(10), 5357–8A.

Seog, Moon-joo (1996) *Music Teaching and Learning Guide for Musical Development*. Seoul: Poong-nam Publishers.

Seog, Moon-joo (1998) 'Portfolio assessment in music classroom', in E. Choi (ed.) *Searching for a New Paradigm of Music Education Research*. Seoul: Hawoo Publishers, pp. 267–8.

Sung, Kyung-hee (1988) *Foundations of Music Education*. Seoul: Eul-ji Publishers.

Sung, Kyung-hee and Baek, Il-hyung (1994) 'A study to improve junior high school music teaching methods (II): development of models for music teaching and learning with focus on concepts, creating, and music listening'. Research Report RR 94–6. Seoul: Korean Educational Development Institute.

Sung, Kyung-hee and Kwon, Duck-won (1992a) 'The sixth music curriculums for elementary, junior high, and senior high schools'. Research Report RR 92–11. Seoul: Korean Educational Development Institute.

Sung, Kyung-hee and Kwon, Duck-won (1992b) *A Study of the Assessment System of Music Subject in Pursuing the Education of the Fundamentals*. Seoul: Korean Educational Development Institute.

Youn, Myung-won (1995) 'Research on creating music in Korean traditional musical style'. *Korea–Research in Music Education*, **14**, 55–89.

North America

Rudolf E. Radocy

North America comprises a vast geographic region. Culturally, striking differences exist between the United States of America and Canada, which developed primarily from British and North-European traditions, and the Latin American countries, developed primarily from Hispanic traditions. This article focuses on various cultural conditions affecting musical development and learning in the USA and Canada, particularly in the context of schools.

Background: historical traditions

Musical development and learning occur within a socio-cultural context, which includes environmental and economic aspects. The beliefs and traditions existing within a society influence that society's educational practices. Several historical and cultural developments influenced the conditions under which music education occurs in North America. All Americans and Canadians either came to North America from somewhere else, or have ancestors who did. Native Americans came from Asia thousands of years ago; waves of Europeans have come over the last 400 years or more; immigration from elsewhere continues today. The sixteenth century saw Spanish explorers searching for gold and souls to convert; much territory of the modern United States was under Spanish or Mexican rule into the nineteenth century. French and English adventurers and settlers came in the seventeenth century in search of economic opportunity, religious freedom, political freedom and conquest.

As the eighteenth century saw Great Britain become the dominant North American colonial power, English, Scottish-Irish and other

European settlers continued to come to North America. The nineteenth century saw a dramatic change in the number and origin of immigrants; increasing numbers of Irish, German and, later, Southern and Eastern Europeans and Asians arrived. The twentieth century saw a major flow of Hispanic and Asian peoples to North America in search of freedom from repression and of economic opportunity. In addition to the willing immigrants, some people, particularly from Africa, became unwilling Americans due to the practice of slavery in the seventeenth, eighteenth and nineteenth centuries.

One must recognize that a wide mix of peoples comprises the United States and Canada; the cultural mix fostered opportunity for sharing musical styles and pedagogical practices as well as preserving traditions brought from elsewhere. Music is a means of cultural transmission and retention, as documented by Merriam (1964), Kaplan (1990) and Gregory (1997), who have categorized music's functions within society. Attempts to preserve particular cultures and subcultures, as well as attempts to build a dominant national culture, affect music education.

A strong 'frontier' tradition existed in the United States and Canada, perhaps as an outgrowth of the nations' relative youth in comparison with European nations. A person's origin usually was less important than the ability to build a life and nation in a challenging environment. Ancestry and social graces, initially, were less important than survival and entrepreneurial skills. Immigrant cultures brought diversity to North America; yet many immigrants abandoned 'old' ways in the interest of assimilation. Schooling facilitated assimilation by developing English language skills and providing common experiences, including an emerging body of familiar music.

As growing nations needed increasing supplies of workers, schools were necessarily concerned with developing practical skills of reading, writing and arithmetic. Music education was important for particular purposes, but often had a lower priority than 'academic' subjects. Community music-making accompanied the nations' growth. Until the onset of recording in the late nineteenth century, there was no way to experience music except by live performance, and it was not until the 1950s that recorded sound actually closely approximated live sound. Music flourished as entertainment as well as an expression of people's life experiences.

Despite the frontier tradition and concern with egalitarian practices, attempts to emulate 'high' society always have characterized some of North American musical life. Concerns for enriching life necessarily influenced the development of formal music education, in private settings as well as in public schools. Religion was important to early settlers, particularly in New England, and they were concerned with improving the quality of singing in worship services. The tradition of the New England 'singing schools', accordingly, was an important tradition in American music education.

Education was for more than survival, especially among families who acquired wealth and influence. Music-making could be seen as important for cultural enhancement and retention, as well as for entertainment. During the nineteenth century, as cities grew, interest in emulating European music grew. Some musicians went to Europe to study. Opera companies and symphony orchestras were established. The United States and Canada therefore represent diverse societal combinations, originating in traditions of building a nation from a 'wilderness', and stressing a common egalitarian experience, yet concerned with building a 'higher' culture. Such a background necessarily led to certain developments characterizing twentieth-century music education.

Competition

Competition, part of the human condition, has been, and remains, a major force in American music education. Band, orchestra and small ensemble contests stimulated the growth of instrumental music education, especially during the 1920s and 1930s. Instrument manufacturers sponsored some contests; a growth in instrumental programmes meant more sales for the manufacturers (Mark and Gary, 1992, pp. 271–4). While national contests eventually became impractical due to growing numbers of competitors, regional contests and festivals expanded.

In many American schools, highly visible musical organizations, especially marching bands, are connected with competitive athletics. In addition to unofficial competition occurring between bands from rival schools during intermissions at football games, much time and effort go to rated marching competitions.

One result of stressing competition is that some music programmes may be driven excessively by the desire to earn recognition for the school and its music teachers by doing well in competitive settings. Marching bands may devote their entire season to presentations of 'the show', learned before the opening of the school year and performed repeatedly throughout the marching band season. Concert organizations may devote most of their rehearsal and performance to a small number of selections presented for adjudication at rated festivals and contests.In addition to restrictions in repertoire, emphasis on competition may stress high-quality performances by a talented few at the expense of more comprehensive musical experiences for the majority of students. Some music 'educators' may value the accolades received from public performance more than the musical knowledge and attitudes of their students.

A passive public

Today, most Americans are involved passively with music. While Gregory (1997) notes that much of the world's music is for something other than independent use of music as music, American musical passivity differs from Gregory's active social roles. Far more listening than active music-making occurs, and much listening is not highly attentive or contemplative. Although virtually everyone listens to music, the listening likely is for entertainment and often occurs in commercial venues, film or television, where the music is incidental to another purpose.

Having relatively few adults involved in music-making means that many 'graduates' of American music education do not continue their active music-making experiences into adult life. Perhaps this is due to lack of desire, or to lack of opportunity. Whatever the reason, a few making most of the music for the many helps make music, primarily, a commodity. This is fine for the 'music business', but it may not inculcate lasting values for music or diverse musical tastes.

Theoretical issues

A behavioural tradition

American teachers, including music teachers, generally are not ideologues regarding schools of psychological thought. Despite psychology being a cornerstone of teacher education, teachers may set psychology aside as they adapt to particular teaching situations (Notterman and Drewry, 1993, pp. 6–7). Nevertheless, behaviourism (i.e. description and prediction of human behaviour on the basis of empirical data) has exerted important influences on music education. Historical stresses on drill and repetitive practice superficially fit Thorndike's (1932) concept of 'stamping in bonds'. More recently, behavioural shaping, management and modification in the tradition of Skinner (1938) have been influential.

Non-behavioural views

Reactions against behaviourism, as well as developments in cognitive psychology, also have had a major influence on American educational thought and music education. The views of John Dewey (1938; 1940) provided considerable rationale for the progressive education movement, a philosophy where learning is an ongoing experience based in 'real-world' problems, rather than preparation for the future. Unit teaching, also called integrated teaching, where a large portion of the school day is devoted to some overall topic such as westward expansion or elections, a vestige of the 1930s, is popular in some American schools today. Some American music educators are concerned that extremes of unit or integrated teaching may make music education strictly in the service of 'academic' learning.

Classical Gestalt theories, exemplified earlier in the twentieth century by Köhler (1929), Koffka (1935) and Wertheimer (1945), have considerable contemporary importance because of concern for musical structures. Facilitating learning by arranging the environment to promote insightful conceptualizations is a logical outgrowth of Gestalt theory. The ability to structure and restructure the musical stimulus in a meaningful way is vital for enhancing musical preference and promoting a desire to learn (Radocy and Boyle, 1997). Hierarchical perceptual structuring, with its development from and into 'deep' structure (Lerdahl and Jackendoff, 1983; West *et al.* 1985), has a logical relationship to Gestalt theory due to the need for 'well-formed' or 'logical' musical structures. While American music educators, generally, may be unaware of underlying Gestalt principles, and may use Gestalt simply in a vague, 'non-behavioural' way, the principles of proximity, similarity, simplicity and common direction address crucial aspects of organization of meaningful musical perceptual structures.

Jean Piaget (Piaget, 1950; Piaget and Inhelder, 1969), with his stages, and conservation, may have been the most popular learning theorist with American music educators (to the extent that any learning theory can be 'popular'), thanks in part to Pflederer's (1967) important work. Of course, Piaget's stages, apparently, are more amorphous and domain-specific than once believed (Gardner, 1993, pp. 20–2), and a seeming lack of conservation (i.e. recognizing that a stimulus may remain unchanged in some fundamental dimension while other dimensions change) may be due to perceptual difficulties (Serafine, 1980). One lingering important service Piaget provided was to show clearly that children are not just miniature adults.

Aims, objectives and policy issues

A bandwagon mentality

Most American music educators do not follow learning theories and other developments in psychology closely, yet they often may follow educational fads or 'bandwagons', where an idea or school of thought becomes popular rapidly, as many people endorse it, often without careful consideration of what the idea really represents or implies. Britton (1958, p. 207) warned that music educators often have been ready to jump on any intellectual bandwagon; that condition has not changed.

Music educators seek constantly to justify music education; music education methods textbooks usually provide rationales for music education. Appeals to music as a sound structure or an aesthetic object, and stressing how all cultures contain some form of music, exemplify music as its own justification. Appeals to better citizenship, building teamwork, enhancing academic achievement and, perhaps, providing 'worthy' use of leisure time exemplify music as life enhancement. Advocates of an enhancement approach must confront the fact that other aspects of schooling promote citizenship, health and achievement; nevertheless, the enhancement approach currently is strong.

Music educators encounter fads arising in other areas of education that may lead to extreme and impractical action when implemented prematurely or inappropriately. For example, the behavioural objectives movement of the 1960s returned in the 1990s as 'outcomes-based' education. A behavioural objective states clearly just what a student is supposed to do under certain conditions; Robert Mager's (1962) pioneering *Preparing Instructional Objectives* helped spur a movement to specify just what students should do to indicate that they had, in fact, learned something.

Music appreciation, a worthy goal, could have many meanings. For example: in what observable behaviour should a student engage to indicate appreciation? Yet writing detailed objectives for all facets of music education was quite impractical, and most music educators were uninterested in obtaining 'canned' objectives, as was possible through the Instructional Objectives Exchange (Kibler *et al.*, pp. 189–90). Enthusiasm for behavioural objectives faded. In the 1990s, however, behavioural objectives, returning as outcomes-based education, a process in which schools identify instructional 'targets', state them in terms of what students will do and plan instruction to meet those targets, often with the contingency that school accreditation will be based on how well the school identifies and meets the designated targets.

American education today contains much discourse regarding brain research and 'brain-based' learning, and some music educators would like to show how music enhances 'brain-based' learning. During the late 1970s and early 1980s, music occasionally was billed as a product of the 'right brain', and a tool for saving education from a 'left-brain' bias (Radocy, 1978). The fact that music is a complex activity that uses many, if not all, brain areas, except in extremely simple situations involving processing of musical stimuli did not deter the true believers.

Many extol the alleged 'Mozart effect', according to which listening to Mozart, supposedly, enhances problem-solving skills. Well-conducted contemporary research, thoroughly grounded in a logical theoretical basis, indicates clearly that listening to structured music in Mozart's style may serve as a type of cognitive 'pump priming' for spatial reasoning tasks (Mountcastle, 1978; Leng *et al.*, 1990; Rauscher *et al.*, 1993, Rauscher *et al.*, 1994, 1997; Sarnthein *et al.*, 1997), but, as with earlier fads, educators generalize way beyond the data (Radocy, 1998).

Recent research has not replicated the effect, even with spatial reasoning (Steele *et al.*, 1999), and suggests that the 'effect' may be more an artifact of arousal, obtainable via other interesting music or stories (Nantais and Schellenberg, 1999). Concerned that music education may be viewed as an educational tool rather than an end in itself, Reimer (1999) states: 'The spatial–temporal argument for the value of music study is perhaps the most extreme that the music education profession has ever faced.' (p. 42).

Bruer's (1999) review suggests that much advocacy for 'brain-based' education is based on folk wisdom and speculations rather than substantive neuroscience. Hemispheric specialization is complex; it is unscientific to place gross categories of behaviours, such as spatial reasoning and musical processing, in one hemisphere or the other. Making an issue of a critical period for generalized brain development during middle childhood is not based on any evidence that the density of synapses or increase in glucose consumption characterizing young brains has any facilitative effect for learning. Bruer concludes with a telling evaluation that is quite pertinent to what Britton spoke of earlier and to the current hue and cry regarding 'brain-based' learning: 'The brain-based education literature represents a genre of writing, most often appearing in professional education publications, that provides a popular mix of fact, misinterpretation, and speculation. That can be intriguing, but it is not always informative' (p. 657).

Some American music educators welcome Gardner's (1993) multiple-intelligence theory because it recognizes a specific musical intelligence: One may make the conceptual leap that if an intelligence exists, education should nurture development of that intelligence. To date, other than various seminars and publications, the influence of multiple-intelligence theory on the practice of music education is uncertain.

During the 1990s, the Music Educators National Conference, the major organization of music educators in the United States, made much of the National Standards for Arts Education (Consortium of National Arts Education Associations, 1994), a set of desired goals and sub-goals for music, drama, dance and the visual arts in elementary and secondary education. Standards fit into the nation's push for 'rigorous' or 'world-class' standards for evaluating educational outcomes. While statements of desirable knowledge are valuable for planning curriculum, instruction and evaluation, the standards may have assumed an exaggerated importance simply because they exist.

After citing claims that music education is necessary to promote spatial-temporal reasoning (Grandin *et al.*, 1998), Reimer (1999) cleverly shows how the much-heralded standards would need consider-able revision if one takes the aforementioned Mozart effect seriously as a major basis for music education. Pursuing music education for enhancing spatial-temporal reasoning necessarily would make tradi-tional parts of a programme irrelevant, such as many ensemble experiences and musical appreciation activities directed at other than 'classical' music in Mozart's style.

Questionable national focus

While there is national concern for education, including sincere concern and political proselytizing, there is no national curriculum in the United States or Canada. Education is largely a function of the states or provinces and, at least in the US, local control of schools is the norm. States, provinces or national governments may strongly suggest or require certain actions as a matter of law or policy where government funds are involved, but local governing bodies set basic policies. As such, music education must sell itself to numerous boards of education and other controlling groups. What is available musically in some schools may be unavailable in others. Despite existence of the standards noted above, there is no compulsion to meet the standards on a national level. Indeed, a national curriculum probably is not politically viable, neither now nor in the near future.

In the United States, there is no national voice for music education that can command the attention of key educational policy-makers and legislators. While the Music Educators National Conference takes public positions in support of music and the other arts in education, and organizations such as the National Association of Music Merchants lend support, MENC is a diverse group, whose members' interests vary. Some are ideologues; some are interested in ideas for instruction; many want their students to be eligible for participation in music festivals where the state-sponsoring affiliate is the state division of MENC. The National Endowment for the Arts (NEA) supports arts education in various ways, but competition is intense, funding from the United States Congress varies and education is but one NEA focus.

Schools are instruments of social policy

Many constituencies consider schools as instruments of social policy and change. A school is a social institution, and affective experiences and resulting attitudes are an inevitable outcome of formal schooling.

Few social forces have been as powerful in American society over the past 45 years or so as racial desegregation, and resistance to desegregation. While legal segregation of races in public schools, once the normative practice in parts of the United States, is long gone, segregation based on housing patterns (the concept of the 'neighbour-hood school' is strong in the United States) remains. Attempts to promote integration by bussing students to particular schools in order to change the racial composition, operating highly visible 'magnet' schools to attract students to schools beyond their residence areas and drawing and redrawing attendance district boundaries have met with mixed success. Music education, occasionally, is seen as a means of enhancing diversity and, in American society, music certainly has been a way for people of diverse backgrounds to work together.

In recent years, schools have assumed functions peripheral to the school's main educational mission, such as providing breakfast, health care, and child care. For many families, where both parents are employed, or for single-parent families, the school is a custodial as well as an educational institution, and any change in school scheduling causes major disruption in the family routine. Seeing the school as a recreational and social services agency is an American vision, in stark contrast to continental Europe (Noack, 1999).

The United States constitution forbids promoting or restricting any sectarian religious practice. Most United States peoples came from a Judeo-Christian tradition, and the practice of religious rituals, including reciting the Lord's Prayer and compulsory Bible reading, was once common in American schools. In recent years, any open espousal of a particular religious belief, or any practice which may appear to compel students to participate in a religious observance, has become severely restricted. A Christmas pageant, or even a Christmas concert usually is forbidden. (A 'winter' concert, however, is all right.) 'Religious' music, such as Beethoven's *Missa Solemnis*, may be studied and performed as music, but the religious message must be subordinate to the music. (Of course, in non-public schools, many of which are organized along sectarian lines, this is not a problem.)

Gender issues are a traditional and contemporary area of concern for American music education. During the nineteenth century, many females were encouraged to become musically proficient, but not overly proficient, lest it peril their social stature; males risked characterization as effeminate if they studied music seriously (Koza, 1990). In the late nineteenth and early twentieth centuries, during the wave of greatest immigration to the United States from Europe, many immigrant parents wanted their children to study instruments, stereotypically the violin for boys and the piano for girls (Rubin, 1973; Tawa, 1982).

The twentieth century saw a paradox in that females predominated in many school performing organizations (Zervoudakes and Tanur, 1994), while, except for certain types of singers, males predominated among performers. Koza (1994) found that, despite high participation in school music, females were under-represented in illustrations contained within middle-school textbooks and were apt to be portrayed as amateurs rather than professionals. O'Neill (1997) concludes that, while positive change has occurred in other educational areas such as sports and mathematics, gender stereotypes persist in music, probably due to the surrounding cultures and, for students, peer pressure.

Ever-increasing exceptionalities

'Exceptional' students, who once would have remained at home or been institutionalized, now attend school, often in regular class settings, including music classes, as a result of policies of 'mainstreaming' or 'inclusion'. Schools must accommodate physical, mental and emotional disabilities. 'Exceptionalities' may include mental retardation, learning disabilities, visual and auditory impairments, physical conditions such as palsy and social maladjustments. Accommodation of exceptional students requires adaptation of facilities, careful curriculum planning and extra attention to individual needs. In the name of mainstreaming, or inclusion, students may be placed in music settings, particularly elementary general music, without adequate planning or resources. Ensemble directors may fear that the necessity to accommodate exceptional students will deteriorate the performance quality of the ensemble. The needs of exceptional students will not vanish; considerable research is necessary to facilitate meaningful accommodation.

Teacher education

Formal preparation, naturally, is a major influence on how music educators study and teach. In the United States and Canada, normal entry to the teaching profession requires completing an approved undergraduate programme. For music education, the student's major field is music education, not general education, the liberal arts, academic music or music performance, although all those areas are part of the programme. The model where a person earns a degree in the cognate area and then receives further education in pedagogical practices is rare. To be sure, some conservatory graduates and other musicians occasionally return to campus for music-education classes, necessary for state licensure or certification, in order to find employment or because of a new interest in teaching.

Accreditation agencies have much to say about the content of teacher-education programmes. Such agencies may be state boards or departments of education, legislatively mandated to set and monitor teacher-education standards, or voluntary participation agencies, such as the National Council for the Accreditation of Teacher Education.

Music-education teacher-preparation programmes are particularly heavy with requirements as curricula reflect the demands of legislative bodies, accreditation agencies and college and university general education requirements, as well as the traditions and beliefs of music-education faculties. Music-education students may receive instruction in teaching reading, adapting multicultural perspectives, awareness of exceptionalities, a wide array of liberal arts and various aspects of 'understanding the school', as well as traditional instruction in music theory, history and performance, ensemble experiences and pedagogical skills.

One may argue over whether or not teaching in American and Canadian schools is a 'profession'. Various regulations and codes of conduct exist, and educators certainly employ a designated body of knowledge. However, entry to the teaching 'profession' is determined by legislative bodies, not professional organizations. Except as they may influence legislative processes, practising educators have little or nothing to say about regulations governing teacher licensure and state approval of teacher-education programmes. Teachers have relatively little to say about conditions of their employment, such as time and length of the school day and organization for instruction within the day. While union-negotiated contracts may address such conditions, the very fact that governing bodies may prescribe work conditions suggests that teaching is not a profession.

Summary

Music learning and development is an individual matter. Yet it occurs within a particular society, filled with opportunities and constraints. In North America, music education is a product of national and regional conditions, the roles schools serve in society, politics and the realities of the conditions under which teachers work. Psychology has much to say about human learning and development but a complete picture of the relevant processes requires recognition of the social milieu in North America, as well as elsewhere.

References

Britton, A. P. (1958) 'Music in early American public education: a historical critique', in N. B. Henry (ed.) *Basic Concepts in Music Education*. Chicago: National Society for the Study of Education, pp. 195–210.

Bruer, J. T. (1999) 'In search of ... brain-based education'. *Phi Delta Kappan*, **80**, 648–57.

Consortium of National Arts Education Associations (1994) *National Standards for Arts Education*. Reston, VA: Music Educators National Conference.

Dewey, J. (1938) *Experience and Education*. New York: Macmillan.

Dewey, J. (1940) 'My pedagogic creed', in J. Ratner and J. Dewey (eds) *Education Today*. New York: Putnam's Sons. (Original work published 1897)

Gardner, H. (1993) *Frames of Mind* (rev. edn). New York: Basic Books.

Grandin, T., Peterson, M. and Shaw, G. L. (1998) 'Spatial-temporal versus language-analytic reasoning: the role of music training'. *Arts Education Policy Review* **99** (6), 11–14.

Gregory, A. H. (1997) 'The roles of music in society: the ethnomusicological perspective', in D. J. Hargreaves and A. C. North (eds) *The Social Psychology of Music*. Oxford: Oxford University Press.

Kaplan, M. (1990) *The Arts: A Social Perspective*. Rutherford, NJ: Fairleigh Dickinson University Press.

Kibler, R. J., Barker, L. L. and Miles, D. T. (1970) *Behavioral Objectives and Instruction*. Boston: Allyn & Bacon.

Koffka, K. (1935) *Principles of Gestalt Psychology*. New York: Harcourt, Brace & World.

Köhler, W. (1929) *Gestalt Psychology*. New York: Liveright.

Koza, J. E. (1990) 'Music instruction in the nineteenth century: views from Godey's lady's book, 1830–77'. *Journal of Research in Music Education*, **38**, 245–57.

Koza, J. E. (1994) 'Females in 1988 middle school textbooks: an analysis of illustrations'. *Journal of Research in Music Education*, **42**, 145–71.

Leng, X., Shaw, G. L. and Wright, E. L. (1990) 'Coding of musical structure and the trion model of cortex'. *Music Perception*, **8**, 49–62.

Lerdahl, F. and Jackendoff, R. (1983) A *Generative Theory of Tonal Music*. Cambridge, MA: MIT Press.

Mager, R. F. (1962) *Preparing Instructional Objectives*. Palo Alto, CA: Fearon Press.

Mark, M. L. and Gary, C. L. (1992) *A History of American Music Education*. New York: Schirmer Books.

Merriam, A. P. (1964) *The Anthropology of Music*. Evanston, IL: Northwestern University Press.

Mountcastle, V. B. (1978) 'An organizing principle for cerebral function: the unit module and the distributed system', in G. M. Edelman and V. B. Mountcastle (eds) *The Mindful Brain: Cortical Organization and the Group-selective Theory of Higher Brain Function*. Cambridge, MA: MIT Press.

Nantais, K. M. and Schellenberg, E. G. (1999) 'The Mozart effect: an artifact of preference'. *Psychological Science*, **10**, 370–3.

Noack, E. G. (1999) 'Comparing US and German education'. *Phi Delta Kappan*, **80**, 773–6.

Notterman, J. M. and Drewry, H. N. (1993) *Psychology and Education: Parallel and Interactive Approaches*. New York: Plenum Press.

O'Neill, S. A. (1997) 'Gender and music', in D. J. Hargreaves and A. C. North (eds), *The Social Psychology of Music*. Oxford: Oxford University Press.

Pflederer, M. (1967) 'Conservation laws applied to the development of musical intelligence'. *Journal of Research in Music Education*, **15**, 215–23.

Piaget, J. (1950) *The Psychology of Intelligence*. New York: Harcourt, Brace, Jovanovich.

Piaget, J. and Inhelder, B. (1969) *The Psychology of the Child*. New York: Basic Books.

Radocy, R. E. (1978) 'Cerebral dominance and music perception: stop the fad', in E. P. Asmus, Jr (ed.) *Proceedings of the Research Symposium on the Psychology and Acoustics of Music*. Lawrence, KS: University of Kansas, 120–30.

Radocy, R. E. (1998) 'Personal perspectives on research: past, present, and future'. *Journal of Research in Music Education*, **46**, 342–50.

Radocy, R. E. and Boyle, J. D. (1997) *Psychological Foundations of Musical Behavior* (3rd edn). Springfield, IL: Charles C. Thomas.

Rauscher, F. H., Shaw, G. L. and Ky, K. N. (1993) 'Music and spatial task performance'. *Nature*, **365**, 611.

Rauscher, F. H., Shaw, G. L., Levine, L. J. and Ky, K. N. (1994) 'Music and spatial task performance: a causal relationship'. Paper presented at the meeting of the American Psychological Association, Los Angeles, August.

Rauscher, F. H., Shaw, G. L., Levine, L. J., Wright, E. L., Dennis, W. R. and Newcomb, R. L. (1997) 'Music training causes long-term enhancement of preschool children's spatial-temporal reasoning'. *Neurological Research*, **19**, 2–8.

Reimer, B. (1999) 'Facing the risks of the "Mozart effect"'. *Music Educators Journal*, **86** (1), 37–43.

Rubin, R. (1973) *Voices of a People: The Story of Yiddish Folksong* (2nd edn). New York: McGraw-Hill.

Sarnthein, J., von Stein, A., Rappelsberger, P., Petsche, H., Rauscher, F. H.

and Shaw, G. L. (1997) 'Persistent patterns of brain activity: an EEG coherence study of the positive effect of music on spatial-temporal reasoning'. *Neurological Research*, **19**, 107–16.

Serafine, M. L. (1980) 'Piagetian research in music'. *Council for Research in Music Education Bulletin*, **62**, 1–21.

Skinner, B. F. (1938) *The Behavior of Organisms: An Experimental Analysis*. New York: Appleton-Century.

Steele, K. M., Bass, K. E. and Crook, M. D. (1999) 'The mystery of the Mozart effect: failure to replicate'. *Psychological Science*, **10**, 366–9.

Tawa, N. (1982) *A Sound of Strangers: Musical Culture, Acculturation, and the Post-Civil War Ethnic American*. Metuchen, NJ: Scarecrow Press.

Thorndike, E. L. (1932) *The Fundamentals of Learning*. New York: Teachers College Press.

Wertheimer, M. (1945) *Productive Thinking*. New York: Harper & Row.

West, R., Howell, P. and Cross, I. (1985) 'Modelling perceived musical structure', in P. Howell, I. Cross and R. West (eds) *Musical Structure and Cognition*. London: Academic Press.

Zervoudakes, J. and Tanur, J. M. (1994) 'Gender and musical instruments: winds of change?' *Journal of Research in Music Education*, **42**, 58–67.

CHAPTER

10

Poland

Wojciech Jankowski and Kacper Miklaszewski

Introduction

In 1918 Poland regained its independence after 123 years of partition and the rules of Russia, Prussia and Austria. Music was a substantial part of education at home and at school in the nineteenth century. Romantic works by great Polish composers (Fryderyk Chopin, Stanisław Moniuszko, Juliusz Zarębski, Ignacy Jan Paderewski) and songs by less well-known musicians helped in developing the national culture and in resisting attempts to assimilate Poles into the societies of the three invaders. This was part of the rapid development of the Polish education system in the time of enlightenment and early romanticism. During Chopin's twenty years in the homeland, the number of schools in Warsaw district grew fourfold, and a Main School of Music (the Warsaw Conservatoire) was founded in 1810.

The authorities of independent Poland considered music education as important for all members of society. Songbooks and method courses were commissioned by governmental agencies, and students at teachers colleges were obliged to develop their singing ability, read music notation and play at least one instrument (usually violin). Social initiatives were encouraged and private and co-operative music organizations developed, organizing concerts for schoolchildren in big cities. The eventual development of specialized music schools after World War II built on projects originated in the 1930s which were interrupted by the outbreak of the war.

Two systems of music education in Poland

Today, 38,650,000 people live in Poland, in an area of 312,000 square kilometres (GUS, 1998). Tradition and cultural policy over the last 50 years have influenced the development of two separate systems of music education, both governed and financed by the state. One of them, which is extensive in its scope, consists of teaching music in general schools, from elementary to secondary level, and is known as the General Music Education system (GME). As with all other subjects, GME is controlled by the Ministry of Education.

The second system, which is intensive rather than extensive, consists of music schools at primary, secondary and university levels, and is known as Specialized Music Education (SME). These music schools are financed and governed by the Ministry of Culture, although the Ministry of Education supervises the teaching of general subjects in them. Table 10.1 shows the number of schools which exist at different levels. Music academies are structured like universities and ruled according to the 1990 Higher Education Act, which governs all higher education institutions in Poland.

Table 10.1 Specialized music schools run by the Ministry of Culture (1998)

Level	No. of schools	No. of students
Primary music schools (6 years)	142	38,584
Primary music schools with general curriculum (8 years)	7	7,940
Secondary music schools (6 years)	41	6,693
Primary- and secondary-level music schools (12 years)	2	
Primary- and secondary-level music schools with general curriculum (12 years)	4	
Music Lycea (4 years)	3	2,315*
Units combining music schools of different type	20	
Music academies	8	4,531
Totals	**227**	**60,063**

Source: Statistical information received by the authors at the Department of Art Schools, Ministry of Culture, June 1998.

*The number includes students of the secondary level from the 12-years schools combining both curricula.

Beside these state music schools, Poland also has nearly 148 non-public music schools, most of which are at primary level. Thirty of these are recognized by the state administration, and their graduates enjoy the same rights as those completing courses at public music schools. There is no state-run system of music education for preschool children, and activities for mothers and newborn children are very scarce and undocumented. However, in kindergartens (children from 3 to 6), teachers are encouraged to play musical games with children, and parents readily pay an additional fee for qualified Dalcroze Eurhythmic instruction, usually twice a week. This kind of activity often forms the foundation of a child's repertoire of songs.

At the time of writing, the system of general education in Poland is undergoing radical structural and curricular reform. The system of providing children with eight years of elementary schooling followed by two to five years of secondary schooling is to be replaced by six years of elementary schooling, three years of junior-secondary school (*gimnazjum*) and three years of comprehensive, senior-secondary school (*liceum*). The first nine years of education are to become compulsory. Furthermore, complex national curricula, which in the past had to be followed strictly by teachers, are to be replaced by 'curricular foundations' which indicate minimal levels of knowledge that all children have to acquire in schools. Teachers will be granted freedom in selecting between various programmes, and are to be encouraged to create their own. Many traditional school subjects like physics and chemistry are also being collapsed into broader areas such as science. These changes significantly alter the position of music in general schools.

Educational outcomes

The musical experiences of pupils trained in these two educational systems differ radically, and the musical development of individuals depends on the opportunity that they have to attend one type of school or another. Despite the existence of SME, Polish children have less chance to acquire good music education than their peers in other countries. GME provides no opportunity for students to intensify their musical experiences should their interest in music develop at school: SME is the only alternative available.

In the 1980s, 90,000 Polish children, representing 0.25 per cent of the country's population, attended primary music schools and music-teaching centres. The corresponding proportion of the Swedish population attending primary music schools was 14.6 times larger. In the United Kingdom during the 1980s, children had the opportunity to elect intensified music training within elementary schools, and 0.9 per cent of the population took this opportunity (Zemła, 1990). The percentage for present-day Poland is even lower, with students of state primary music schools constituting only 0.12 per cent of the population (although the number of children attending non-public schools is not known). One possible cause of this concerns the unequal distribution of primary music schools across the country: the number of state schools per thousand of the population varies from 0.001 to 0.015, depending on the region in question (Jankowska, 1990).

Aims and objectives

Before World War II, music was considered an important subject in general schools. However, for fifteen years after the war it was suppressed almost to the point of extinction. One priority of educational policy at that time was to prepare people for the technical reconstruction of the economy and for so-called 'democratization', as communist indoctrination was called. Similarly, the 'cultural advancement of masses' during the 1950s was realized by a network of specialized music schools organized exclusively for gifted children (Jankowski and Zemła, 1999).

The 1960s saw more favourable conditions for the development of GME. Music as a compulsory school subject came back to all general public schools and a selection of vocational schools. The 'Polish concept of music education' had been developed (Przychodzińska, 1979), and a complex music education curriculum, textbooks, teachers' guides and a set of LP records were prepared. Teachers were served by a series of methodological aids and a philosophical introduction by Jankowski (1970). The most important change was that music was now assigned two hours a week in grades one through three (one hour a week in all remaining grades), and school principals felt quite free to finance extra-curricular musical activities such as choirs and ensembles. Unfortunately, these positive developments could not reverse the neglect of music in previous years (Rakowski, 1986).

The beginning of the 1990s brought Poland rapid democratization and a free market. The radical economical reforms of the decade limited the amount of money allocated to all kinds of schools by government agencies. The first subject to suffer was music, with choirs and ensembles in general schools being refused financial support almost entirely.

Current educational reforms do not allow music to be taught as a separate school subject in the elementary grades: in grades four through six, music is taught in the 'block' called Arts. In new junior- and senior-secondary schools (*gimnazjum* and *liceum*) music is given the status of an 'activity whose form is elective'. Students can decide to attend general music classes *or* a choir *or* an ensemble, although the content of music lessons still maintains a close relationship with other arts and cultural issues. Students are expected to develop skills rather than collect knowledge, and teachers are encouraged to be creative in developing their own curricula and textbooks.

General music education

Until now the main educational objectives of GME had been to provide students with experience in music performance, the opportunity to produce simple forms of creative work, and the necessary knowledge to allow them to participate in so-called high musical culture. General music education was also expected to develop both musical abilities (such as a sense of tonality and harmony) and interests, particularly those which push children to sing in a choir or play in an ensemble. The new curricular foundations call for generally similar objectives (MEN, 1998) and set schools similar tasks, but stipulate that music should be taught with more reference to other traditional subjects such as literature, history and languages.

Musical literacy has not been a single unified goal in the GME curriculum. Programme documents refer to 'score-aided singing': this is rote learning with a score at hand to help memorization of lyrics and melody, rather than reading music at sight from a score. New curricular foundations leave this objective unchanged despite intensive lobbying by musicians who wanted the sight singing to become a priority. It is also worth noting that competencies which could allow general school graduates to transfer to SME schools or to enrol in music academies are at no point mentioned in the GME curriculum.

Specialist music education

Music schools cater for those people (aged 7 to adulthood) who are gifted and interested in music. These primary and secondary music schools aim to provide students with basic and advanced musical skills which allow the further development of artistry, mastery and maturity in music academies. The system also trains competent music instructors who go on to work in general schools, cultural centres, clubs etc. It is assumed that the graduates of the SME system will work in musical professions.

Students enrolled in primary music schools encounter music notation at their very first lesson and are presented with theoretical concepts and musical terminology quite early on. Also, most students are encouraged to associate notes on the staff with fingering when learning their instruments (which usually occurs through private lessons held twice weekly). Students learn to sing, to read music and to move to music in small groups, though they are not expected to improvise, either vocally or instrumentally. They also listen to the basic classical repertoire in courses on music history and musical forms. Young pianists and string players enrol in secondary music schools after graduation from the primary level. They continue their private instrumental instruction, participate in ensemble performances and attend advanced music history and theory courses. Some of them achieve real mastery in recognition of musical structures by ear and in singing. However, it is also possible to enter secondary music school without former training, particularly in specialisms such as wind instruments, double bass, operatic singing and percussion. These students follow intensive ear-training and theory classes but quite often fail to achieve the level of competence comparable with their more experienced peers.

Educational outcomes

Today's GME and SME satisfies neither its organizers nor its graduates. In GME, the curriculum aims to integrate students into Polish musical culture systematically, but consequently neglects individual preferences, the varying musical aptitudes of different children and the role that music plays in their lives. Furthermore, only very well trained teachers tend to be able to follow the complex curriculum, and many schools have no such staff member.

In SME schools there is heavy emphasis on musical professionalism from the very beginning. Students experience selection stress and are forced to learn music which is often too difficult for them. Much of this teaching might well violate modern methodological principles which require the formation of sound concepts before the introduction of verbal terms and music notation. Private instrumental instruction, furthermore, does little to plug the gap in terms of ear training and music theory. As a consequence of this, many SME students become disenchanted with music and some face psychological disorders. However, despite this criticism, the creation of an SME system, its service to gifted children, and the high level of musicianship it produces should be recognized as successes.

Recent surveys show that 99 per cent of elementary- and secondary-general school students express an interest in music, and that for a majority of them music is an 'important or very important factor of life' (Kamińska and Manturzewska, 1999). However, only 20 per cent of elementary-school students declare any interest in classical music. Although this interest increases in secondary general school pupils (35 per cent), pop and rock music is the predominant interest of young people attending GME classes. Students in specialized music schools, in contrast, are interested mostly in classical genres. Of SME school students, 75 per cent, and all members of a group of pupils defined as 'extraordinarily gifted' in the research sample, expressed a preference for classical music.

Contents and methods

Curricular foundations for GME

The current curricular foundations define some minimum, general obligatory activities in music. In grades one to three, children have to experience differences in timbres of instruments and different voices, start to realize what rhythm and tempo are, sing, play simple instruments and move to music. They also have to recognize elements of humans' acoustical environment and listen to musical compositions. In grades four to six children are introduced to 'musical terms necessary to talk about music', the 'abundance of musical forms' (e.g. domestic and music from other nations) and values transmitted by classical, folk and popular music. The junior-secondary school (*gimnazjum*) continues with these activities, while in the senior-secondary school (*liceum*) students learn about the 'historical development of European music … music in rituals, magic and religion; music in film, theatre and media'. They are also expected to discuss music as a non-verbal means of communication and 'to create musical structures' (MEN, 1999).

Centrally developed curricula for SME

In the system of specialized music schools, aims and educational objectives are clearly specified. Centrally developed curricula for all schools guarantee a uniform level of training across the country. Secondary music schools which offer combined music and general education help musically gifted young people to prepare for General Certificate of Education exams, which are a strict prerequisite for studying at college level.

In the primary music schools (grades one to six) all children are required to attend private instrumental instruction, in addition to classes concerning ear training, eurhythmics and musical knowledge. Students in grades four to six are also required to participate in some group music-making (e.g. a choir or an orchestra). Most of the primary music schools offer major instruction in piano, violin, cello and accordion. Some also offer wind instruments and percussion.

The curriculum for secondary music schools consists of private lessons in all musical instruments (and, in many schools, voice) as well as Dalcroze's eurhythmic method and music theory. The core set of courses includes ear training, four-part harmony, rudimentary instrumentation and counterpoint, history of music and analysis of musical form. Obligatory subjects also include choir and vocal ensembles, chamber ensembles and orchestras. Electives are often also available, which may cover elementary conducting and composition.

Students who attend primary music schools that do not combine music training with general education spend six to twelve afternoon hours a week on music, in addition to time spent rehearsing at home. The corresponding figure for secondary music school is 12 to 20 hours which, if added to over 30 hours of secondary general school duties and (much) practising, means that musically gifted Polish adolescents work very hard indeed.

Teaching technology

The availability of teaching technology in both GME and SME is quite poor. Well-equipped music laboratories are scarce, and the rapidly developing music-recording industry has had no impact on school practice. In our informal survey of 42 music teachers and instructors from teacher-training institutions, 88 per cent reported using portable tape machines or portable CD-players in their classrooms, and 21 per cent had hi-fi equipment at their disposal. Only two persons had access to a collection of more than 100 CDs.

Assessment

No system of assessing attainment in music education is adopted at national level. In general schools, music teachers are obliged to follow general instructions concerning how they should assign marks, as, for example, in geography or mathematics: neither standardized achievement tests nor well-defined assessment procedures have yet been developed. However, music achievement tests for SME have been developed by the Warsaw-based Institute for Research in Music Education, Chopin Academy of Music. Over 60 years of research has resulted in Polish adaptations of the music ability and aptitude tests by Bentley, Drake, Wing, Gordon (IMMA, PMMA, MAP) and Zenatti, and the development of the Institute's own music achievement tests.

These include 'The Music History and Music Heritage Test' by Kamińska (1984), for general secondary school seniors, and the 'Solfeggio Test' by Kielanowska (1985), for candidates for advanced music studies. The most ambitious is the 'General Music Knowledge Test' (TWOM: Kotarska, 1995b, 1997) which is designed for four levels, i.e. after 6, 8, 10 and 12 years of specialized music training. To date, the tests for the third level have been developed, standardized and normalized, and there is growing interest in the test among Polish SME teachers of music theory and history. The contents of this are shown in Table 10.2.

Table 10.2 Content of the General Music Knowledge Test battery, level III (Kotarska, 1997)

	No. of items
I. Music material (four sub-tests), total	**206**
Intervals	48
Scales	24
Melody	4
Metre and rhythm	49
Harmony	58
Texture	9
Notation (clefs)	4
Tempo, dynamics, articulation marks	10
II. Culture and a composition (two sub-tests), total	**110**
Texture	3
Performing apparatus	9
Components of musical form	20
Creation of a form	6
Components in a form development	5
Forms and genres	15
Aesthetic programme	4
Music repertoire	20
History of music and musical thesaurus	23
Recognition of music from other countries	5
III. Contemporary musical life (one sub-test), total	**131**
People acting in music	60
Musical institutions	32
Music in the press and music periodicals	27
Knowledge of contemporary music	9
Music in radio and TV	3
Grand total	**447**

Non-classical music

The inclusion of world and pop music in general schools depends mostly on a teacher's interest and competence. There was little coverage in the previous music-education curriculum, but in the present climate, in which teachers and schools enjoy more freedom, the proportion of teachers using pop songs in the classroom and referring to music from other cultures may increase. However, few Polish secondary and music schools offer training in pop music (although the Szymanowski Music Academy in Katowice is a notable exception). Similarly, no Polish music school offers specialized training in the performance of music from non-western cultures.

Educational outcomes

The musical aptitude of young Poles seems to be similar to that of their peers in other countries. Kotarska (1995a) found that the mean Gordon's *PMMA* score obtained by one hundred 7-year-olds from an elementary school in Warsaw was identical to that obtained by 280 American peers belonging to the test standardization group (both means = 32.0), and Kamińska and Manturzewska (1999) found that the mean score of 343 Polish students from various types of school on Wing's Standardized Tests of Musical Intelligence (parts 1–3) was almost the same as the British standardization group mean (40.2 and 40.5 respectively).

Normative contents and achievements in GME

Lipska and Janowska (1984) found that before the introduction of the new curriculum, students at the highest grade (15 years), during a school year, sang an average of eight songs, performed five instrumental pieces and tried five times to solve the creative problems of improvising music to a simple poem. Teachers in 40 per cent of schools taught by rote, and music notation was taught by rote learning in 36 per cent of schools. Students listened mostly to romantic music, and the most popular work was Franz Schubert's *Erlkönig*. The number of compositions listened to during the year ranged between three and fourteen. Students knew how to describe the features of music written in particular historical periods. Verbal tasks of this kind, which do not involve any listening or performing experience, were easy for about 60 per cent of subjects, while matching titles of compositions with the names of Polish contemporary composers appeared to be quite difficult for all but 27 per cent of the participants. The majority of the students were able to sing melodies which contained 10–13 notes accurately, while the poorest singers were able only to sing melodies containing 4–6 notes. While they managed to use music notation during the performance of simple instrumental pieces, they had difficulty in doing so for sight-singing.

In 1985–7, 2470 eighth-grade students from 100 schools in ten regions of Poland were surveyed to see how their skills changed following the introduction of a new curriculum (Hoffman-Lipska and Jankowska, 1988). Students taught by the 'old' curriculum were most successful in verbally describing music they listened to, i.e. at identifying instruments and describing musical mood and character: over 70 per cent of such tasks were correctly solved. Fifty per cent of questions about knowledge of music (its form, composer's name, style) were answered correctly, while the expected level of musical skills (singing, using musical score, playing musical instruments) was acquired by only 23 per cent of students. Students were generally good at aurally recognizing musical instruments and Polish folk dances (about 70 per cent correct answers in both cases), but had difficulty in recognizing foreign composers (only 8.7 per cent correct answers). While 60 per cent of students managed to quote a definition of three-part form (ABA), only 15 per cent were able to sing a song at sight.

Two years later the study was repeated in the same 100 schools, covering 2536 young people trained according to the *new* curriculum. The differences between students taught by the new and the old curricula were not very great. Listening remained the easiest task (73 per cent met the expected standard), skills (music reading and writing) was the most difficult (22 per cent) and musical knowledge was still intermediate (55 per cent). This was despite 87 per cent of the teachers claiming that they had worked on the development of reading and singing skills. Sixty-four per cent of students correctly recognized sounds of musical instruments, 44 per cent knew about Polish composers, but only 15 per cent had the expected degree of knowledge of historical epochs and foreign composers (Hoffman-Lipska and Jankowska, 1990). It appeared that changes in curriculum and teaching methods were much too small to modify educational outcomes. It also became clear that formation of such skills as music reading and writing needs more intensive training than one hour a week. A recent study by Kamińska and Manturzewska (1999) suggested that the current situation remains unchanged. They administered Kamińska's 'Music History and Music Heritage Test' to 145 seniors from general elementary schools. Only about 28 per cent of the test items were answered correctly, and the scores of 84 lyceum students were not much higher.

Lewandowska (1978) matched the developmental curves of scores on Bentley's *Measures of Musical Abilities*, collected in Argentina, Hungary, and the UK with those in Poland. While eight-year-old children gained similar results in all countries, Polish thirteen-year-olds scored ten test points lower than their peers in other countries. Kamińska (1997) studied the singing ability of children attending general elementary schools. Her precise measurement technique showed that 14-year-olds actually appeared to be poorer singers than were 11-year-olds, but intensive music education (i.e. participation in the first Polish Kodály group, meeting their music teacher five times a week) helped to overcome this tendency. She suggested that this decline in singing skill may be related to the change of interests in early adolescence and that systematic and attractive music experience may help young people to overcome feelings of shyness caused by an inability to perform music skilfully.

Our own experience tells us that almost no-one who learns music exclusively in a Polish general school is able to sing simple songs at sight, play simple music on an instrument from the score, write down a tune or improvise. Furthermore, there are no songbooks with music notation in Polish Catholic churches (where the majority of the population gathers at least once a week), and people do not sing from scores in pubs, scout camps or during family reunions. Non-professionals who do use music notation belong to the rare group of dropouts from specialized music education; and so the ability to read notation is something that needs to be addressed urgently.

Normative contents and achievements in SME

Intensive training in specialized music schools orients students towards professionalism in music at an early stage. Although we have found only a few primary music-school graduates who are able to play accompaniments to the most popular Christmas carols at sight, most of them are able to learn simple pieces after a few days of rehearsal from the score. Their level of attainment is illustrated by average scores on the Australian Test for Advanced Music Studies, Part II (Polish version) achieved by applicants to the Chopin Academy of Music. Despite the differences between applicants to various departments, the mean total score of 202 Poles (19.4, S.D. – 4.4) is higher than the corresponding score achieved by Australian applicants to music departments (16.4, S.D. – 5.4; Meyer-Borysewicz, 1995).

Music-school graduates are also expected to give recitals on their major instruments (or voice). A pianist completing primary music school is expected to perform studies, a simple classical sonata, a Bach Three-Part Invention or an easy fugue, and a miniature. The secondary school calls for an almost professional performance, lasting for about 40 minutes, of a 'serious' sonata (e.g. Beethoven) or a concerto with orchestra. Academies of music formulate no specific requirements for students' final recitals, although each instrumentalist is obliged to give two solo performances from within the standard concert repertoire, each consisting of no less than 90 minutes of music. Improvising skills are rare, however, and training in musical creativity is only given to students by departments of composition, organ and eurhythmics.

Student issues

Gender

Gender does not seem to influence students' opportunity to study music in general school: the same general music classes have been obligatory for both sexes for a very long time. However, because boys' voices change in early adolescence, the majority of higher-elementary-grade choirs consist primarily of girls.

There is an even balance of girls and boys in music schools. In 1970/71, girls comprised 53 per cent of the 26,177 students in state music schools (Campbell Trowsdale, 1973). There is little to suggest that this has altered significantly since then, although the precise gender distribution varies over time and according to the particular subject of specialization. This variability is illustrated by our own data based on graduate lists published in the fiftieth anniversary books of two Warsaw music schools, which show that more and more girls study typically 'male' instruments like winds (flute is now dominated by girls) and accordion.

Gifted children

Gifted children and youths have an opportunity to enter specialized music schools regardless of their socioeconomic status. Primary music schools advertise recruitment to their first grade each year. The entrance tests consist of checking song repertoire, voice quality, musical interests and, in some cases, the ability to learn music quickly. All state music schools are free of charge, and students from low-income families receive a subsidy on the rental of musical instruments.

In music academies, scholarships are available on the same principles as in all higher-education institutions. Very successful music school students are assisted by the Polish Government's Children Fund (*Fundusz na Rzecz Dzieci*), which also organizes summer courses and performances. Music schools effectively select children and adolescents with outstanding musical aptitude. The lowest score in Wing's 'Standardized Test of Musical Intelligence' (parts 1–3), gained by students of music schools, was still four test points higher than the mean value obtained from students of the same age group attending general schools (Manturzewska and Kotarska, 1990). Kamińska and Manturzewska (1999) also found a 'substantial growth' of scores on Wing's test in secondary music-school students as compared with comparable data collected in the 1970s.

Careers in music

The crisis stemming from the very rapid social transformations of the 1990s limited traditional career opportunities: opera houses and orchestras have suffered serious financial difficulties in recent years. However, political freedom has resulted in the appearance of many small groups, performing a range of musical styles. As a consequence of this, concert life in Poland is now even more active than during the communist regime, and there are still career opportunities in music. About ten small companies issue CDs with classical recordings by Polish musicians. Many of these activities are sponsored by local authorities and by industry. Perhaps the greatest threat to this musical prosperity is that very low wages are offered to music teachers in both GME and SME, which results in a decreasing number of musicians who also identify themselves as educators.

Until today, professional music schools have not developed any institutional support for young musicians at the beginning of their professional careers. There is no impresario office to organize and support debut performances, nor do music academies promote their graduates. Although no surveys have been conducted currently on this problem, it seems that many music academy graduates find jobs abroad or work in non-musical professions.

Conclusion

Despite more than 40 years of a communist regime which claimed to create equal educational opportunities followed by ten years of the development of 'western' democratic relationships, the wide gap between professional music training and mass music education has increased in Poland over this period. Both systems urgently need reform.

The professional system needs to adapt to changing labour-market conditions, to stylistic discoveries in European music, to the music of other cultures and to psychological constraints on human development. The amount of work required to meet the high standards forced by competitors can have adverse effects if pupils are attending two schools at the same time, or spending all afternoons rehearsing.

The Polish general music education system seems to be at real risk. Parents who have missed a good introduction to music in their own education can neither encourage nor support their own children's musical development, and may not see the value of high-level arts and music teaching. School principals, unpressurized by parents and with small financial resources, do not hesitate to cancel extra musical programmes and to limit compulsory music classes to the legal minimum. The introduction of young people into a valuable musical heritage needs an attractive and cost-effective educational system which could be common for both streams at least at the elementary-school level.

Attaining such a goal is certainly difficult, but may not be impossible given the achievements of psychology of music and music education research. There is a developing Polish literature in these fields, starting with Lissa's (e.g. 1933) early publications. These have been followed by Manturzewska's fundamental studies of the psychological determinants of success in music (Manturzewska, 1969, 1974) and life-span development in music (Manturzewska, 1995), and by adaptations of the Zoltán Kodály and Edwin Gordon music education systems, as well as by Kamińska's (1997) study of children's musical development. The problem now is how to transfer theoretical knowledge of human music behaviour into effective educational practice.

References

Campbell Trowsdale, G. (1973) *Public Institutions in Music Education: A Profile of the Polish Music Schools*. Vancouver: University of British Columbia.

GUS (1998) *Rocznik Statystyczny R.P.* [Statistical Yearbook of Polish Republic]. Warszawa: Main Office of Statistics.

Hoffman-Lipska, E. and Jankowska, L. (1988) 'Stan przygotowania muzycznego młodzieży szkół podstawowych (na podstawie badań) [Music preparation of young people from elementary school (research report)]. *Wychowanie Muzyczne w Szkole*, **32** (2), 93–105.

Hoffman-Lipska, E. and Jankowska, L. (1990) 'Stan przygotowania muzycznego młodzieży szkół podstawowych (na podstawie badań – II etap)' [Music preparation of young people from elementary school (research report – II stage)]. *Wychowanie Muzyczne w Szkole*, **34** (1–2), 28–34.

Jankowski, W. (1970) *Wychowanie Muzyczne w Szkole ogólnokształcącej* [Music education in a general school]. Warszawa: PZWS.

Jankowska, M. (1990) *Szkolnictwo Muzyczne w Polsce. Materiały Statystyczne* [Music schools in Poland: Statistical data]. Warszawa: Chopin Academy of Music.

Jankowski, W. and Zemła, A. (1999) (eds) *Pierwsza szkoła umuzykalniająca w powojennej Warszawie* [First music school in post-war Warsaw]. Warszawa: Kolberg Music School.

Kamińska, B. (1997) *Kompetencje wokalne dzieci i młodzieży – ich poziom, rozwój i uwarunkowania* [Vocal competencies of children and youth – their level, development and developmental conditions]. Warszawa: Chopin Academy.

Kamińska, B. and Manturzewska, M. (1999) 'Określenie przesłanek psychologicznych i socjologicznych postaw i oczekiwań młodzieży w odniesieniu do muzyki w szkole' [In search of psychological and sociological bases of young people's attitudes and expectancies toward music in school], in J. Kurcz (ed.) *Kształcenie Nauczycieli Muzyki: Stan Obecny in perspektywy* [Training of music teachers: the present state and perspectives]. Kraków: Cracow Academy of Music.

Kielanowska, Z. (1985) *Test Solfeggia Zofii Kielanowskiej* [Zofia Kielanowska's Solfeggio Test]. Warszawa: Chopin Academy of Music.

Kotarska, H. (1995a) 'Podstawowa Miara Słuchu Muzycznego (PMMA) i Średnia Miara Słuchu Muzycznego (IMMA) E. Gordona, Wyniki badań prowadzonych pod kierunkiem Katedry Psychologii Muzyki w latach 1991–1994' [Gordon's PMMA and IMMA: results of studies undertaken under the supervision of the Chair of Psychology of Music], in E. Zwolińska and W. Jankowski (eds) *Teoria Uczenia się Muzyki Według Edwina Gordona* [Music Learning Theory by Edwin Gordon]. Bydgoszcz: WSP.

Kotarska, H. (1995b) 'Music tests in Poland', in M. Manturzewska, M. Meyer-Borysewicz, K. Miklaszewski and A. Białkowski (eds) *Psychology of Music Today*. Warszawa: Chopin Academy of Music.

Kotarska, H. (1997) *Testy Wykształcenia Ogólnomuzycznego. Poziom III. Podręcznik* [General Knowledge of Music Tests. Level III. Manual]. Warszawa: CEA/ Chopin Academy of Music.

Kotarska, H. and Kamińska, B. (1984) *Testy Osiągnięć dla Młodzieży Szkolnej* [Achievement tests for school youth]. Warszawa: WSiP.

Lewandowska, K. (1978) *Rozwój Zdolności Muzycznych u Dzieci w Wieku Szkolnym* [Development of Musical Abilities in School Children]. Warsawa: WSiP.

Lipska, E. and Jankowska, L. (1984) 'Nowy program muzyki klasy VIII szkoły podstawowej w świetle badań wdrożeniowych' [New music education programme for grade 8 of elementary school in the light of developmental research]. *Wychowanie Muzyczne w Szkole*, **27** (4–5), 237–49.

Lissa, Z. (1933) 'Twórczość muzyczna dziecka w świetle psychologii i pedagogiki' [Musical creativity in children as viewed by psychology and pedagogy]. *Muzyka w Szkole*, no. 5.

Manturzewska, M. (1969) *Psychologiczne Warunki Osiągnięć Pianistycznych* [Psychological Determinants of Pianistic Success]. Wrocław: Ossolineum.

Manturzewska, M. (1974) *Psychologiczne Wyznaczniki Powodzenia w Studiach Muzycznych* [Psychological Predictors of Success in Music Studies]. Warszawa: COPSA.

Manturzewska, M. (1995) 'A biographical study of the life-span development of professional musicians', in M. Manturzewska, M. Meyer-Borysewicz, K. Miklaszewski and A. Białkowski (eds) *Psychology of Music Today*. Warszawa: Chopin Academy of Music.

Manturzewska, M. and Kotarska, H. (1990) 'Zdolności muzyczne, ich rozwój i związek z działalnością muzyczną w świetle wyników badań testowych' [Musical abilities, their development and relationship to musical activity as viewed through test results], in M. Manturzewska and H. Kotarska (eds) *Wybrane Zagadnienia z Psychologii Muzyki* [Selected Issues in Psychology of Music]. Warszawa: WSiP.

MEN (1998) *Reforma Systemu Edukacji Narodowej* [The Reform of the System of National Education]. Warszawa: Ministry of Education.

MEN (1999) *Załącznik do Rozporządzenia Ministra Educacji Narodowej* [Enclosure to the Decision of the Minister of Education]. Warszawa: Ministry of Education.

Meyer-Borysewicz, M. (1995) 'Candidates for the Chopin Academy of Music in Warsaw as tested with the "Australian Test for Advanced Music Studies" by Doreen Bridges', in M. Manturzewska, K. Miklaszewski and A. Białkowski (eds) *Psychology of Music Today*. Warszawa: Chopin Academy of Music.

Przychodzińska, M. (1979) *Polskie Koncepcje Powszechnego Wychowania Muzycznego* [Polish Concepts of Mass Music Education]. Warszawa: WSiP.

Rakowski, A. (1986 edn) *Podstawowe Uwarunkowania Dostępu Dzieci i Młodzieży do Kultury Muzycznej* [Fundamental Determinants of Children and Youth Access to Musical Culture]. Warszawa: Chopin Academy of Music.

Zemła, A. (1990) 'Kwestia dostępu do kształcenia muzycznego w aspekcie porównawczym' [A problem of the accessibility of music education as viewed in comparative perspective], in A. Rakowski (ed.) *Podstawowe Uwarunkowania Dostępu Dzieci i Młodzieży do Kultury Muzycznej, tom II b* [Fundamental Determinants of Children and Youth Access to Musical Culture, vol. II b]. Warszawa: Chopin Academy of Music.

Portugal

Graça Mota

Historical perspective

Although Portuguese music education has undergone considerable change and improvement over the past few decades, the prevailing ambiguity and lack of clear direction is best understood in terms of its historical background. The first Royal Conservatory (later National Conservatory) was created in Lisbon by the Portuguese writer Almeida Garrett in 1835. For at least 80 years it was the only place where music was taught in a systematic way, and the Conservatory produced some of the most significant musicians of the period.

From 1878 there were regulations concerning the inclusion of choral singing in the school curriculum during the first years of primary school. A document written in 1909 states that 'music helps to build the unity of the people in every act of public life, and when that country is ruled by a democracy that praises the principle of equality, then choral singing should be the best form to express its feelings' (Arroyo, 1909, p. 17). These words, written one year before the end of the monarchy and the beginning of the First Republic, and about twenty years before a dictatorship was installed for 48 years, still embody the spirit of the French Revolution and its 'Marseillaise'. In fact, however, music education immediately before the Salazar dictatorship was described by Real Costa (1923) as being part of the curriculum 'just on paper', and as having little or no importance attached to it by administrators or by students.

Later, the function of choral singing in the Portuguese educational system was to convey national ideology, though it was never one of great importance. In the whole of the curriculum choral singing played a very minor role, being taught mainly by untrained teachers who felt unable to motivate their pupils. Its significance was mostly restricted to the National Youth organization, in which the singing of heroic hymns formed part of public rallies. Although it is acknowledged that such singing did not contribute to the general musical development of young people, its impact on their relationship with music-listening and -making was not actually negative.

The year 1968 saw the wholesale reform of Portuguese music education as a result of the international emphasis on the arts in education, as well as several visits to Portugal by prominent music educators who were philosophically close to Orff, Willems, Dalcroze and others. Choral singing was replaced by a system of music education based on broader concepts of teaching and learning: notably that musical practice should always precede musical theory. The Gulbenkian Foundation and the Associação Portuguesa de Educação Musical (APEM) played a major role outside the state system, organizing seminars, conferences and music courses that brought to the country musicians and educators such as John Paynter and Murray Schaefer, and their ideas concerning music education.

Further change occurred after 1974, when dictatorship changed to democracy: a society in search of its identity in every domain of the citizen's life began to discuss what should constitute education in the context of a democratic political framework. At that time, music was definitely not an educational priority, although it did have a social and political role. Many of the young people of the time identified with what might be called a 'politically engaged music' which employed words that reflected the everyday issues of Portuguese society, and which was heard and played everywhere as part of the revolution. Interestingly, some of that music also found its way into the classroom, and even today is still performed by pop groups (albeit in modified form, and less motivated by the revolutionary flame). Several pop groups have recently begun to explore their Portuguese musical roots, which in some cases has led to wide international recognition.

The Portuguese colonization of Africa ended in 1975, leading to political problems and wars in many of the countries concerned. As a consequence, natives of Angola, Mozambique, Guinea, and Cape Verde came to Portugal in search of employment. Portuguese society was subject to a sudden cultural change that was most noticeable in Lisbon, but also manifest more or less all over the country. The richness of the African musical styles that came to prominence (e.g. mornas, coladeiras, funanás) now forms part of the music which is heard daily in Portugal. Though still consumed mainly by African people, these styles have proved popular with many young people. Some younger teachers have begun incorporating this music and its powerful rhythms in their music lessons, a new direction in Portuguese music. In fact, while 500 years of colonization failed to bring European and African cultures closer together, the post-revolutionary times have seen this happen in another context. The influence of this new direction on young children's musical development should be carefully followed and researched.

This chapter does not attempt to make a comparative study of the Portuguese and Spanish music education systems, although this is an important area in its own right: the histories of both countries are strongly intertwined, and it appears that there is considerable potential for joint projects and development strategies. Unfortunately, apart from some initiatives taken by the Portuguese and Spanish sections of the International Society for Music Education (ISME), there are as yet no signs of real sharing between the two music education systems.

In 1978, Spanish democracy went through a process of restoration, and Parliament approved a new Constitution that opened up the possibility of autonomy for Spain's very different regions. This change had an impact on the educational system, especially regarding 'the defence and promotion of everyone's right to education as a plural and non-discriminative public service ... based on the participation of all members of the school community' (Mateus, 1992, p. 120). The 1990 approved Law for the Organisation of the General Educational System confirmed the system which already existed, namely that music should be present in the whole Spanish curriculum of Basic Education (which lasts for eight grades). According to Mateus, however, 'music education has been and still is – apart from honourable exceptions – completely abandoned' (p. 139). Since the content of the Spanish music curriculum is very prescriptive, describing age-specific targets in considerable detail, recent efforts have been devoted to the questions of how the curriculum might actually be implemented, and to the appointment of specialized music teachers (which was contrary to government policy until 1975).

Finally, it is worth mentioning that there has been a systematic concern with modern issues in music education in Spain, which has been promoted by the publication of translated versions of the work of the most important authors in this area. This has made Spanish music educators aware of the most relevant research produced in recent decades, and has also enabled a wider public to have access to writings in music education.

The music curriculum today

In discussing music education in present-day Portugal, we will distinguish between general music education and specialist music education. These two parts of the system are less co-ordinated than they might be, which could, unfortunately, have negative consequences for Portuguese children.

General music education

General music education has changed significantly as a result of the last national reform of the educational system, and the introduction of music degrees by polytechnic schools of education in 1986. Over the last decade, discussions concerning the new music curriculum for general education contributed to a broadening of perspectives towards what constitutes music education and corresponding teacher education. These discussions also introduced Portuguese music educators to contemporary Anglo-American educational trends (e.g. Reimer, 1970; Swanwick, 1979; Thomas, 1979). Both these aspects of the preparations for reform indicated that music education had to begin to relate to students' musical experiences: this in turn meant asking students to listen, perform and compose.

Music education had been dominated for decades by the development of performing skills and/or factual knowledge of music history. The curriculum reforms meant that the preparation of music teachers was one of the most important and delicate issues. However, the Portuguese Ministry of Education, while accepting publicly that music should be present through the whole curriculum, reverted in practice to an ambiguous position in which important decisions were systematically delayed.

The Portuguese school system develops through three cycles in terms of compulsory schooling, which go up to the ninth grade: grades 1–4 (first cycle); grades 5–6 (second cycle); grades 7–9 (third cycle). There are also further secondary schools which go up to the twelfth grade. In the first cycle, one classroom teacher is in charge of all curriculum subjects, including music. After that, teaching is based on specific disciplines, with maybe one teacher for two curriculum subjects. At present, music is part of the Portuguese National Curriculum, and is statutory for all children up to the age of 11 (first and second cycle). From ages 11 to 14 (third cycle), music appears in the curriculum as an optional subject. The same happens at secondary level, with very few schools in the country as a whole offering courses in music.

In the first cycle, music is not taught in a systematic way. Classroom teachers, who teach all subjects in primary school, are expected to include music. However, this expectation is not fulfilled properly, since classroom teachers undergo very limited musical instruction in their own training programmes, and consequently lack confidence. The music curriculum guidelines for primary schools (1990, Programa do 1º ciclo Ensino Básico) exacerbate the problem by being vaguely formulated, and by failing to present a consistent pattern of the sequential developments expected from pupils. Furthermore, the curriculum lacks a framework that enables schools to plan, assess and evaluate their music programme according to the resources available. The musical development of children at this level has thus been more or less left to chance, or to the particular interest of parents, engaged teachers and the community. I will return to this topic when discussing specialist music education.

In the second cycle, music education has a regular place in the curriculum: it is allocated up to three hours a week and is taught by a music specialist. The music curriculum is more coherent and organized sequentially at this stage, although children are still relatively undeveloped, with respect to music, for their age. This could be attributed to the lack of music provision in the previous four years of schooling, to too many children in a classroom or to the general shortage of musical equipment. However, it is necessary to recognize that a significant number of children are sufficiently motivated by their experiences during these two years of music education to pursue further optional study. A few interested music teachers readily grasp the opportunity at this stage to build up singing and instrumental groups which can lead to regular musical practice in schools (e.g. public performances and school music clubs).

Two further critical points should be made, however: first, a great many of these instrumental groups are strongly bound to the Orff tradition; this, combined with a lack of teacher expertise as well as limited access to different instruments and to music technology (Mota, 1997), leads to a restricted repertoire. Secondly, although the curriculum clearly prescribes the three areas of composing, listening and performing, composition is largely excluded. Children, instead, do a lot of notation, music reading and aural-training activities which often diminish their motivation to continue learning music (*ibid.*). This is exacerbated by the way in which some teachers who have difficulty managing the classroom environment use these activities as a means of controlling pupils: other, more interesting musical activities, such as composing and performing, are thus perceived as being of secondary importance.

In the third cycle, music education is an optional subject. It, correspondingly, faces a shortage of music teachers, and the restriction that a minimum of fifteen pupils are required to start a programme. The document *School Network 96/97*, from the Departamento de Gestão de Recursos Educativos (DEGRE) indicates that of the more than 850 state schools in Portugal, only 104 were offering music education.

In secondary level (up to the twelfth grade), those institutions which do offer courses in music enjoy a more or less free approach to it, and need the approval of senior music educators (which follows from the presentation of a coherent course plan) and the existence of the necessary human and material resources.

To sum up this section, although several factors restrict the access of Portuguese children to music education, several musical activities involving young people occur outside the formal education system, sometimes as an extension of it and sometimes in spite of it. In the meantime, it is interesting to note that the Portuguese Ministry of Education itself recognizes the 'importance of generalizing access to arts education for all children and young people'. Since 1991 (Despacho 187/ ME/91) it has allowed joint projects between specialized music schools and extra-curricular musical activities. Although few schools have taken advantage of this opportunity to date, some notable successes have occurred when music academies have teamed up with first-cycle schools.

Specialist music education

In specialist music education there are two types of schools which co-exist within the system: conservatories and music academies (which are run both by the state and privately) and professional schools (which are run privately with state support).

Conservatories and music academies became subject to government regulation in 1983, ending the system whereby the training of musicians was carried out within a vertical framework which included secondary and college education. Instead, higher music education fell under the auspices of polytechnic institutes (colleges of music and colleges of education) and universities. The innovative aspect of the 1983 regulations was the notion that the undergraduate training of a musician should integrate a high-quality specialized music curriculum (involving advanced instrumental and compositional techniques) with educational sciences (including methodological issues as well as cultural and aesthetic issues in music).

The professional schools of music began in 1989. They were intended to widen the provision of training (a) by providing incentives for private agents in the system and (b) by promoting the curricular and pedagogical autonomy of the schools concerned. These goals reflect clearly the political zeitgeist of the time: they came to light in the context of a 'change and modernisation of the social tissue that [was] present not only in Portugal but also in the European Community and in countries of the OECD' (Departamento do Ensino Secundário, 1996, p. 8). The main idea of these schools was to make a clear break with the other specialist music schools in an attempt to prepare instrumentalists capable of joining Portuguese orchestras. These orchestras were (and to a certain extent still are) surviving through the recruitment of a large number of foreign musicians.

In the beginning, the professional schools were mostly concerned with the preparation of string players and appeared to be almost pure 'string schools'. Other directions have been taken more recently, such as the percussion section of the professional school in Espinho, which has enjoyed considerable academic and public acclaim. In these schools there are two types of courses, namely level 2, which takes students up to the ninth grade, and level 3, which lasts until the end of secondary school. At each level, the curriculum demands 3600 hours of teaching over a period of three years and is divided into two components such that 50 per cent of students' studying is devoted to socio-cultural subjects and the remaining 50 per cent to technical, technological and artistic subjects.

The professional schools of music represented an important and positive addition to Portuguese music education. However, the syllabus of these schools, and also that of the other specialized music schools to some extent, follows a strict traditional structure. There are few or no points of interdisciplinary convergence, and little space for experimentation and the promotion of creativity and innovation. It is unclear whether such an approach can reflect the needs and values of today's society. Ten years after their appearance it seems necessary to evaluate the musical development of their young musicians and the impact they have had upon Portuguese music and society.

Today, innovation in the Portuguese music education system will have to take into account two central questions: do Portuguese young people receive the essential guidelines for making musical options throughout life?; and, does the system produce active and conscious listeners, performers and composers? I would argue that some of the very best Portuguese performers and composers, as well as critical audiences, are for the most part a product of special circumstances and particular biographies. In terms of general music in the classroom, musical creativity, improvisation and composition are underdeveloped areas of the curriculum with little or no significant output. The most promising results are to be found in performance, although mostly as a product of informal, out-of-school practices. In spite of the significant efforts of a few isolated institutions, both at secondary and college levels, the aims, processes and products of music education in general need to be reassessed.

Music teacher education

A consideration of teacher training for the different institutions mentioned above highlights some positive changes in the system and also some points that require improvement. Ten years ago, music teachers for the general school system were still recruited directly from conservatories into classroom practice. Although these teachers could apply to a two-year, in-service training course, no college or university offered a degree in music education. The vast majority of current Portuguese music teachers are of this kind.

In 1986, the schools of education within the polytechnic institutes began a curriculum in music education that was designed to produce music teachers for the first two cycles of the Portuguese general education system. In some schools this curriculum has a half-generalist, half-specialist format, while in others it prepares specialist music teachers for the whole of compulsory schooling. This development has brought a significant renewal in general class music, at least for pupils up to eleven years of age. Although there are no systematic studies of the relationship between general class music and subsequent attendance at specialized music schools, the fact that so many Portuguese children apply today for music conservatories and music academies may well result from the improved and more motivating music teaching in general schools.

The training of teachers for specialized music schools seems to be more fragile. In 1989, the University of Aveiro began an undergraduate degree producing graduates qualified to teach instruments, composition and music theory: and Évora University followed the same path in 1996. However, these two courses have been unable to produce the quantity of graduates required by a specialized music school network consisting of six state music conservatories, 60 private music academies and nine professional music schools (source: Ministry of Education/Secondary Schools Department, 1996/97).

Most music schools, therefore, survive by employing untrained teachers who are often themselves still in training. This means that the student often enters full-time teaching immediately after the completion of training, and has not had the time to develop the self-concept and perhaps the technical sophistication of a 'true musician'. The elitist notion that people become music teachers because they lack the talent to become performers is very unhelpful for the recruitment of good teachers. Unfortunately, the immediate switch from being a student to being a teacher means that such a prejudice is often internalized by Portuguese music teachers themselves, which can have devastating consequences for their own self-esteem and classroom practice.

Music learning outside the classroom

It is important to recognize that a great deal of Portuguese musical development and learning takes place in contexts outside the formal school curriculum (Perdigão, 1979). One of these contexts is the Portuguese *bandas de música*. The *banda* is an instrumental group (mostly comprising woodwind and brass instruments) that differs from those found in many other cultures through its repertoire and through the role it plays in a very specific cultural context. These groups exist in most small rural towns in Portugal, as well as in other southern European countries like Spain and France. Men and women of all ages form part of a strong hierarchy in which musical knowledge is passed on from grandparents, to parents, to grandchildren, in a very disciplined and traditional way. To be in the band involves playing at least every other weekend, and on every special occasion for that particular region. This is particularly the case during the summer, when there are many open air festivals. In many situations two or three bands compete and are judged according to the ambitiousness of their repertoire and the sophistication of their technical skills. In addition to the folk music repertoire of each region, the bands play arrangements of well-known classical pieces as well as popular hits of the moment.

Many children begin their music education with these bands and remain attached to their first *banda* throughout their lives. College students or professionals living in the city often come back to play side-by-side with family members, former peers and new participants. The *bandas*, as typical working- and low-middle-class attachment groups, allow people to learn how to read music, write music, play an instrument and perform in public events almost simultaneously, and independently of their age, gender or level of musical ability.

Another significant source of young people's musical development, as in many other cultures in the western world, is the peer group. Like other countries in Europe, Portuguese children are consumers of popular

Anglo-American musical culture. The musical learning process, whether of an instrument or voice, occurs interactively: older children 'teach' the younger ones, far from the culture of formal schooling or parents. In many instances there is direct contradiction between the instruction provided by these two sources of influence.

Perhaps the most significant aspect of this mode of learning is that it provides young people with a sense of attachment to a peer group that values music and musical activities. The summer of 1999, for example, saw at least seven big rock festivals in Portugal. Groups of young people organize their school holidays according to these events, travelling around the country for about a month. Performers at these festivals are predominantly American and British, although they are supplemented by a handful of Portuguese bands which mostly, but not always, perform in the Anglo-American tradition.

The whole system of Portuguese formal music education consciously ignores this other side of pupils' musical life. There is a clear distinction in pupils' minds between 'our music' and 'their music'. The National Curriculum guidelines clearly state the need to bring popular music into classrooms. However, my own systematic observation of music teaching in classrooms found that teachers either do not follow this instruction because they are unacquainted with pop music, or that they bring popular music into their classroom in an uncritical manner, based on the assumption that 'pupils like it'. This is an issue that clearly needs to be addressed.

Careers in music

The sources of musical employment in Portugal are similar to those in all other western countries. The most significant employers are music education institutions: even those whose primary employment intentions concern performance or composing find it difficult to survive without a supplementary teaching income. However, whereas parents might have been worried if their children wished to become musicians in the past, the present-day situation is much more attractive, and several possibilities are available (Mota, 1997).

General classroom music still faces a shortage of teachers. While there is almost no such problem in the bigger cities, many countryside schools systematically employ untrained music teachers. This problem is exacerbated by the current nature of teacher training: in order to confer degrees in music education, schools of education must integrate a music department containing staff with postgraduate music qualifications. Music education in the Portuguese general school system should therefore be considered to be an area that is still expanding. Specialist music schools suffer from much the same problem: the growing market for private music academies means that demand for specialist teachers far outstrips supply. However, regulations issued by the Ministry of Education make funding for specialist schools conditional on teachers possessing a college education. This shortage of teachers in both the general and specialist systems is clearly an area that requires urgent attention from administrators.

Young musicians enjoy performance opportunities that would have been unthinkable just twenty years ago, and there are three main sources of these. First, a growing number of small cultural societies and festivals (some of them attached to local authorities) have promoted the growth in performance of many different musical styles. Secondly, a growing CD industry is yet to become a major employer, but does help to boost the visibility of Portuguese performers in the media. Thirdly, major orchestras in Porto and Lisbon have tended to employ foreign instrumentalists in the absence of qualified Portuguese musicians, and these orchestras represent an obvious future employment market for native performers. This process has already begun in the field of composition, where young Portuguese composers are being commissioned for specific festivals and events. This tradition was started by the Gulbenkian Contemporary Music Festival in Lisbon, and is now followed by other institutions and the local authorities.

Finally, a whole new area for music careers is in the field of technology. Portuguese colleges (e.g. the Polytechnic Institute in Porto) have recently begun offering degrees in music technology. Although there has been little investigation of the likely future impact of this development, the innovations described above seem to indicate the need for young people qualified in music technology.

Conclusions

One of the major criticisms of the whole Portuguese education system, and, by implication, Portuguese music education, is the absence of any real assessment of its institutional agents, curricula and syllabuses. Although reforms have continued unabated since 1930, a logical first step would be to establish some key areas in which their effects can be evaluated. As far as general music education is concerned, there are three main areas in which such evaluation might take place. These are (a) the relationship between aims, methodologies and results, with particular attention to the issue of process versus product; (b) the ways in which music teachers are addressing the tension between old and, more recently, emergent musical styles, and the question of what *can*, instead of what *should*, be taught by the typical music educator; and (c) the relationship between teaching methodologies and the different social and cultural contexts in which they are adopted.

While all of these questions might also be applied to the specialist music teaching system, there are still other significant issues to be tackled in this specific domain. It seems urgent first to evaluate how the professional schools of music have influenced the development of new performers, composers, orchestras, chamber groups etc. The next question is the extent to which the work done in these schools, especially those outside the main cities, has helped to build new audiences for music, and whether it has had a significant effect on the type of music being consumed by young people and the general public. To evaluate the organizational, curricular and cultural models of these schools is of great importance for any future decision-making in specialist music education. Another important issue is the relationship between training institutions and their former students, and, in particular, the students' opinions about their teachers.

A better understanding of musical development in Portugal must account for the huge cultural contrasts within the country. We must arrive at a policy for music education that clearly rejects the idea of a single model of musical learning and development and, instead, acknowledges the existence of many different cultural values.

References

Arroyo, A. (1909) *O canto coral e a sua função social*. Coimbra: França Amado.

Departamento do Ensino Secundário (1996) *Dinâmicas, memórias e projectos das escolas profissionais*. Porto: Autor.

Mateus, M. C. (1992) *Por una educación musical en España*. Barcelona: PPU.

Mota, G. (1997) 'Determinants of children's musical development in the early years of general classroom music instruction'. Unpublished doctoral dissertation, University of Keele.

Perdigão, M. (1979) *Ensino artístico. In: Sstema de ensino em Portugal*. Lisboa: Fundação Calouste Gulbenkian.

Real Costa, C. (1923) *O ensino da música em Portugal*. Lisboa: Tipografia do Comércio.

Reimer, B. (1970) *A Philosophy of Music Education*. Englewood Cliffs, NJ: Prentice-Hall.

Swanwick, K. (1979) *A Basis for Music Education*. London: Routledge.

Thomas, R. (1979) *MMCP Synthesis*. Bellingham: Americole.

CHAPTER
12

Post-USSR countries

Maris Valk-Falk and Marina Gulina

Introduction: Music and society in the former Soviet sphere

In central and eastern Europe, both folk and classical music have featured prominently within national cultures, sometimes as a unifying influence, sometimes emphasizing diversity. Folk music was sometimes manipulated in subtle ways to draw together disparate ethnic groups (a strategy exploited effectively by President Tito in the former Yugoslavia), though elsewhere, particularly in the former Soviet states, it was generally considered unhealthy to allow local folk music to proliferate, lest it should provide a dangerously strong ethnic signature. The population movements within Russia during Stalin's time had the (deliberate) effect of breaking up local ethnic groupings, and with them, their musical cultures.

Nevertheless, it was official policy at the time to include token representatives of minorities in musical concerts, which would often incorporate popular formal songs (*estradnaya musica*) having a regional flavour. (Shortly after the 1917 revolution, Lenin had written of the need to avoid *velikorusski* [Greater Russian] chauvinism.) Folk music of the village variety (*narodnaya musica*) only remained prominent in the republics and regions. Throughout the former USSR, traditional religious, village folk, and gypsy music were actively replaced by patriotic national songs. For all ages, in kindergartens, Young Pioneer camps and *komsomol* (young communist) groups, such singing was mandatory, and an important part of collective cultural life. Songs were state-commissioned and recommended to teachers. Nevertheless, opposition to the state in the latter part of the Soviet era was also expressed effectively in music, for example via the obliquely ironical, tongue-in-cheek, intellectual humour, satire and expression of singers such as Bulat Okudzhava.

In Soviet times, classical music (and other arts) were employed in the service of social engineering: factory workers in cities were often taken, sometimes unwillingly, to ballet, opera and orchestral performances in an attempt to widen cultural appreciation, although exposure was to a prescribed and heavily censored musical repertoire. Among educated Russians, it is almost sinful to be labelled *nekulturnii* (uncultured); knowledge of the arts was considered an important route via which all citizens, even manual labourers, could be elevated to universally high levels of cultural sophistication. State ideology had a profound impact on musical style and content, as in other countries with centralist governments such as China (see Chapter 3). Lenin and Stalin were well aware of the potential of the arts as powerful means of moulding political attitudes, and it was necessary for music and musicians to conform to the demands of the state. Indeed, Dmitry Shostakovitch and Aram Khachaturian were commanded in the 1930s and 1940s to stop writing 'bourgeois music' (Moore and Parry, 1974, pp. 23–4); Sergei Prokofiev was effectively subjected to social exile, and the music of Nikolai Rimsky-Korsakov was derided. Music was considered degenerate if it did not conform to Soviet criteria of realism and patriotism.

Despite these constraints, for musical as well as other forms of culture, few societies have been richer and fuller than Russia and the former Soviet Union. The Moscow and St Petersburg Conservatories are particularly distinguished. The St Petersburg Conservatory, established by Anton Rubinstein in 1862, represents the Russian national school, characterized by the work of Mikhail Glinka, Modeste Mussorgsky, Nikolai Rimsky-Korsakov, Mitrofan Belaiev and Alexandr Borodin. It is worth noting that the conservatory was considered too academic by some Russian composers; commenting on the influential group based around the free-thinking Mily Balakirev in the mid-nineteenth century in St Petersburg, Tchaikovsky wrote that they 'believed it was not necessary to study ... that schooling kills inspiration, dries up creativity ...' Russian culture represents a curious amalgam of free expression and romanticism on the one hand and tight, rehearsed virtuosity on the other. The Moscow Conservatory, established by Anton's brother, Nikolai Rubinstein, in 1864, has traditionally represented a broader international style than its St Petersburg counterpart, characterized by the music of Piotr Tchaikovsky, through Sergei Taneiev and Sergei Rachmaninoff.

Theoretical background

As in many countries, music education in Russia and the former Soviet Republics can be considered at two levels: first, the general teaching of music as part of the ordinary school curriculum and, second, the specialist teaching of music within dedicated music schools whose aim is to produce expert orchestral musicians, music teachers and international concert performers. Underpinning all these aspects of music education was a strong theoretical basis, in particular that advanced by the Russian aesthete, musicologist and composer Boris Assafiev (1884–1949). Assafiev was well known as the composer of two major ballets: *Plamya Parija* (Flame of Paris) and *Bakchisaraiskii Fontan* (Bakchisareiski Fountain). He wrote extensively about music education and, in particular, the concept of musical 'intonation' (see Assafiev, 1955–57; Orlova, 1984).

It is important to note that the use of the term 'intonation' in this context extends beyond the concept of 'judgement of pitch', which is the usual definition in western musicology. Assafiev's use of the term translates as the appreciation, memorizing and expression of musical form (including pitch judgement), but, particularly, the sophistication and subtlety of musical expression. In order to better understand the development of the theory of intonation and its great significance in Russian music education, it is necessary to consider Assafiev's views on the development of musical form.

Music perception and expression, according to Assafiev, involve a continuous process of detecting similarities and dissimilarities among successive sound patterns; this requires that the individual possesses, in advance, an internalized set of sound patterns called, collectively, a 'glossary of intonation'. A consequence of the persistence of such mental sets is that music is enjoyed more when familiar patterns outnumber unfamiliar ones. Music with prevalent intonations that are not yet assimilated can be more or less completely perceived, but only if the listener makes a conscious effort. Unfamiliar forms of music, when heard for the first time, may not only give rise to feelings of disjunction among their components, but may even be experienced as formless – as noise or chaos. When heard repeatedly, the intonations become clearer – they are said to 'crystallize' – at which point they can be used to accommodate subsequent novel intonations (in a process not unlike Piaget's general epistemological principle of adaptation, involving 'assimilation' and 'accommodation'). The understanding of music is therefore said to begin from (a) the correspondence of relatively familiar sounds with the existing content of consciousness, and (b) from their comparison with less familiar sounds. When listening to music, the greater the rhythmic and intonational differences between any two elements, the stronger is the tendency to make comparisons between them. According to Assafiev, these processes of selection and comparison lead to the acquisition of musical form.

As a result of a protracted analysis of the notion of intonation, Assafiev arrived at the conclusion that music as an independent manifestation of intonation develops in parallel with, or is closely intertwined with, the qualities and forms of the particular 'musical intellect' which is fixed in the collective mind of a community that shares the same musical 'expression'; that is, their traditional and distinctive musical forms. Accordingly, in their particular environments, different groups of people possess different sets of intonations. Assafiev placed particular emphasis on intervals in musical intonation, since these confer distinctive qualities. He noted that the choice of intervals in different musical cultures is such that not every interval that is possible acoustically is used with the same frequency (e.g. 'energetic' fourths and 'sad' minor thirds). Assafiev believed that it is the difference in the frequency with which particular intervals are employed that gives each musical culture its own particular distinctiveness.

Assafiev's views have been extremely influential both in theory and practice within Soviet and Russian music and music education. In the 1920s, for example, when the state demanded 'musical enlightenment' to educate new audiences throughout the Soviet Union, Assafiev argued that music had become an important means by which the masses could express their emotional state (Assafiev, 1957; Malinkovskaya, 1990). He asserted repeatedly that every individual possesses a natural musical aptitude and that educationalists must take this seriously, ceasing to make unnecessary and artificial distinctions via the use of such labels as 'artistic people' or 'people born for the stage'. In his study *A Personal Crisis of Creative Work*, he expressed the essentials for music education. He wrote that, 'If there are many people among us who play and sing without talent and without gusto, then a considerable part of the fault lies with those who change the genuine aim of music education, [viz] the awakening and establishing of musicality, [in favour of] the excessive demonstration of one's achievement and performance-activity as the peak of one's dreams' (Assafiev 1957, p. 23). In this early Soviet period, individual virtuosity was ascribed less importance than musical expression as a common, societal medium.

Musical education: regular schools

The study of music and the arts generally received greater emphasis within the former Soviet Union than in the west, at all levels of education. In Soviet kindergartens, expert pianists were engaged to accompany singing and dance lessons; it was considered important that children were exposed, from the earliest age, to the music of great classical composers. Music education in schools was seen as an aspect of character building, although it was generally limited within the school curriculum to the singing of patriotic songs and classical musical appreciation, i.e. to promote musical literacy.

In a recent publication, *Russian Music in Schools*, directed toward music teachers, Sergeeva and Shmagina (1998) provide a guide to the teaching of music appreciation. Verbatim transcriptions from class lessons are used to illustrate good didactic style. The text is particularly interesting in so far as it reflects the influences on music teaching of more general changes in Russian society, differing in several telling ways from equivalent texts available prior to *perestroika*. The authors include eight chapters, each devoted to the study of the music of a different Russian composer. Six of these would have featured in Soviet times (namely Mussorgsky, Borodin, Tchaikovsky, Sveridov, Rachmaninoff and Prokofiev) but, now, Berezovskii and Kalinnikov have been added. Pupils were formerly taught to regard Mikhail Glinka as the father of Russian classical music, since he was said to have composed the first Russian opera *Zhizn za Czarea* (The Life of the Czar) in 1836, yet teaching now emphasizes that the first true Russian opera was actually *Demafont*, composed in the 1760s by the religious musical composer Maxim Berezovskii. Note that while this text is devoted to Russian music, Bach, Mozart, Rossini, Beethoven and Chopin have always been prominent in the curriculum as well.

Teachers have high expectations of pupils at all levels; the in-depth study of individual composers begins when children are six to seven years old. Taking Mussorgsky as an example, year 1 (6–7 years) children study songs, dances and marches taken from his operas *Boris Gudunov*, *Khavanchina* and *Pictures at an Exhibition*. In year 2 (7–8 years), children study the historical development of musical form; they also consider variations on themes within one particular movement (*progulka*) taken from Mussorgsky's *Pictures at an Exhibition*. In the third year (8–9 years), children study motifs of Russian folk music, and Mussorgsky's incorporation of Polish and Persian styles in his operas. In later years, children are expected to identify parallels between music and other art forms (such as literature and painting); to understand the contribution of music to dramatical construction (that is, to appreciate 'the story behind the music') and to appreciate the characteristics of certain musical 'personalities' via the analysis of famous arias, again taken from the work of Mussorgsky. It can be seen from this example that the teaching of musical appreciation requires a child to adopt adult musical terminology from an early age. Music education is not child-centred, but is geared to adapting the child to the musical world of the cultured adult.

In conclusion, with the exception of kindergartens, where there are dance and musical expression lessons, music education in ordinary schools is essentially a passive activity. The traditionalism and sense of history that pervades Russian teaching has meant that modern electronic keyboards and synthesizers, which are used frequently in classrooms elsewhere in the world, are deemed to be disadvantageous and are used reservedly in Russian schools at present. Schools tend to be proud of their rather strict programmes, and will usually claim that attempts to experiment with children's 'creativity' have had a negative impact on their achievement of what Assafiev termed musical 'intonation'.

Music education: specialist music schools

In Russia (and in the former Soviet Union and its republics generally) children have not learned musical instruments in ordinary schools; the teaching of instrumental music is exclusively the realm of the specialist music school (or musical high school). In Soviet times, such schools were available outside regular school hours for those children who showed great musical aptitude, and also for those whose parents benefited from the patronage of the communist party. However, such schools were not a communist invention, predating the communist era by some 60 years. The first, providing free education, was set up in St Petersburg in the early 1860s by Balakirev, and a similar school opened in Moscow shortly afterwards. The schools trained children in choir and opera, independently of the conservatory structure, adopting the teaching methods that were pioneered by Rimsky-Korsakov. (These methods remained undocumented until formalized by such writers as Assafiev (see above).)

The first music school, in St Petersburg, still bears the name of Rimsky-Korsakov (and did so throughout Soviet times, even when his music was scorned). Balakirev also set up a school for boys in the St Petersburg Kapella, concentrating on church music, though children were also taught to play musical instruments. Music schools proliferated in the 1920s; the state policy of 'musical enlightenment' required that artistic cultural education in ballet and music was expanded, targeted particularly at children from poorer families. They became the 'feeders' for the major academies and conservatories, and thus the sources of expert musicianship with which Russia, particularly, has become associated. In Soviet times, such special musical education was almost free (parents paid only 1 per cent of their salary). Music schools have endured and have remained highly subsidized, the state paying for some instruments and their repair, though it is necessary for parents now to pay considerably higher fees (perhaps 10 per cent of their salary).

Soviet music schools had high expectations; they strove for excellence in performance which would reflect well on the communist party at home and abroad. Teaching followed a fixed and nationally universal procedure; assessment was via nationwide examinations conducted by external examiners, which always incorporated stage performance. The basic structure remains in place today. The curriculum, which also remains essentially the same, consisted of six main elements, namely a first instrument (five years for wind and string instruments; eight years for piano), a second instrument (most often piano), theory of music (history and science), solfeggio (note literacy and vocal training), orchestra, and choir. The emphasis was primarily on musicality (i.e. interpretation of music, the use of an instrument to express depth of feeling, conceptualizing what a composer intended) and only secondly on virtuosity (i.e. technical ability). In particular, it was argued that music by particular composers, such as Brahms and Schumann, could not be played properly by a musician who is merely technically competent. Nevertheless, technical skill was considered a priority in early musical training, which began at six to eight years of age. Creativity was deemed to become possible only when technical skills had been mastered. The main principles adopted in Soviet times still remain in Russian music schools today. (Information on the history of music schools is kindly provided by R. K. Klochkova (personal communication).)

Since *perestroika*, and since increasing commercialization began, all aspects of Russian music education, from university research to school music teaching, have suffered, in common with all publicly funded activities, due to a lack of financial support. Nevertheless, attendance at musical concerts and general knowledge of composers (both Russian and non-Russian) remains at an impressively high level among Russian and central- and eastern-European schoolchildren.

Training musicians: educational policy and practice

In contrast to many other countries, music schools in Russia do not make a strong distinction between the training of professional music teachers and of performing musicians; these functions are regarded as occurring in parallel. According to Assafiev, being an educator demands the mentality of a theorist, historian, ethnomusicologist and performer, and also, of course, possession of the corresponding skills (Assafiev, 1955). Music teaching benefited from the emphasis on the instilling of fundamental skills, reflected by perfection in performance and musicians' striving for spirited, artistic intonation. The selection of music turned out to be crucial in the educational process. Musical scores were carefully selected: in particular, it was deemed important that students' repertoires should be broad, incorporating character pieces and works of both classical and modern styles. The aim of this was to create greater intonational richness in the musical consciousness of the people. Indeed, 40 years of research were devoted to the issue of music selection for instrumental training (Malinkovskaya, 1990).

As a result of this music teacher-training programme, (a) a large number of professionally educated music teachers emerged; (b) the need for new music primers arose all over the central and eastern European region, and tutoring manuals were prepared professionally and issued in mother tongues; (c) teachers of instrumental performance were themselves good performers, making it possible for 'performing before students' to be used as a teaching method; and (d) students became very adept in musical performance, preparing the way for an era of outstanding success in international competition.

Regarding instrumental training in music schools, a range of teaching methods have been adopted in order to maintain a balance between an emphasis on emotional experience (musicality) and the process of technical development (virtuosity). Instrumental training in Russia and the former USSR has, traditionally, emphasized education at pre-liminary levels. It should be clear from the description of Assafiev's theory (see above) that early musical training and experience was regarded as crucial for the later development of higher levels of musical intonation and, therefore, musicianship.

The preliminary course provides the bases for the development of professional playing techniques. For example, teaching methods call particular attention to small details, and a recommended aim is to physically free the player's body, especially her/his back and shoulders, elbows, arms and hands. At the same time, attention is paid to the player's feeling of the weight of his/her hand, the strengthening of fingers and to the autonomy of different fingers, since these are the means by which players instil their performances with intonation. Pupils then begin to develop fingering techniques and a feeling for their chosen instrument (e.g. its dynamics). More complex techniques are soon added and applied to a repertoire that is increasingly complicated from both a musical and a technical perspective. At the next stage, attention is devoted to scales, transposition exercises and hearing skills.

Vocal training

The tradition of teaching singing is one of the oldest in Russian music education, since it embodies the teaching of old Russian/Slavic church hymns, while covering the whole period leading to the modern vocal methods used today. One particularly notable aspect of the latter concerns the revitalization of formerly neglected traditions and attempts to apply their virtues to the teaching of choral music. The traditions are treated in their appropriate historical context, although stylistic, physiological and psychological fundamentals of vocal experience are also introduced. This subject is dealt with in more detail by Nikolskaya-Beregovskaya (1988). As a result of her arguments, different professions in Russian music education are beginning to be integrated: for example, the roles of practising artists and music teachers are linked closely.

Informal music

Contact with the West since *perestroika* has meant that young people in Russia and the republics are now exposed to a great deal of modern western music which was forbidden in communist times. School pupils form groups and bands and learn to play instruments to do so, including guitar styles such as rock and blues. Most of the groups they hear are English-speaking (from the UK and US in particular), but Russian groups increasingly imitate western styles while singing in Russian, and in other former Soviet republics native pop groups prefer singing in English. The CDs of these groups sell well, encouraging other young people to imitate them. Indeed, school concerts now often feature in-house pop groups.

Furthermore, Irish folk music is especially popular among young people, and English folk music is gaining in popularity. Jazz clubs have opened (one sponsored by the local Pulkovo airline), and in a few centres, such as some cultural institutes, tuition is given in jazz and blues music. In St Petersburg, the House of Culture (*Dom Kulturi*) offers young people opportunities to take professional lessons in guitar for only one dollar per hour, while another centre (based within the Rimsky-Korsakov school) offers extra-mural music tuition in any instrument, for people of all ages.

The role of folk music

Over recent decades, writers and educators in the Baltic states (and other countries) have particularly emphasized the role of folklore in children's musical development. Deliberate attempts to introduce elements of folk music into the classroom have opened new opportunities for teaching fundamental musical abilities, as well as developing childrens' emotional experiences. This has been particularly the case at the preliminary and elementary stages of music education, although it must also be said that the optimal use of these materials is at present hampered by the level of teaching skill available (Pullerits, 1999). It is clear that in the present socioeconomic climate it would be utopian to expect that folk music could immediately assume the same significance it enjoyed in times past. Yet, equally, the essential characteristic features of traditional folk music should not be allowed to disappear (Liimets, 1999a).

One particular example of the use of folk music in post-USSR music education concerns Estonian runic songs. These songs are 'catchy', featuring a high degree of repetition (Pullerits, 1999), prominent rhyming and rhythm and frequent examples of alliteration and assonance (see Päts and Kõlar (1975) for examples). Estonian teachers at the elementary level use runic songs to encourage (a) children to count out rhythms and (b) monophonic and polyphonic singing. Pupils are asked to produce a variety of 'natural' musical sounds (e.g. clapping, stamping, stepping, jumping) to develop their emotional expression, and also to reduce their fear of performing. Such activities also develop an appreciation of rhythm and metre and encourage discrimination of sound volume and timbre.

Another particular advantage of the use of folk music concerns its role in developing improvisation skills. Lippus (1981) suggests that wide-ranging experience of folk songs allows children to learn different musical patterns as well as the rules for connecting, combining and deriving them. The ability to express one's particular ideas in more complicated forms should grow as the number of patterns and rules to be acquired increases (in keeping with Assafiev (1955–57), discussed earlier). Of course, exposure to classical music might also provide similar skills, but the advantage of employing folk music to such ends in Baltic cultures is that this music typically employs uniform and regular schemes, with one-line and two-line melodies being the most common forms. This obviously facilitates learning of musical patterns, particularly among younger children, and perhaps goes some way to explaining the particular interest that has arisen in the educational utility of folk music from the region.

Conclusion

Educational policy

Modern music-education practice in Russia and the former Soviet republics emphasizes the importance of deep emotional experience and sensual satisfaction, perhaps more so than anywhere else in the world. These aspects are regarded as being equal to, or greater in importance than, strenuous practice and technical competence, such that emotions are considered as perhaps the most relevant aspect of music education. As such, it is easy to see why general music education places so much emphasis on musical experience, perhaps at the expense of developing musical performance skills. This approach to music stems from the writings of Assafiev, who emphasized the manner in which music is processed by the perceiver. However, the divergence between Russian music education and more recent trends within the developmental psychology of music should, obviously, be lessened. Existing forms of Russian music education also fail to take into account more pupil-centred factors such as each individual's musical needs, expectations, talent and level of knowledge; as well as the particular roles of music in the surrounding community.

Folk music education

Employing folk songs and improvisations based upon them provides a natural device for improving pupils' intonation skills. However, longitudinal research on school pupils' lifestyles has shown that few continue their interest in folk music. In the light of this, Liimets (1999a, b) asks whether east European educators will ever really be able to justify a heavy emphasis on folk music in the curriculum. Nevertheless, she gives an affirmative answer to this question. Her argument, rooted in developmental psychology, is that early experiences of folk music determine the individual's emotional attitude towards the world: the world outlook found in folk music sustains the musical mother tongue of a people and their culture more generally. The issue of ethnic identity, is of course, of crucial importance in the countries of the former USSR, and music education will clearly play as much of a role in this in the future as it has done in the past.

Acknowledgements

The authors and editors would like to express their thanks to Professor Nigel Foreman and to Regina Konstantinova Klochkova for their invaluable help in the preparation of this chapter, and to Kristin Sarv for help with the translation.

References

Assafiev, B. (1955–57) *Izbrannye trudy (Selected Works)*, 1–5. Moscow: Izdatelstvo Akademii Nauk SSSR.

Liimets, A. (1999a) 'Rahvamuusika ja isiksuse terviklikkus' (Folk music and integrity of personality), in M. Vikat (ed.) *Child and Folklore*. Tallinn: TPÜ Kirjastus, pp. 21–31.

Liimets, A. (1999b) 'Folk music as a factor of personality development', in A. Liimets (ed.) *Past and Present of Music Education*, pp. 42–3.

Lippus, U. (1981) 'Lastele sobivad improvisatsioonivõtted, mida pakub regilaulu stiil' (Providing, via runic music, ways of improvisation suitable for children), in M. Valk-Falk (ed.) *Klaveriõpetuse metoodika küsimusi*. Tallinn: EKKM, pp. 45–50.

Malinkovskaya, A. (1990) *Fortepianno-ispolnitelskoye intonirovanie (Representative Piano Intonation)*. Moscow: Muzyka.

Moore, H. T. and Parry, A. (1974) *Twentieth-century Russian Literature*. London: Heinemann.

Nikolskaya-Beregovskaya, K. F. (1998) *Russkaya vokalno-horovaya shkola IX–XX vekov (Russian Choir Singing from 9th to 20th Centuries)*. Moscow: Jazyki Russkoi Kultury.

Orlova, E. (1984) *Intonatsionnaya teoria Assafieva kak utshenie spetsifike muzykalnogo myshlenia (Intonation Theory by Assafiev as Science of Musical Thought)*. Moscow: Muzyka.

Päts, R. and Kõlar, L. (1975) *Klaveriõpetus: Algosa (Piano Tutor: Elementary)*. Tallinn: Eesti Raamat.

Pullerits, M. (1999) 'Kõnekeelest regilauluni' (From verbal language towards runic songs), in M. Vikat (ed.) *Laps ja folkloor (Child and Folklore)*. Tallinn: TPÜ Kirjastus, pp. 45–51.

Sergeeva, G. P. and Schmagina, T. C. (1998) *Russkaya muzika v'schkole (Russian Music in School)*. Moscow: MIROS.

CHAPTER
13

Scandinavia

Bengt Olsson

Introduction

The 1960s saw a growing political interest in music education in Sweden as well as in the rest of Scandinavia. There was general agreement among school authorities and politicians about the importance of musical skills and knowledge in education. At the same time, local community music schools expanded all over Scandinavia. From a historical perspective, the development of music teaching and learning within different educational institutions, along with the rise of the media during the last 30 years, amounts to what might be called the 'music revolution of the twentieth century'. Music and music education have never involved more people, and musical activities have never been more important than during this period.

Since music education is very important to a great many Scandinavians, educational institutions play a key role in shaping the nature of musical development. In general, music is a compulsory subject in school for the first six years, followed by compulsory courses, in combination with optional courses, at the secondary and tertiary level. At the same time, almost every community in Scandinavia has some kind of community music centre for instrumental tuition outside the school. Furthermore, musical leisure activities are important through the strong community support to youth centres and other kinds of cultural arts centre. Those involved in this work think it likely that more people are active as amateur musicians outside than within musical institutions in Scandinavia, although systematic research would be needed to support this impression.

These activities represent what might be called 'music networks', which involve interactions which cross the boundaries between school and the community. School music teachers, for example, are local conductors and leaders of ensembles and bands of the community, school buildings are locations for rehearsals and concerts of all kinds, schoolchildren participate as musicians in local musical life, and so on.

This chapter presents some core issues concerning musical development and learning primarily from a Swedish perspective, but with some reference to the rest of Scandinavia. First, aims and objectives are discussed in the light of curriculum development. How are the aims and objectives contained in different Scandinavian curriculum documents concerning music education transformed into practice, and what are the consequences for music education of 30 years of increasing decentralization? In contrast to the United Kingdom during the 1990s, for example, Sweden is moving away from national control of the curriculum towards local autonomy, and this has clear implications for the goals of music teaching.

A second issue concerns assessment and its role in music education. At the same time as the Nordic governments are stressing the advantages of local interpretations of the music curriculum, they also emphasize the need for assessment in terms of national standards. In political terms this standard is formulated as a strong 'target orientation', although the learning process is relatively unregulated. Put simply, the policy is that 'you can learn whatever you want as long as you achieve the necessary skills and knowledge requested in the attainment targets'. This position raises crucial questions concerning the musical and didactical values that are implicit in the assessment criteria, and the extent to which the concept of learning is informed by psychological and educational theory.

Finally, the chapter addresses one main issue concerning assessment and learning in music; namely, how teachers resolve the possible contradiction between their identities as teachers and their identities as musicians. Different tutors and colleges seem to have their own view of what is and what is not important in music education, and this has a strong influence on the identity formation of the student teacher. This third part of the chapter summarizes the preceding arguments, i.e. how different views of aims, objectives and assessment in music education can interact within different educational contexts.

Aims and objectives

Arguments within curriculum theory (Lundgren, 1979) illuminate how music teaching takes shape in Scandinavian schools and in society at large. This approach emphasizes the school as an institution, and how it is (at least partly) responsible for the cultural reproduction of society and the recreation of human knowledge, values and symbols over a historical period (Sandberg, 1996). The concept of the 'curriculum code' describes how education is influenced by significant tendencies in society; that is, how society's notions concerning what is important affect how knowledge is selected, organized and conveyed via schools and education. Within the field of music education, this includes artistic, aesthetic and musical dimensions (such as the notion that pop music either is or is not inferior to classical music, for example).

Stålhammar (1995) emphasizes different aspects of the curriculum code in a review of Swedish music syllabuses from the late 1960s until the present day. In particular, traditional aesthetic aims and objectives have been challenged during the 1980s and 1990s by musical pluralism and the growing significance of musical activities during leisure time. Consequently, the past 30 years have given rise to a gradual development from 'school-type music' to 'real music in schools'. Similarly, Swedish classroom music teaching has increasingly recognized the multi-faceted nature of 'musical knowledge'. Nielsen (1998), in a Danish review, described this connection between the classroom and music in everyday settings as 'ethno-didactic'.

During the same period there has also been a shift in Sweden from centralized, directive curricula to local, decentralized guidelines, so as to strengthen the connections between schools and society. Local authorities are providing increasing support for municipal orchestras and choirs, certain forms of municipal teaching for elementary-school pupils, and other forms of instrumental tuition arranged by the community.

The shift toward increased freedom of choice for local school authorities has led to a more open organization of school activities, although these changes have illuminated discrepancies between curricular intentions and actual practice (Sandberg, 1996). These probably arise because the curriculum is produced by decision-makers from a structure-oriented, 'top-down' perspective, but is implemented by teachers from what is, by necessity, a 'bottom-up' perspective. Political visions have to be interpreted by teachers, and this is not always a straightforward process. Indeed, interpretations and actions of the local teachers are characterized by a high degree of autonomy, and a certain level of independence from the decision-making process.

Nielsen (1998) discusses five modes of activity which exemplify changes in the Scandinavian process of musical development and learning during the last three decades:

1. production (to create, to compose, to arrange and to improvise music);
2. reproduction (to perform and to recreate existing music);
3. perception (to perceive sounds as music);
4. interpretation (to analyse and to interpret music, to express understanding in a non-musical way such as in language, art or movement);
5. reflection (to investigate and to value music in relation to styles and genres.

Analytically, these five modes might explain how changes in the Scandinavian curricula have influenced music education practice. The curricula in the 1960s and early 1970s were dominated by a focus on reproduction, perception and reflection: on teaching pupils to sing, perform and listen, mainly to historical music. Pupils were expected to internalize the music of the great masters as well as traditional folk music. These older curricula represented a strong emphasis on the development of specific skills and knowledge in music. During the 1980s and 1990s, however, greater emphasis was placed on production and interpretation. For example, the curriculum authorities began to talk about 'composing' rather than 'composition' in order to signify that this was an activity in which students should participate actively. This 'participant ethos of contemporary music education' asserts that students can be expected to be capable of any musical activity, just as they can be expected to read and write (Cook, 1998).

One example of this development has occurred in Norway in the reformulation of two previous activities, namely 'movements' and 'creative music-making', into, respectively, new activities called 'dance' and 'composing' (Jørgensen, 1982; Det kongelige kirke-, 1996): the aim is to stress the artistic intentions behind them. Nielsen (1998) discusses these changes in the Danish curricula from a didactical perspective, arguing that they represent a movement from the content aspects of education to those more concerned with learning *per se*. This is also shown by the focus on 'rhythmic music' (i.e. pop and rock music) in those aspects of Danish education concerning performance and dance.

Productive and interpretative activities now have equal status with other skills, and this raises a number of issues. Perhaps the most important is that of authenticity, which has been the subject of lengthy discussion by Cook (1998). Authenticity is connected to the idea that some music is more 'natural' than other music – it is so familiar that it is experienced, in its context, as 'musical common sense'. When we speak of music, Cook says, we are really talking about a *multiplicity* of activities and experiences: it is only the fact that we call all of these 'music' that suggests they belong together.

In Scandinavia, as in many other countries, the main challenge of authenticity is the recognition of musical activities outside the school system. All kinds of music are performed, although rock music predominates among teenagers. Rock music produces new kinds of learning experiences, and youngsters are, in effect, educating each other about the skills and knowledge of the styles they are interested in, rather than learning from teachers in formal settings. This is related to the current argument about the extent to which styles such as the blues are more 'from the heart' and more 'real' than comparatively 'artificial' styles such as classical music. Cook also suggests that pop music performers lack authenticity, since they are puppets of the music industry, whereas rock performers control their own destiny. A prevailing value system within our culture seems to place innovation above tradition, creation above reproduction and personal expression above the market-place. Music must be authentic; otherwise, it is hardly music at all.

At the same time, authenticity has more direct implications for Swedish general education. Two of the main principles behind developments in Swedish progressive education concern 'authentic learning' and 'authentic learning environments'. Although progressive education has, in the past, been grounded within individually-based psychological learning theories (Broady, 1992), the new approaches are linked to theories of contextual learning and socially shared cognition (Rogoff, 1990; Lave and Wenger, 1991; Carlgren, 1997): they emphasize collective, authentic, contextual and informal teaching. The outside world is seen as more efficient at teaching than schools, since the latter are regarded by pupils as meaningless and out of date (Stålhammar, 1995; Cook, 1998; Nielsen, 1998).

Similarly, phrases like 'guided participation' and 'interactionism' have become important in Swedish music education. Guided participation is an apprentice-like teaching in which education is closely linked to a certain practice. Interactionism stresses the 'appropriation of meaning' through participation and social interaction: you don't learn the rules first and then how to perform them; instead, you learn the rules through the collaborative performance of tasks. Both of these concepts represent a shift from regarding learning as an aspect of the individual to regarding it also as part of the environment. Consequently, it is not possible to separate the prerequisites of learning from the act of learning itself, nor to separate the content of knowledge from its actual application.

To summarize, participation in authentic musical activities is the key principle underlying the aims and objectives of contemporary Scandinavian 'communicative curriculum codes' (Ödman, 1995). This leads to an interest in pupils' motivation, and how their everyday musical experiences can be used in the school to develop their knowledge of music. Another implication of this line of thought is that musical talents and gifts are viewed in a relativistic manner: everyone is capable of composing, performing and appraising. As long as pupils are 'natural and true to their own musical ideas', their activities should lead to the positive development of musical talent.

Assessment

In Scandinavian music curricula during the 1990s, the discussion of assessment issues has focused on activities such as performance, singing a capella and part-song, appraisal, knowledge of musical styles from different periods and cultures, the verbalization of listening experiences, knowledge of music theory and the ability to use this in creative activity. Attainment targets related to pupils at different age levels are formulated for each of these aspects.

Historically, Scandinavian music teachers have opposed strongly all forms of assessment as being inappropriate and undesirable since they are antithetical to the activity itself. This attitude was strengthened further by arguments about the relativism of musical values: that the performance of different musical styles cannot be evaluated by any single set of assessment criteria, and that performers themselves are the only people able to judge a performance. On the other hand, classically-trained music teachers have a long tradition of assessing pupils' skills and knowledge. As in many other countries, certain pieces have constituted a reference canon from which assessment criteria have been derived. Judging the quality of musical performances is a matter of evaluating a set of technical and interpretative attributes.

Few contemporary Scandinavian music educators deny the importance of assessment and feedback, and one clear guiding principle is the distinction between 'formative' and 'summative' forms of assessment (Francke-Wikberg and Lundgren, 1985; Heiling, 1995). The former refers to the long-term evaluation of the process by which a particular product evolved, whereas the latter refers to an 'overall evaluation of a piece of work which has been undertaken over a period of time, taking into account the final artistic product' (Hargreaves, Galton and Robinson, 1996, p. 3). These approaches are complementary and each has its own strengths and weaknesses.

Summative assessment can involve the problem of devising formal written criteria that are able to accommodate a wide range of different musical activities and individual outcomes. In short, how can teachers avoid reducing the 'quality' of a performance to a set of technical and interpretative attributes? Similarly, how can teachers devise guidelines that encapsulate the notion of progression and include in these all the multi-faceted ways in which children can develop? The problems lie not in finding appropriate verbal descriptors but in identifying objective definitions. At the same time, the desire to be objective can lead to criteria that are too precise and detailed. This is a particular problem in Scandinavia, in that the aims and objectives of music education are so open and activity-based. Indeed, the adoption of specific assessment criteria can narrow the scope of the aims and objectives to focus on classical art music rather than popular music or jazz, and this might effectively constitute a 'hidden curriculum'.

Formative assessment should cover all aspects of the process which lead to the final artistic product. This is strongly connected to the progressive movement and to beliefs concerning the individual, creativity and self-expression which flourished in Scandinavia during the 1970s and 1980s (Olsson, 1992; 1993). Formative assessment grew in popularity for two main reasons. First, it promoted the integration between different aspects of musical (and indeed non-musical) activities. Secondly, it was more palatable than a system of summative assessment that could only ever be based on ethnocentric criteria of musical quality.

However, a major problem with the formative approach lies in the way in which the 'learning process' is defined. In general terms, it seems to involve all the skills and knowledge involved in a particular activity during a certain period of time. This all-inclusive approach makes quantitative assessment difficult (Francke-Wikberg and Lundgren, 1985; Olsson, 1992). Put simply, how can a teacher assign one single mark to a multifaceted activity? A second problem concerns how both musical and non-musical aspects of a task can be included within the same assessment model. In considering a group composition, for example, a teacher may want to assess the quality of the musical ideas proposed by group members as well as that of verbal interactions within the group, and these two aims may be incompatible.

Since 1994, the Swedish curriculum has reduced the formative aspect of assessment to a discussion of pupils' general musical development. The Norwegian curriculum places a stronger emphasis on the pupils' involvement in assessment through what is called 'assessment as learning', which can be seen as a process-based approach to assessment.

However, as in Sweden, assessment still prioritizes products rather than processes (Det kongelige kirke-, 1996).

Lindström (1998) has introduced an alternative portfolio method for assessing arts education. This was developed by the Arts Propel and Spectrum projects at Harvard University, which emphasized formative, holistic assessment of the process of production. In addition to submitting portfolios of work, the pupils are involved in reflective conversations that investigate their creative intentions and their ability to evaluate their own work. Involving pupils as well as the teachers provides a more reliable and valid form of assessment which is more likely to be perceived as impartial.

Given the advantages of the formative approach, we might ask why Scandinavian assessment tends to be based on summative, performance-based approaches. This is probably because these serve functions in the modern curriculum other than that of assessment. Assessment might indeed be regarded as a hidden form of control of the decentralization process. The use of summative assessment, based on nationally-determined standards, keeps a check on the degree of local autonomy: local freedoms are limited through the need to meet national assessment criteria. Formative assessments (e.g. through portfolios) would prevent the imposition of nationally-determined attainment targets, however: they could only be carried out relative to the locally-determined aims and objectives of music education.

Assessment and learning

The tension between aims, objectives and assessment criteria has advantages and disadvantages for pupils. Children and teenagers interested in learning how to perform classical music in the traditional way are promoted within the current system, while pupils concerned with other musical styles and ways of learning are at a great disadvantage. Some contemporary Scandinavian studies of musical development and learning, particularly, reflect the need for Nordic countries to adopt new approaches to assessment in music.

Saar (1999) discussed how the context can influence children's learning, and analysed their experiences of the educational context in terms of 'six types of situated learning'. Saar points out two particularly important frames of experience, each of which serves a different function:

> ... in what I have described as a musically framed activity, performance is flexible, and so are the rehearsal routines and the

songs. Instead of reproducing music and concert forms, this direction consists of actions that aim at producing new knowledge and also actively involve the musician in different aspects of performance. In contrast, the activity with a pedagogical framing was described as an out-distancing and objectifying of the music, the instrument and the body. Musical knowledge is accumulated through analysis and diversification of the music. (*Ibid.*, pp. 171–2)

Our earlier discussion of authenticity or decontextualized teaching and learning is closely connected to these two forms of framing. Musical and pedagogical framing are related to each other in the sense that they contextualize two complementary ways of teaching, but the pedagogical emphasis comes to the fore in assessment. This is partly because pedagogical framing has a strong foundation in musical references, like a traditional canon of instrumental works and pieces.

A second study by Bouij (1998) uses role identity theory in focusing on the professional socialization of music teacher-training students. Bouij discusses role identity from the point of view of the professional roles that students see ahead of them (teacher or musician) and what degree of musical comprehensiveness they see as being adequate for this professional role – he refers to 'broad' and 'narrow' musical comprehensiveness. During teacher training, the roles of 'performer' and/or 'content-centred teacher', which are based on narrow musical comprehensiveness, are acknowledged and supported much more than those of 'all-round musician' and/or 'pupil-centred teacher', which are based on broad musical comprehensiveness. Bouij shows that institution-alized teacher training tends to focus on the roles of narrow mainstream performer and/or strong teacher identity, and thereby neglects others.

This confusion of role identities also occurs in the domain of assessment in music education. For the teachers in the lower grades – the generalists – assessment is not considered to be important. Small children are supposed to play and have fun with music, and these aims provide primary teachers with freedom to treat the assessment criteria in a more liberal way. However, specialist music teachers are subject to different conditions that are grounded in the old conservatoire tradition (Olsson, 1993). The values of the western cultural tradition are emphasized through auditions for entrance to specialist teacher training, individual instrumental tuition, the use of codified musical scores, weekly practice and specialized performance occasions. Other values, such as those concerning music as a means of personal expression, challenge the aims and objectives of the compulsory school curriculum.

Indeed, these hidden controls in the Scandinavian curricula effectively unite the school authorities' need for efficiency and quality with the hegemony of western aesthetic values that exist within conservatoires and colleges of music.

These circumstances within teacher training might explain why production and performer-oriented values are closely connected to a pedagogical frame, whereas process-oriented values are more closely connected with a musical frame. These consequences arise precisely because objective assessment criteria are used in relation to a certain musical canon within teacher training. The aims of teacher training in music are more dominant than the aims of the curricula in general music education. In other words, music teachers reproduce their own teacher training to a greater extent than interpreting the options in the curriculum (Olsson, 1993).

Conclusion

Scandinavian school authorities clearly regard music education as important. Music has played an important role in the curricula of compulsory schools over the last 40 years, and instrumental tuition within community music schools has been equally important. The aims and objectives of contemporary curricula have changed with the musical life of the region. Music education now encompasses a range of styles and modes of activity such as production, reproduction, perception, interpretation and reflection.

At the same time, contemporary curricula are limited by certain in-built obstacles, one of the most prominent of which is assessment. Current assessment criteria focus only on certain activities while others are neglected. The main reason for this imbalance seems to be the school authorities' desire to control educational outcomes on the one hand, and music teachers' desire to find objective and measurable grounds for assessment criteria on the other. The dominant reference system for these evaluative criteria is western art music, which predominates in teacher-training departments. Styles and activities outside this reference system are either evaluated from inappropriate perspectives (e.g. criteria based on art music are used to assess rock and jazz music) or neglected as unworthy of assessment.

Music teacher training highlights this tension between aims and objectives on the one hand and assessment on the other. In the socialization of the music teacher, role identities like 'performer' and 'content-centred teacher' are acknowledged, while others connected to non-western art-music styles and activities receive little support. There is an obvious need to work out new and more comprehensive assessment criteria that are in line with the current aims and objectives of Scandinavian music education.

The connection between artistic/musical and pedagogical framing might serve as the foundation for this change. By involving recognized musicians from many different styles and traditions in education, music teachers will be challenged by other aesthetic value systems and other forms of framing. A fruitful dialogue might evolve from this in which assessment criteria are based on the real-life musical experiences of today, and not the norms and values derived from a minor part of musical society. The power of music and music education in Scandinavian society as a whole is so strong that the evolution of a new musical landscape is inevitable, and music education must keep pace with these changes.

References

Bouij, C. (1998) *Musik – mitt liv och kommande levebröd. En studie i musiklärares yrkessocialisation* (Music – My Life and Future Profession: A Study in the Professional Socialization of Music Teachers). Diss, Göteborg: Göteborgs Universitet, skrifter från institutionen för musikvetenskap, Goteborgs Universitet, no. 56.

Broady, D. (1992) 'Bildningsfrågan: ett återupplivningsförsök'. *Ord & Bild*, **1**, 3–26.

Det kongelige kirke-, utdannings- og forskningsdepartement (1996) *Læreplanverket for den 10-årige grunnskolen*. Oslo: Nasjonellt læremiddelscenter.

Carlgren, I. (1997) 'Klassrummet som social praktik och meningskonstituerande praktik' (The classroom as social practice and meaning-forming culture). *Nordisk Pedagogik*, **17**, 8–27.

Cook, N. (1998) *Music: A Very Short Introduction*. Oxford: Oxford University Press.

Francke-Wikberg, S. and Lundgren, U. (1985) *Att värdera utbildning. En introduktion till pedagogisk utvärdering*. Stockholm: Wahlström & Widstrand.

Hargreaves, D. J., Galton, M. J. and Robinson, S. (1996) 'Assessment of primary children's classroom work in the creative arts'. *Educational Research*, **38**, 199–211.

Heiling, G. (1995) *Bedömnings- och utvecklingsfrågor i musikutbildningar*. Malmö: Lunds Universitet, Musikhögskolan i Malmö.

Jørgensen, H. (1982) *Sang og musikk. Et fags utvikling i grunnskolen fra 1945 til 1980*. Oslo: Ascheschough & Co.

Lave, J. and Wenger, E. (1991) *Situated Learning: Legitimate Perpiheral Participation*. Cambridge: Cambridge University Press.

Lindström, L. (1998) *Portföljvärdering av elevers skapande i bild. Allmän del*. Projekt inom ramen för Skolverkets utvärdering av skolan. Unpublished manuscript.

Lundgren, U. P. (1979) *Att organisera omvärlden*. Stockholm: Publica.

Nielsen F. V. (1994, 1998) *Almen musikdidaktik*. København: Akademisk Forlag, 2. Reviderede og bearbejdede udgave.

Ödman, P.-J. (1995) *Kontrasternas spel. En svensk mentalitets- och pedagogikhistoria*. Stockholm: Norstedts.

Olsson, B. (1992) 'Musikämnet i nationell utvärdering', in G. Svingby (ed.) *Engelska, musik, matematik, omvärldskunskap: NO. Instrumenten i den nationella utvärderingen granskas. En rapport inom det Nationella Utvärderingsprogrammet*. Göteborg: Göteborgs Universitet, Institutionen för Pedagogik, no. 21.

Olsson, B. (1993) *Sämus – en musikutbildning i kulturpolitikens tjänst? En studie om en musikutbildning under 70-talet*. Diss, Göteborg: Skrifter från musikvetenskap, no. 33, Musikhögskolan i Göteborg.

Rogoff, B. (1990) *Apprenticeship in Thinking*. New York: Oxford University Press.

Saar, T. (1999) *Musikens dimensioner: en studie av unga musikers lärande* (Göteborg studies in educational sciences). Diss, Göteborg: Acta Universitatis Gothoburgensis, no. 133.

Sandberg, R. (1996) *Musikundervisningens yttre villkor och inre liv: Några variaioner över ett läroplansteoretiskt tema* (The External Conditions and Inner Life of Music Education: Variations on a Curriculum Theme). Diss, Stockholm: Stockholm Institute of Education, Department of Educational Research.

Stålhammar, B. (1995). *Samspel. Grundskola – musikskola i samverkan: En studie av den pedagogiska och musikaliska interaktionen i en klassrumssituation* (Interplay – School and Music School in Collaboration: A Study of Pedagogic and Musical Interaction in a Classroom Situation). Diss, Göteborg: Göteborgs universitet, skrifter från den musikvetenskapliga avdelningen, no. 41, musikhögskolan i Göteborg.

Utbildningsdepartementet (1998) *Läroplan för det obligatoriska skolväsendet, förskoleklass och fritidshemmet*. Stockholm: Fritzes offentliga publikationer.

Vinther, O. (1997) *Musikkonservatorierne og musikskolerne: En relationsanalyse. Med teoretisk perspektivering af Frde V. Nielsen*. Aarhus: Det jydske musikkonservatorium.

CHAPTER

14

South America

Alda de Jesus Oliveira

Context, contents and methods

The South American context of music education is varied and diverse.
The racial and cultural mixture of the continent makes the music of its
people one of the most exciting in the world. There exists a great range
of music from a multicultural repertory, in the folk and artistic
traditions, all of which shows signs of vitality. Formal music education
tends to value foreign-oriented approaches and theories, however, and
although informal music teaching and learning structures abound in the
continent, they have only recently been the subject of more systematic
study. The context and contents of Latin American musics do show signs
of success, particularly in commercial music genres, although formal
music education seems to follow political and religious tendencies. With
the development of knowledge, documentation, communication and
discussion concerning these contexts and contents, Latin American
music education should progress in more balanced and appropriate
ways.

The role of music in South American countries

South America has approximately 324.9 million inhabitants, with Brazil
the most populous country. The Latin American countries were
colonized mainly by the Spanish and the Portuguese. Members of
ecclesiastical orders began settling the area from the late sixteenth
century with the aim of converting the native population to
Christianity. The interaction of sacred and secular cultural influences,
in addition to the pre-existing racial mixture, generated a great cultural
diversity in South America. For example, the Jesuits used educational-

artistic works called 'autos' to convert the native population and teach them European culture.

During the seventeenth and eighteenth centuries, the Jesuits had a strong impact on South American cultures through their missions in Paraguay, Bolívia, Argentina and Brazil. Indians and mestizos became part of choirs and small orchestras, and Indian dances were allowed for religious services and processions. The Jesuits provided the students with notations of the work of Europe's best musicians. Musical instruction in Paraguay, for example, reached such an impressive level that it was mentioned by Pope Benedict XIV in his 1749 encyclical *Anus qui hunc vertetem*. Indeed, the Jesuits were the educational leaders in Brazil before their expulsion in 1759, and from Spanish America as a whole, in 1767 (Béhague, 1979).

During the second half of the eighteenth century, music education advanced rapidly in Latin American territories: music continued to be used by missionaries as a means of teaching Christianity to the native populations. Music instruction at the Colegio de San Andrés (Quito, 1550–81), for sons of Indian chiefs, used Gregorian chant and later canto de órgano or polyphony. However, prejudice and political care must have influenced the colonizers. Although the Indians were considered very skilful musicians, they never led the musical life of the area (with the exception of some Mexican and Peruvian mestizo musicians).

In the eighteenth century, music was used mainly for Catholic services in the cathedrals, not only in Latin but also in vernacular forms. The church was the centre of the community and controlled education at all levels, fostering intellectual and artistic activities. Musicians worked directly for the Church and also supplied the needs of the viceroyal palaces. The most important positions at the cathedrals were the chapelmaster and the organist, who were European or Europe-trained musicians, with the responsibilities of 'selecting repertory, rehearsing the musicians and conducting the music services throughout the year ... [along with] writing original compositions and teaching the choirboys' (Béhague, 1979, p. 6). However, the cathedral archives which survive in Latin America 'represent only a small proportion of the riches they once boasted' (*Ibid.*, p. 7).

The archives of the cathedral at Bogotá are 'the richest repertory in the New World of European sixteenth-century polyphony and Baroque music' (*Ibid.*, p. 29). For example, the chapelmaster of Bogotá, Gutierre Fernández Hidalgo (1553–1620), wrote the *Libro de Coro*. During the sixteenth and seventeenth centuries, José de Cascante and Juan de Herrera worked as composers associated with the cathedral, producing mostly villancicos. Herrera's permissive music-education practices are recorded in the cathedral documents, which blame him for the students' lack of intelligence as well as the poor quality of their voices.

Until the eighteenth century, Peru was the main administrative centre of Spanish South America and developed an extraordinary artistic and cultural life during the colonial period, mainly in the cities of Cuzco and Lima. The Cuzco Cathedral library had music personnel and a collection of choral books, and these resources allowed it to found the Seminario de San Antonio de Abad, the first in the New World, which taught polyphonic and instrumental music (*Ibid.*, p. 35). In Lima, the capital of Peru, which was founded in 1535, the first church was inaugurated in 1540. Although it became the see of an archbishop in 1549, it was not until the seventeenth century that its music became organized on a regular basis. Various regulations governed the responsibilities of chapel members, singers and the chapelmaster, including composition for the latter, and specified the musical repertory for the liturgies at various occasions. A typical chapel orchestra would contain Peruvians, Indians or mestizos and, by the end of the colonial period, blacks and mulattos.

By 1624, Bolivia possessed one of the most distinguished universities in Spanish America, the San Francisco Xavier University (*ibid.*). The La Plata Cathedral became an archepiscopal seat in 1609, and its present archive at the Sucre Cathedral is one of the richest on the continent, containing documents dating from 1564. In 1569 a school for music and dancing was opened under the initiative of Juan de la Peña Madrid and Hernán Garcia. At around the same time, the first school of music in Argentina was founded by Father Pedro Comental (1595–1665), and among the best music teachers were Juan Vasseau (of Belgium), Luis Berger (of France) and Antonio Sepp (of Austria).

Although musical activities in the country decreased considerably after the expulsion of the Jesuits, a revival began when Teatro Colón and other theatres opened in 1857, which transformed Buenos Aires into an important world centre for opera. The nationalist composer Alberto Williams (1862–1952) founded the Conservatório Williams and wrote theory texts. During the sixteenth and seventeenth centuries, dramas were written mainly for the didactic purposes of the Church, but these musical forms began to find their way into theatres, opera houses and the local repertory.

Independence from colonial rule spread throughout Latin America between 1810 and 1830. National music institutions and conservatories began to develop, as did the building of theatres for opera performances. This period saw the rise of opera and light musical theatre, songs and piano music and, later on, symphonic and chamber music, even though foreign performers tended to predominate. Salon music dominated sheet-music publishing and Argentina, in particular, had a much more prominent musical life during the nineteenth century than it had during the colonial period, enjoying 30 important musical societies promoting symphonic, choral, chamber and stage music.

The twentieth century has witnessed the rise of multiculturalism and changes in educational policy in musical organizations. South American music educators met for the first time to discuss these issues during the first Latin-American Music Education Meeting, organized by the Brazilian Association of Music Education and the International Society for Music Education in 1997. It became apparent at this meeting that although significant problems persist, the continent enjoys a great musical richness in both formal and informal contexts. The 82 presentations included work on music in the regular schools, the development of the professional musician, special education problems and alternative and informal music education. Participants spoke about Latin American problems, musical memory, linguistic development through music activities, interdisciplinarity and multiculturalism, and music and society (Barbosa, 1997), and a second meeting was successfully organized in Venezuela in 1999.

As Anthony Seeger affirms,

> The Americas have seen a creative fusion of styles whose vigour and beauty have made their music known throughout the world. This process continues daily as musicians continue to create and perform. As old traditions are revived or new ones are created, music repeatedly serves as a resource for social group formation. On the other hand, musical performances of a particular genre or style often are the hallmark of a given group. Musical performances are used by composers, performers, audiences, critics, governments, oppressors, and liberators (in sum, by all social actors) in ways they find meaningful, which are not (for them) mixed up at all. And while each group may be characterised by one kind of music, a given individual may claim membership in various groups and perform a variety of musical styles appropriate to them. Musical performance is thus part of larger social processes – among them oppression, resistance, and the creation and affirmation of social identities. (in Béhague, 1994, pp. 12–13)

If we accept Seeger's view that musical identity forms just one part of broader social processes, music education in South America can be seen as developing, albeit slowly, in a positive direction. The growing tendency both in education and society as a whole is towards growing respect for the whole diversity of musics. Although the number of postgraduate courses in music in Latin America is small compared to Europe or United States, there is significant growth, particularly in Brazil and Argentina.

Brazil

The Federative Republic of Brazil has 27 states. It occupies almost half of the geographic region of South America and has 174.8 million inhabitants. Perhaps because informal music-making has flourished in Brazil since colonial times, music education has followed a pattern of frequent reform and lack of continuity. Brazilian superior-level education has 41 graduate courses in music, aproximately 150 courses in artistic education and seven postgraduate programmes in music.

During the first three centuries after the country was discovered by the Portuguese in 1500, music was tied primarily to religion. Between their arrival and ultimate expulsion in 1759, the Jesuits were extremely concerned with education, leaving eleven *colégios* and six seminaries behind them. The work of the Jesuits brought European musical practices to the colony, employing these as a means of facilitating education in general. The Jesuits took advantage of the native inhabitants' musicality to teach the Portuguese language and moral code. In addition to the natives, almost 5 million African slaves were brought to Brazil from Africa between 1538 and 1888, and the Jesuits also provided formalized music instruction for these people from as early as the 1600s.

The Jesuit José de Anchieta may be considered the forerunner of Brazilian education and Father Antônio Rodrigues (1516–68) the patron of Brazilian music educators, because he taught European music to the native inhabitants and taught education through music from 1556 (Perrone and Cruz, 1997). The Jesuits' broad concept of education included music, dance and theatre for the natives and their children, which served to awaken their artistic senses and to develop instrumental skills. Despite the lack of a university and printing press, Brazil produced a significant literature during this period, including names such as Manoel da Nóbrega, José de Anchieta, Antonio Vieira, Gregório de Matos, Claudio da Costa and Tomás Gonzaga.

European musical styles of the time were assimilated, in particular the pre-classic homophonic style. The first opera houses appeared in Bahia in the early seventeenth century, although theatrical presentations with music are known to have taken place earlier. The local repertory reflected that of Lisbon, staging essentially Spanish plays. Since Bahia, the first capital, was the major slave centre of the South American Atlantic Coast, it was rapidly populated by blacks and mulattos, and several black musicians flourished there. Professional conductors from sugar plantations organized private choruses and orchestras comprising slave musicians, which resulted in the formation of several colonial groups of mulatto composers and musicians. Native composers also began to appear: Álvares Pinto, chapelmaster at the church of São Pedro dos Clérigos in Recife, completed the treatise *Arte de Solfejar* in 1761, and this may be the earliest known work by a New World-born author.

During the nineteenth century, including the proclamation of the Republic in 1822, Brazil saw the rise of a bourgeoisie, and the rise of urbanization and industrialization. In 1847, Francisco Manuel da Silva founded the Music Conservatory of Rio de Janeiro, the second capital. Prior to this, music instruction was almost non-existent, and the conservatory represented the first attempt in Brazil to create music as a true profession. The Conservatory's music curriculum included voice and solfège, string instruments, woodwind and brass, harmony and composition.

The twentieth century brought modern movements in the arts and music such as the creativity movement of the 1960s, the integrated arts movement of the 1970s and the postmodernist movement of the 1990s. The influence of the media and global communications on musical development continues to grow in the absence of a formal structure for school music education. Consequently, the musical repertoire of children and teenagers emphasizes pop music and music from the most popular festivities, such as Carnaval and São João.

From 1930 to 1937, Getúlio Vargas' regime promoted nationalism, and Anísio Teixeira created the SEMA council (Superintendency of Musical Artistic Education) in 1932 to implement the orpheonic singing movement initiated by Villa-Lobos in Sao Paulo. Formal music education became a compulsory part of the school curriculum, based on four principles which emphasized (a) the exact place – in time and space – that music should have in education; (b) music education as a collective enterprise; (c) the integration of the artist into society; and (d) the composer as a reflection of the soul of the people (Menegale, 1969).

Villa-Lobos' programme worked basically with the human voice. He organized a preparatory course for teachers as well as many student concerts which attracted huge crowds of up to 40,000 people. The key aspects of Villa-Lobos's approach to music education were the defence of musical literacy, compulsory government-funded musical education, the potential socializing effects of music such as citizenship, altruism, fraternalism and humanitarism, the integration of different social classes, the importance of beginning musical learning in very early childhood, the importance of the voice and the use of Brazilian folk music or high-quality composed music. Music education was intended to mimic the way a child learns to speak, so that the process began by merely exposing the child to music before the introduction of musical rules and symbols. Teachers also used the manossolfa method (special hand signs developed by Villa-Lobos) to aid improvisation and special effects.

Luciano Gallet, Mário de Andrade, Liddy Mignone and Sá Pereira were working towards the improvement of Brazilian musical production and education, and used orpheonic singing and musical initiation methodologies (Fuks, 1991). The latter were inspired by the progressive methodologies of Dalcroze, Orff, Kodály and, later, Willems, and were mainly organized in specialized schools. However, the public schools taught music through more traditional oral techniques. The modernist influence decreased in the 1940s, and because Villa-Lobos was no longer involved with the SEMA, active music-making declined in the schools (*ibid.*).

This period was followed by the creativity movement, which was inspired by child-centred pedagogies. The theories of Dalton, Montessori and Lubienska were promoted in Brazil by the later 1950s, and educators from the left, such as Paschoal Lemme and Paulo Freire, promoted this new pedagogy, emphasizing its benefit for the whole population (Giraldelli, 1994). In later years it was developed and refined by other liberal educators as a result of the work of theorists including Dewey, Kilpatrick, Piaget, Bruner and Lauro de Oliveira Lima.

The military regime, from 1964–85, inhibited this, as well as many other potentially new and interesting educational developments, and had a deleterious effect on the general state of Brazilian education. In 1983 the Brazilian population included 60 million illiterates and semi-literates. In implementing what it called a 'social peace', the regime smothered civil organizations and controlled the media, schools, political parties and labour unions. This centralizing tendency was apparent in Law 5692, passed in 1971, which implemented policy in artistic education (*ibid.*).

While the bourgeoisie fought to maintain its power, other social classes were fighting to democratize Brazil's development and modernization. Students were engaged in educating the people, and music was a very important medium for this. Many musicians became involved with new teaching techniques and some worked for the Centros Populares de Cultura (CPCs), the Movimentos de Cultura Popular (MCPs) and the Movimento de Educação de Base (MEB). Arts and music helped to promote political awareness and to raise consciousness about the individual's role in history. For example, Paulo Freire promoted a dialogical method in which the real-life problems and knowledge of students were considered in an attempt to develop their consciousness.

By the 1980s, the informal music scene was also very active: Tom Jobim, Caetano Veloso, Gilberto Gil, Chico Buarque de Holanda, Maria Betânia, Gal Costa, Tom Zé, Toquinho, Moraes Moreira and other musicians were creating a new Brazilian musical profile. The Bossa-nova, the Tropicália, and later, the Novos Bahianos opened new possibilities, embellishing the traditional samba or other musical structures such as marcha-rancho and baião. Exchange between formal and informal music practices was frequent. For example, some of the Bahian pop musicians attended orchestral concerts, and attended the *Seminários de Música* in Bahia to meet erudite musicians such as Lindembergue Cardoso, Jamary Oliveira, Fernando Cerqueira and Ernst Widmer.

Although these exchanges between formal and informal music practices were beginning to develop, there remains a gulf between them even today. The educational system considers pop music to be rather exotic, perhaps because of its use of improvised techniques or its lack of flexibility. Many of the musicians involved use local repertoires, mostly from rural areas or belonging to specific urban identity groups, and these approaches have only recently been studied by ethnomusicological educators such as Conde, A. Oliveira, Rios, Prass, Borges, Gomes and Stein.

Following Nogueira's (1987) pioneering work, a group of postgraduate music students organized a symposium in Paraíba, in 1988, to discuss general problems of research and education in music: this developed into the National Association for Research and Post-Graduate Studies in Music (ANPPOM) and the Brazilian Association for Music Education (ABEM), which organizes annual meetings to discuss the general problems of music in Brazil. ANPPOM and ABEM have sought governmental support for the visits to Brazil of some important international researchers such as Gerard Béhague, David Hargreaves, Judith Jellison, Clifford Madsen, K. Nketia, Keith Swanwick and others. These scholars participated in discussions about research in specific problems related to music and music education theories and practices.

Discussions within the music community indicated that one teacher could not be responsible for teaching several art forms, that one hour a week was well below the average time required to allow any work to develop properly and that the existing system hampered children's opportunities to follow a career in the arts. The educational context began to change after 1995, when curricular reforms became needed after the new *Lei de Diretrizes e Bases da Educação Nacional* (LDB) (December, 1996), which recognizes the teaching of Art (Art. 26), which includes music, dance, theatre and visual arts. The Arts and Design Specialists Commission and the Music Specialists Commission of the Ministry of Education developed documents to guide the curriculum reforms of all university courses related to music.

Availability and consistency of provision in Brazil

According to recent data (Pestana, 1999), the general proficiency of Brazilian students at the fundamental and medium level of education is beginning to improve. However, this general pattern disguises a considerable amount of economic, geographical and social heterogeneity. There is as yet no consistent provision of music education activities in schools, although music is at least present in all schools by means of festivities and other activities. There exists a general belief within Brazilian society that music is needed at schools mainly for non-musical purposes (see, for example, Hentschke *et al.*, 1999). There are two caveats to this rather gloomy picture, however. First, it is worth noting that with the approval of the new LDB (December 1996), new educational guidelines have been developed for all levels of education. Secondly, the tropical climate ensures that informal musical activities – in bars and carnivals, for example – stay in a very healthy state.

Teacher training for music education does not provide enough competencies to deal with the problems of the socio-cultural reality of the regular schools. At the same time, the regular educational system does not provide a solid training in music. When students arrive at university for teacher training, they consequently have to acquire not only the usual pedagogical skills, but also a proficiency in music. Brazilian universities offer two categories of undergraduate course for students interested in becoming music educators: one concerns general arts education or music education, and the second deals with music performance, composition and conducting. As a result, two kinds of music professionals emerge: the first is trained to teach the arts or music, but has little specific knowledge in music, while the second is trained to perform, compose and/or conduct, but has no pedagogical training to teach general music. Consequently, formal music education in regular schools does not generally go beyond singing or experimenting with vocal and instrumental sounds. Professional training in music generally takes place in the conservatories, with private music teachers or university community workshops.

In summary, we might conclude that Brazilian music educators currently face five problems in reintroducing music into schools, namely (a) the short duration of the music lesson (45 minutes, once per week); (b) the lack of an adequate infrastructure for music lessons; (c) the tendency to organize the school calendar around festivities, visitors, educational trips or other such events; (d) the high level of truancy, and (e) teachers' competence to teach music.

Aims and objectives

Brazilian music education and culture

It is already clear from the foregoing section that Brazilian music education is rooted in the country's ethnic and cultural background. One manifestation of this is the strong position of oral literature, the Capoeira providing an interesting musical example. It was brought to Brazil from Angola as a fight, and during the twentieth century was transformed into a choreographic game involving music and dance. The Capoeira songs are accompanied by the berimbau, a one-string instrument, and other percussion instruments. The Capoeira players simulate a fight, following the tempo of the songs, which accelerate progressively. Recently, the Capoeira has become one of the most popular folkloric and educational attractions in certain regions of Brazil. Indeed, many schools have adopted the Capoeira as an event for school social activities and even, in some cases, as a curriculum component.

Another cultural influence on Brazilian music education has been a historical lack of governmental interest in education. More recently, some attempts have been made to rectify this. The new LDB (Law 9394) has generated quality control documentation by specialist committees covering issues such as (a) national curriculum standards; (b) the registration, governmental recognition and evaluation of new courses; (c) the introduction of national exams for all students at the end of their courses; and (d) new directions for professional courses. Since 1995, the Arts Specialists Committee of the Ministry of Education and, in 1997, the Music Specialists Committee, have developed two important documents aimed at improving art and music standards, entitled

'Quality Standards for Undergraduate Music Courses' and 'Curriculum Directions for Undergraduate Music Courses'. This new system is already being used in the whole country.

Regulation of the music profession comes via Federal Law 3857, from 1960, which created the Musicians Order of Brazil. It is interesting to note that although there exists a conflict between formal and informal aspects of music education, the Musicians' Order does not reflect this. It recognizes as professionals not only individuals with school or conservatory qualifications, but also 'any musicians of any genre or speciality working in any professional activity' as well as people who pass the Musicians' Order exam. Such liberal legislation has both positive and negative consequences. On the plus side, it allows those who learn music informally to exercise the profession, but, at the same time, it fails to provide an incentive for these people to enter music schools or work towards improved musical literacy. It is easy to see how this tolerance for informally-acquired musical skills might have evolved from a history of music education which, as described earlier, has always emphasized universality of access.

Music in and out of Brazilian schools

Interest in *in*formal music is another important aspect of the aims and objectives of Brazilian music education. A number of recent post-graduate studies have concerned music both in and out of schools, and the relationship between these two forms of musical learning and development. For example, Oliveira and Hentschke (1999), Hentschke *et al.* (1999) and Oliveira and Costa Filho (2000) considered the testing of a curriculum model, the relationship between the school and the music class, and the formation, production and administration of different musical groups respectively. Studies have also been made of the relationship between theory and practice in curriculum development; the balanced musical development of students in performance, appreciation and composition; motivation through the choice of repertory; teachers' knowledge of the teaching and learning processes; and music materials in specific musical groups (Conde, 1980; Oliveira, 1986; Silva, 1995; Tourinho, 1996; Bastião, 1997; Borges, 1997; Rios, 1997; Ben, 1998; Prass, 1998; Stein, 1998; Gomes, 1998; Arroyo, 1999; Marques, 1999; and others). Schools need this information in order to prepare students and music teachers for the diverse musical activities they might encounter, both within and outside formal settings.

Although the teaching of the arts is enforced by law at the basic level, the methods by which Brazilians learn music are mostly directed by social and contextual factors, rather than being school-oriented. These methods include (a) empathy and osmosis, with consequent repetition of musical motifs and gestures resulting from observation, imitation and improvisation; (b) musical games and plays; (c) group interactions which have strong implications for the identity of the participants (e.g. family musical reunions, peer musical gatherings, neighbourhood and inner-city musical bands, commercial business choirs etc.); (d) experiencing music for personal enjoyment (e.g. in bars, night clubs, theatres, beaches, community associations etc.); (e) programmes for the development of disadvantaged communities; (f) religious activities; and (g) private music lessons.

Specific issues

Identity and educational processes

In conclusion, informal music practices abound in Brazil, perhaps because there is a lack of formal music education in the schools and, in particular, an insufficient number of music teachers to reflect the great diversity of music listening and performing practices. In addition to this lack of school provision, private music lessons are expensive and teachers' salaries are very low, which must, presumably, hamper recruitment. Despite these problems there remains a growing tendency for the younger generation to engage in musical activities, particularly those from disavantaged social classes. There are some recent signs that music is being used increasingly as a means of identity development, particularly among people of African descent (e.g. the Pracatum School in Bahia). In many contexts, musical development results from processes of creolization or black nationalism, although most music teachers have yet to incorporate Brazilian musical identities into school music practices.

As Béhague (1994) affirms, 'black ethnicities often adopt the ideology of négritude as the essence of their cultural, sometimes class, identity. In so doing, they naturally develop counter-hegemonic strategies towards the ultimate elimination of their political and economic subordination and exploitation. In this struggle, aspects of expressive culture such as music function as highly effective symbolic means of vindication' (p. vi). However, music teachers are often not prepared to acknowledge pupils' identities and so classroom musical practices are frequently distant from students' informal musical experiences. Factors such as this must be introduced into teacher preparation courses, because even within a single community members may have a number of different potential identities.

Let me conclude by emphasizing six important features that future research studies and pedagogical practices should incorporate. They should (a) study the formal and informal music learning and teaching structures and processes in different South American and Brazilian contexts, in order to improve teachers' musical skills; (b) adopt interdisciplinary perspectives which reflect the relationship between formal and informal musical practices; (c) prepare teachers to deal with the different musics and musical identities which exist in the classroom and in community settings; (d) enhance professional musicians' knowledge of the process of producing music in order to improve the whole system, and to pursue professional excellence; (e) exchange ideas, personnel, publications and practices in order to increase the effectiveness of music education programmes; and (f) increase support for community music activities, and enhance the links between these and school practices. By taking these steps, music education in Brazil and South America as a whole can draw further on the rich cultural diversity on which it is based and develop the quality of provision towards which it aspires.

References

Arroyo, M. (1999) 'Representações sociais sobre práticas de ensino e aprendizagem musical: Um estudo etnográfico entre congadeiros, professores e estudantes de música'. Unpublished doctoral dissertation, Universidade Federal do Rio Grande do Sul, Instituto de Artes.

Barbosa, J. (ed.) (1997) *Anais do I encontro Latino-Americano de educação musical ABEM – ISME*. Brazil: ABEM.

Bastião, Z. (1997). 'Reações dos alunos ao ensino de música: Análise de comportamentos registrados em video decorrentes da aplicação de um planejamento para a 1a série do 1o Grau'. Unpublished master's thesis, Universidade Federal da Bahia, Escola de Música.

Béhague, G. (1979) *Music in Latin America: An Introduction*. Englewood Cliffs, NJ: Prentice-Hall.

Béhague, G. (ed.) (1994) *Music and Black Ethnicity: The Caribbean and South America*. London: Transaction Publishers.

Ben, L. M. D. (1998) 'A utilização do modelo espiral de desenvolvimento musical como critério de avaliação da apreciação musical em um contexto educacional Brasileiro'. Unpublished master's thesis, Universidade Federal do Rio Grande do Sul, Instituto de Artes.

Borges, A. (1997) 'O processo de transmissão do conhecimento musical no Ilê Apô Afonjá'. Unpublished master's thesis, Universidade Federal da Bahia, Escola de Música.

Conde, C. (1980) *Significado e funções da música do povo na educação* (partial report). Brasília, Brazil: Instituto Nacional de Estudos e Pesquisas Educacionais.

Fuks, R. (1991) *Discurso do Silêncio*. Rio de Janeiro: Enelivros Ed. Ltda.

Giraldelli Jr, P. (1994) *História da Educação*. São Paulo: Cortez.

Gomes, C. H. S. (1998) 'Formação e atuação de músicos das ruas de Porto Alegre: Um estudo a partir dos relatos de vida'. Unpublished master's thesis, Universidade Federal do Rio Grande do Sul, Instituto de Artes.

Hentschke, L. , Oliveira, A. and Souza, J. (1999) 'A relação da escola com a aula de música' (partial research report). Brasília, Brazil: Conselho Nacional de Pesquisa e Desenvolvimento Tecnológico.

Marques, E. F. L. (1999) 'Discurso e prática pedagógica na formação dos alunos de licenciatura em música em Salvador, Bahia, 1998'. Unpublished master's thesis, Universidade Federal da Bahia, Escola de Música.

Menegale, H. (1969) *Villa-Lobos e a Educação*. Rio de Janeiro: Artes Gráficas da Escola Técnica Federal.

Nogueira, I. (1987) *SINAPEM*. João Pessoa: Universidade Federal da Paraíba – Departamento de Música. MEC (SESU/CAPES) – CNPq.

Oliveira, A. (1986) 'Frequency of occurrence of specific music elements in Bahian folk songs, using computer and manual analysis: suggestions for music education'. Unpublished doctoral dissertation, University of Texas at Austin.

Oliveira, A. e Costa Filho, M. (2000). 'Educação e trabalho em música: estudo 1'. *Quaderni della SIEM*, **16**, 234–9.

Oliveira, A. and Hentschke, L. (1999) *Um estudo longitudinal aplicando a teoria espiral de desenvolvimento musical de Swanwick com crianças Brasileiras da faixa etária de 6 a 10 anos* (Final Research Report). Brasília, Brazil: Conselho Nacional de Pesquisa e Desenvolvimento Tecnológico.

Perrone, M. da C. C. and Cruz, S. B. A.(1997) *Instituto de Música: Um Século de Tradição Musical na Bahia*. Salvador: Gráfica da Universidade Federal da Bahia.

Pestana, M. (1999) *SAEB 97: Primeiros Resultados*. Brasilia: MEC, Instituto Nacional de Estudos e Pesquisas Educacionais.

Prass, L. (1998) 'Saberes musicais em uma bateria de escola de samba: uma etnografia entre os "Bambas da Orgia"'. Unpublished master's thesis, Universidade Federal do Rio Grande do Sul, Instituto de Artes.

Rios, M. (1997) 'Educação musical e música vernácula: Processos de ensino e aprendizagem'. Unpublished master's thesis, Universidade Federal da Bahia, Escola de Música.

Silva, W. M. (1995) 'Motivações, expectativas e realizações na aprendizagem musical: Uma etnografia sobre alunos de uma escola alternativa de música'. Unpublished master's thesis, Universidade Federal do Rio Grande do Sul, Instituto de Artes.

Stein, M. R. A. (1998) 'Oficinas de música: uma etnografia dos processos de ensino e aprendizagem musical em bairros populares de Porto Alegre'.

Unpublished master's thesis, Universidade Federal do Rio Grande do Sul, Instituto de Artes.

Tourinho, C. (1996) 'A influência do repertório de interesse do aluno na aprendizagem de violão em grupo'. Unpublished master's thesis, Universidade Federal da Bahia, Escola de Música.

United Kingdom

Graham F. Welch

Introduction

In any consideration of musical development and learning, context will be significant. Neither development nor learning occurs in a vacuum; both are located socially and, arguably, socially constructed (because that which counts as learning is, primarily, socially defined). Moreover, musical behaviour is a product of three generative elements in which the socio-cultural context interfaces with the developing anatomical/physiological history of the individual, and 'music' as defined within the culture (Welch, 1998; 2000b). The functioning of this basic cognitive architecture is shaped temporally by socio-cultural factors that facilitate the reproduction and transformation of musical behaviour. Such socialization determines which particular groupings of perceived sounds are classified and valued as 'music' within the culture, which is therefore learned and not absolute (Finnegan, 1989; Burns, 1999; Carterette and Kendall, 1999). At the level of the individual, similarities and differences are evident in the development of musical behaviour. These arise from an interaction that has inherent potential tensions between the musical 'pathways' (Finnegan, 1989) that groups and societies utilize in order to induce, foster, perpetuate and transform musical traditions across successive generations, and the some-what more idiosyncratic developmental 'routes' (Welch, 1998) actually taken by individuals through such pathways.

The socio-musical and cultural context for school music

In the case of contemporary UK society, at least part of the socio-cultural context for musical development and learning can be seen in the population's leisure activities, as these frame significant experiences from childhood through to adulthood. The latest government statistics for 1996/7 reveal that children aged 4 to 14 average just under six hours a week listening to radio (Office for National Statistics, 1998). In 1996, nearly 160 million CDs were sold in the UK, as well as over 78 million singles. Eight in ten people regularly listened to music on CD, tape and/ or records (but only six out of ten in Northern Ireland). As far as 'high culture' was concerned, 12 per cent of sampled adults reported that they regularly attended classical music concerts, compared to 7 per cent attending ballet and 6 per cent opera. In contrast, 27 per cent of adults aged 16 and over reported regular attendance at a disco or night club.

These lifestyle statistics show that contemporary UK citizens spend a lot of their leisure time each week engaged with the sonic world through a diverse variety of media, both technical and sensory. Music, in all its various guises, is a significant part of people's lives, irrespective of social or ethnic grouping. Within the UK's South Asian community, for example, recent research has revealed a multiplicity of musical genres and practices (Farrell *et al.*, 1999). The Indian, Pakistani and Bangladeshi population of 2.5 million (which forms a majority of the total 3.4 million (6%) ethnic minority population in the UK), embraces many different musics and at least five major linguistic communities (Modood *et al.*, 1997). For adults and children, two particular musical genres predominate, namely north Indian classical music and *filmi* song (songs from popular movies). Yet many links between the two (and between 43 other identified genres) are evidenced, alongside a preference by the younger population for variations of their own popular music, *bhangra*. Each of these musics is an integral element in the framing of personal and group identity (Finnegan, 1989; Baumann, 1990; Baily, 1995; Crozier, 1997; North and Hargreaves, 1997; 1999; Farrell *et al.*, 1999).

Given the rich diversity of musics that co-exist in contemporary Britain, embracing many different genres and sub-strands, it is self-evident that the contemporary child is born into a complex and varied sonic world. Whilst it is possible to argue that this has always been the case and that childhood was never 'silent', previous generations were not born into a global musical village in which modern technologies are utilized to such a degree to bring such a diverse array of musics into both the home and the outside world.

Yet such diversity presents a particular challenge to the formal school system because certain musics (and musical practices) have customarily been part of the curriculum to the exclusion of others (Wiggins, 1996; Cope and Smith, 1997; Kwami, 1998), particularly in the case of the musics associated with adolescence (Durrant, 1999). For example, when 704 young people aged 14 to 24 were asked to reflect on their secondary-school arts experiences, negative experiences were more evident among ethnic minorities (Harland *et al.*, 1995), which suggests a mismatch between (sub-)cultural expectations and their experience of 'school' music. Furthermore, less than half (48 per cent) of those who reported taking music as an option for the General Certificate of Secondary Education (GCSE) examination at age 16 years saw the subject as 'creative' or 'imaginative' (Harland *et al.*, 1995).

Similar negative findings are reported in two large-scale surveys of secondary-aged pupils (Ross, 1975; Ross and Kamba, 1998). Despite a gap of 25 years, the least popular curriculum subject in each study was music (along with physics). This lack of popularity increased with the age of the groups surveyed, but girls always tended to be more positive than boys. Similar levels of increasing disenchantment with music in secondary school emerged in a three-year longitudinal study by Swanwick and Lawson (1999), but with evidence of some positive impact on attitudes for pupils who were able to work additionally with professional musicians outside the school context.

Such mixed experiences of music as a school subject probably underlie the relatively low proportion of young people entering for GCSE music examinations. Although there were 50,000 music GCSE entries in 1995/6 (DfEE, 1998a), this represents only 1 per cent of the total GCSE entries across all subjects. Not surprisingly, given the attitudinal data above, more girls than boys take these examinations and achieve better results. Subsequently, just over one in ten of these young people go on to take music at an advanced level two years later (aged 18).

There is some evidence (Harland *et al.*, 1998) that success in school music relates to the degree of formal musical knowledge that pupils bring with them into the classroom. Children who undertake specialist instrumental tuition are provided with certain technical skills and knowledge that are valued by the school system and useful for the successful engagement with school music (see Aims and Objectives, and Content and Methods below). Yet, perhaps paradoxically, there has been a downward trend in the provision of such instrumental instruction as part of the school day, which is one of the outcomes of changing budget priorities of local education authorities and schools. Approximately only 1 per cent of pupils receive tuition in England and Wales (TES, 1998) and between 5 and 8 per cent in Scotland (Hall, 1999).

It is from the relatively small pool of musical 'experts', defined by school and conservatoire examination syllabuses of musical literacy, that the next generation of school music teachers is drawn. There is limited opportunity for higher education, subsequently, to redefine or expand this expertise because English primary (elementary) initial teacher education (ITE) has a statutory bias in time, resource and staffing towards the 'core' subjects of English, mathematics, science, and information and communications technology (DfEE, 1998b). Consequently, the other statutory school curriculum subjects, such as music, have relatively little time available (an average of sixteen hours' tuition for music education on a one-year primary ITE course and 30 hours on a four-year course (Rogers, 1998)). This means that any intending teachers who enter primary ITE courses with particular instrumental skills and knowledge are more likely to have these developed pedagogically during their pre-service preparation. On qualification, they will return to the classroom and so complete a cycle that suggests an implicit socio-musical and contextual bias in the definition, design and delivery of music in schools. Although there are some exceptions (cf. Naughton, 1998; Farrell *et al.*, 1999), the current formal education system provides pupils and their new teachers (including secondary music teachers who, customarily, have a conservatoire-type background) with relatively little opportunity to engage with specialist experts from the wider range of musics available within the UK.

Aims and objectives: a 'National Curriculum' for music

Schools are powerful agents in the formalization of musical development, as well as in attitudes to, and definitions of, musical competency. But in terms of lifelong musical experiences, the school contributes only one part to an individual's musical development and learning. The years before formal schooling are characterized by many musical encounters, beginning with the prenatal development of the auditory system (Lecanuet, 1996; Papousek, 1996). As a result, children enter the school system already exhibiting a wide variety of musical behaviours. They have a developing mastery of certain aspects of pitch, melodic contour, rhythmic patterning, tonality and song structure, alongside a growing knowledge and performance repertoire of musical fragments from the dominant culture(s) (Hargreaves, 1996; Welch, 1998; Dowling, 1999).

Consequently, one of the key criteria by which any school music curricula should be judged is the extent to which young children's existing and growing musical competencies are recognized and provided for by the statutory requirements. However, because education is a contested concept, the statutory curriculum for schools in the UK has been subject to much critical debate and change. Prior to 1988, there was no formal legislative prescription of the curriculum, only 'guidance' (with the exceptions of religious instruction – although not strictly treated as a curriculum subject – and sex and political education (Harris, 1989)). That year, however, saw the introduction of a National Curriculum for Schools in England and Wales (ERA, 1988). Scotland and Northern Ireland continued to operate their own national systems, with curriculum 'guidance' for music in the former and a version of the National Curriculum in the latter. The phasing-in of the National Curriculum over a number of years from 1989 meant that music was not introduced until 1992. It was then revised fully in 1995 for children aged 5 to 14, but became optional and non-statutory for pupils aged 14 to 16 (DFE, 1995b).

With regard to the statutory aims and objectives of the music curriculum, the original music curriculum working group sought to promote music in schools as 'an activity' (Ward, 1998; Pratt and Stephens, 1995). Ministerial diktat determined, however, that there should also be a strong 'knowledge about' music component. Consequently, the 1992 curriculum was framed under two 'attainment targets': Performing and Composing, and Listening and Appraising, with the notional time allocation for each being two-thirds and one-third respectively. (Wales, in contrast, was allowed three elements: Performing, Composing and Appraising.) The subsequent effect of the 1995 revision to the National Curriculum was largely cosmetic, with some changes in emphasis contained within a much 'slimmer' document. The same two attainment targets were maintained, but were meant to be brought together 'wherever possible' (DFE, 1995b).

The latest (third) version of the music curriculum (DfEE, 1999a; 1999b) commenced in September 2000. It only has one Programme of Study – Knowledge, Skills and Understanding, which is an amalgamation of the two former (1992 and 1995) components. The subtext states that 'Teaching should ensure that **listening, and applying knowledge and understanding** are developed through the interrelated skills of **performing, composing and listening**' (DfEE 1999a, pp. 124–6; 1999b, p. 172 – emphasis in original). This latest statutory text for the rather global, undifferentiated aim for music is subdivided into four content areas, namely: (a) 'Controlling sounds through singing and playing – performing skills'; (b) 'Creating and developing musical ideas – composing skills'; (c) 'Responding and reviewing – appraising skills'; and (d) 'Listening, and applying knowledge and understanding'. The text contains little specificity, other than such statements for five- to seven-year-olds such as 'Pupils should be taught how to create musical patterns' [and] 'to play tuned and untuned instruments' (1999a, p. 24). More detail is included within the nine 'levels' of the 'attainment target[s] for music' (1999b, Annex, pp. 44–5). These are organized hierarchically in a linear format, with each succeeding level designed to indicate the DfEE's view of progression and growing mastery.

Music in the preschool curriculum

In addition to the statutory National Curriculum for pupils aged 5–14, the government has now introduced a new version of its preschool guidance, titled *Early Learning Goals* (QCA, 1999), officially considered to be the 'Foundation Stage' for the National Curriculum. The Goals include a section on 'creative development' (cf. DfEE, 1999c), which subsumes musical development. The aims for music are as follows:

By the end of the foundation stage, most children will be able to:
(e) recognise and explore how sounds can be changed, sing simple songs from memory, recognise repeated sounds and sound patterns and match movements to music;
(f) use their imagination in . . . music;
(g) express and communicate their ideas, thoughts and feelings by using . . . a variety of songs and musical instruments.

Not surprisingly, there is a degree of overlap between the specification of the music Early Learning Goals and attainment level 1 of the statutory National Curriculum. This appears to be because the former are meant to be applicable to children up to the age of 6, whereas the statutory curriculum applies to children from age 5 upwards.

Alternative curriculum perspectives across the UK: Northern Ireland and Scotland

The National Curriculum for Northern Ireland was introduced in 1989 and its format resembles closely that for England and Wales. The current version dates from 1996 and the next major revision is planned to commence in September 2002. Music is part of the 'Creative and Expressive Area of Study' and applies to pupils aged 4 to 14. Unlike the rest of the UK, post-primary education is still selective (based on a public examination at 11). Major concerns that affect the quality of teaching and learning outcomes for this age phase are a general shortage of music teachers, as well as a lack of musically qualified staff. One third of respondents in a major survey of post-primary music teachers did not have a first degree in, or including, music (Drummond, 1999). Furthermore, three out of ten music teachers did not have any recognized teaching qualification. As in other parts of the UK, adolescent pupil dissatisfaction is evident in the non-GCSE classes, particularly among boys. With regard to the wider range of musics in the Irish community on both sides of the border, however, there is evidence that Irish traditional music continues successfully as part of an oral culture, with the 'teachers' being seen as the best performing musicians within the community (Veblen, 1996).

In Scotland, there is no statutory curriculum. Instead, the Scottish Office Education and Industry Department (SOEID) provides 'guidance' for the 'progression and performance' of children. Music is part of their 'expressive arts' guidance (alongside art and drama) for pupils aged 5 to 14, but is not included post-14. 'Expressive arts' are expected to account for 15 per cent of curriculum time. With regard to preschool provision, there is an explicit creative and exploratory focus to the 'expressive and aesthetic' component of the Curriculum Framework for Children aged 3 to 5 (SCCC, 1998).

Summary of underlying trends in official aims and objectives for music

- There has been a general movement towards an 'outcomes-based' curriculum design, with the 'process' subsumed into specified learning goals. In the latest version of the English National Curriculum for music (DfEE, 1999a; 1999b), however, the text is specifically more teacher-focused, with the aims and objectives specified in terms of teacher as well as pupil behaviours. This is in contrast to the Early Learning Goals (QCA, 1999) which continue an earlier tradition of specifying what pupils should be able to do (as opposed to being taught to do).
- Each of the constituent countries of the UK has a slightly different approach to the curriculum. Nevertheless, the general aims and objectives for music are similar, despite the official wording, whether statutory (England, Wales, Northern Ireland) or as guidance (Scotland).
- Notwithstanding its various incarnations, the curriculum is conceived essentially as the promotion of musical learning through action. Action is characterized and framed by such textual terminology as: 'performing' (including singing, performing, practising, rehearsing), 'composing' (improvising, exploring, developing, producing, extend-

ing), 'appraising' (analysing, evaluating, comparing, communicating, adapting, refining) and 'listening and applying' (listening, identifying, applying).

- The re-introduction of attainment 'levels' in the latest revision of the statutory curriculum for music (they were originally included in the 1991 draft proposals, but left out of the 1992 and 1995 statutory versions) reaffirms official support for the notion of 'norms' in musical attainment. In accordance with all other subjects, pupils are expected to attain level 2 in music by the age of 7, level 4 by the age of 11 and levels 5/6 by the age of 14 (DfEE, 1999b, Annex, p. 1). With regard to musical literacy, for example, notation and music reading are seen as evolving from the children's own graphic representations of sound (level 2), through to 'performing from simple notations' (level 4), to using 'relevant notations' for 'different genres and styles' (level 6). (This is despite recent Welsh research evidence that three- and four-year-olds are capable of learning pitch notation (Tommis and Fazey, 1999).)
- There are few obvious links with findings from music education research, nor from the psychology or sociology of music, despite the UK government's commitment to education as a 'research and evidence based profession' (TTA, 1997). The flavour of the latest (1999) attainment target wording appears essentially to be based on the 'craft knowledge' of practitioners, particularly as the levels ascend into the secondary age phase. Although this is not necessarily a weakness, the normative nature of the curriculum design assumes that all musical development is (a) sequential and even and (b) fully encompassed by the official wording.
- At the macro level, there is a general concordance between the philosophy that underpins the music curricula design (cf. DfEE, 1999a) and the dominant philosophical stance exhibited by the UK research community in recent years. In both cases, musical development is regarded as normal: all children are considered to be capable of learning and achieving musically. Closer inspection of the detail, however, suggests that the hierarchical linearity of the curriculum is simplistic as compared with the research evidence (cf. Dowling, 1999).

Content and methods

The implicit message from the National Curriculum designers is that musical development is facilitated and enhanced within a supportive environment. However, it is the research evidence that makes this explicit. For example, researchers have commented on the importance of:

- the amount of time spent learning (Hallam, 1998);
- self-perception as 'musicians' (O'Neill and Sloboda, 1997);
- partnerships through specialist input (Cottrell, 1998);
- appropriate pedagogic language use (Mellor, 1999);
- ensuring a 'match' between the musical task and current abilities (Swanwick and Franca, 1999; Tommis and Fazey, 1999; Welch, 2000a);
- 'the amount of formal practice, the degree of parental involvement and pupil–teacher relationship' (Sloboda and Howe, 1999, p. 52).

So far, the government has not drawn formally on such research evidence to provide any specific pedagogic guidance for teachers, although 'Schemes of Work' were expected to have been published by the DfEE in March 2000. Instead, it has relied on school inspection reports from OfSTED (the Office for Standards in Education; a non-ministerial government department) to create a general commentary on attainment, illustrated by specific examples of 'best' (as against 'weak' or 'unsatisfactory') practice.

The content of the statutory music curriculum has become increasingly minimalist across its three versions (1992, 1995, 1999). The apparent intention has been to provide a condensed text that can be utilized successfully by the musically 'naïve' primary school teacher, whilst allowing the more musically 'expert' teacher (whether primary or secondary) a degree of freedom in the exercise of invention and imagination. As outlined above, the principal *content* of the formal school curriculum for music has, essentially, been concerned with performing, composing, listening and appraising (DFE, 1995; DfEE, 1999a; 1999b). Each of these elements acts as an umbrella term for subsets of related activities (termed Programmes of Study) for three separate age phases, namely lower primary (5–7), upper primary (8–11) and lower secondary (12–14). Under 'composing', within the upper-primary phase, for example, the Programme of Study states that pupils should be taught how to '(a) improvise, developing rhythmic and melodic material when performing and (b) explore, choose, combine and organise musical ideas within musical structures' (DfEE, 1999a, p. 126). The corresponding attainment outcome wording for the average 11-year-old (level 4) is that they are able to 'improvise melodic and rhythmic phrases as part of a group performance and compose by developing ideas within musical structures' (DfEE, 1999a, Annex, p. 35).

Musical development and learning: the inspection evidence

The school inspection evidence from OfSTED (OfSTED, 1998; 1999a) for England and Wales suggests that the quality of musical development and learning has improved between 1994 and 1998 for both primary and secondary phases in relation to the specifications of the 1995 National Curriculum. However, there are differences between the various sectors.

Primary and preschool provision

In primary schools, OfSTED reports that high standards in singing, playing instruments, composing, listening and appraising are now found more frequently and that fewer pupils leave with low musical attainment (OfSTED, 1999a). Yet for a minority of schools where there is a concern, the most neglected aspect of the music curriculum is 'composing' (OfSTED, 1999b). Similarly, concerning provision for under-fives, it is the 'creative' rather than the reproductive aspects of music which cause concern. Although 'most institutions are good at giving children opportunities to listen to different sounds, and to explore different ways of making them' (OfSTED, 1999e, para. 46), less progress has been made in children's opportunities to make and perform music.

OfSTED collected evidence on primary peripatetic instrumental lessons separately from class music lessons. It reports that 'many children learn to read staff notation during instrumental lessons' (cf. Harland *et al.*, 1998). Overall, OfSTED reports that there is greater coherence to the primary music curriculum provided by both specialists and non-specialists.

Secondary provision

Although there has been a similar sustained improvement in standards in secondary schools since 1993, music 'continues to compare poorly to other subjects with respect to standards [of attainment] and teaching' (OfSTED, 1998, p. 153). In particular, standards are 'unsatisfactory in one-fifth of schools' (OfSTED, 1999c, p. 1), in part because their music curriculum 'has ossified and is remote from pupils' interests' (OfSTED, 1999c, p. 2). Nevertheless, inspectors report a significant improvement in singing, with the provision of a more suitable repertoire, and more pupils using their voices in composition (OfSTED, 1998, p. 153). There are ongoing issues of coherence and continuity in the curriculum (Mills,

1998), such as when pupils transfer between primary and secondary schools, as well as inappropriate flexibility of the curriculum to match particular children's needs, both musical and general (e.g. literacy needs).

The paradox of these findings is that secondary-school music is predominantly taught by graduate musicians. However, it is apparent that having extensive subject knowledge does not in itself guarantee pedagogic excellence (Alexander *et al.*, 1992). Moreover, the oldest pupils to receive the statutory curriculum (aged 14, year 9) are those that are subject to the most variable teaching quality (OfSTED, 1998). Such 'unsatisfactory teaching' resonates with the increasingly negative attitudes to school music exhibited by many such pupils, particularly boys (cf. Ross and Kamba, 1998; Harland *et al.*, 1998). Yet, post-14, when music becomes an optional subject for GCSE, OfSTED is very positive about both attainment and the quality of teaching. Inspection evidence suggests that such pupils have chosen to continue to study music because of their earlier positive experiences and, consequently, are likely to be more motivated to succeed.

Provision in special schools

Pupils were only making satisfactory progress in one-third of special schools (OfSTED, 1999d). Elsewhere, progress was either unsatisfactory, or there was insufficient music tuition seen for OfSTED to make a judgement. Once again, provision and attainment were better for primary-aged pupils. Where progress was regarded as good, inspectors comment positively on primary pupils learning to sing in tune, recognizing rhythm and pulse, playing untuned percussion to accompany their singing and listening attentively to music. However, progress in composing and appraising was less satisfactory and very few special schools made 'effective use ... of ICT in music sessions' (OfSTED, 1999d, p. 23). Furthermore, progress in the secondary phase was weaker because 'the earlier work had not been developed' (p. 23). Inspectors also noted that schools for pupils with severe learning difficulties (SLD) 'often used music in lessons in other subjects, including sensory sessions, and music was also played sometimes to set a calming atmosphere' (p. 23).

Surprisingly, none of the recent OfSTED summative reports mention the use of ICT for music in mainstream (primary and secondary) schools. Inspectors express a general concern about the appropriateness of accommodation, with additional concerns about resources for music in some schools. But there is no specific mention of ICT, notwithstanding the 1995–97 DfEE-initiated Music/IT Support Project (Mills, 1997) and the growing body of research evidence on the potential of ICT and music technology (Colley *et al.*, 1997; Bray, 1997; Webster, 1998 (for a review)).

In Scotland, 70 per cent of pupil attainment in music is regarded as 'satisfactory' or better; the majority of schools were providing courses that were 'good' or 'very good'. Nevertheless, similar concerns surface as for England and Wales regarding composing. 'Pupils sang and performed well, but their ability to apply their knowledge and practical skills to inventing their own music was weak' (SOEID, 1999).

Content and methods in the curriculum: other evidence

Aside from the official inspection data, empirical research evidence suggests that musical development is more complex than that made explicit within the National Curriculum model. With regard to performing and composing, for example, a study of lower-secondary pupils indicated that higher-order musical thinking was observed in 'composing' activities as compared to the same pupils' 'performance' behaviours (Swanwick and Franca, 1999). The authors argue that there is 'a difference between performance skills in composition and in performance itself', with the latter being related critically to the extent to which the chosen performance repertoire allows pupils 'to reveal the quality of their musical thinking' (p. 13).

Similar concerns arise from critiques of the underlying pedagogic competencies required from teachers by the design and wording of the curriculum. These include:

- the primary music curriculum's requirement for specialist technical knowledge of music by teachers (Thomas, 1997);
- the model for assessment (Swanwick, 1997);
- teachers' own limited abilities as 'composers' (Paynter, 1997);
- a pedagogic model that is insufficiently 'reflexive' (Ross and Kamba, 1998) and 'aesthetic' (Finney, 1999);
- the curriculum's simple hierarchy of singing development compared to the complex realities of vocal development from childhood into adolescence (Cooksey and Welch, 1998).

Student issues: equal opportunities

There has been considerable interest in the UK in various aspects of equal opportunities in relation to musical development and learning.

With regard to *gender*, mention has already been made of the differences between boys and girls in musical achievement in the formal GCSE examination (DfEE, 1998a). Overall, examination success across subjects favours girls, a trend that first became discernible in the late 1980s (Arnot *et al.*, 1998). Boys' underachievement in music is echoed in the English examination data, but not in science, whereas mathematics performance is similar to that of girls. Research evidence suggests that there are clear differences between boys and girls regarding preferences for (a) music and musical activities and (b) musical instruments, with certain instruments perceived as more 'gender-appropriate' (such as flute for girls, or music technology for boys) (O'Neill, 1997).

These differences derive from the nature of the interface between socio-cultural 'pathways' for music within the community and the developmental 'route' of the individual (Welch, 2000). Green (1999) argues that, because classical music in schools is practised successfully by females, it comes to delineate femininity, whereas popular music delineates masculinity. For example, notwithstanding their general underachievement in GCSE music, boys appear to be more confident than girls, as they get older, in the new area of music technology (Colley *et al.*, 1997). A related, but contrasting, example is the traditionally gendered membership of English cathedral choirs. There were no opportunities for girls' participation until a 1991 initiative at Salisbury cathedral. The customary argument was that only boys' voices were capable of producing the archetypal cathedral timbre required in the performance of the sacred music repertoire, presumably on the premise of a tradition that stretches back over 1300 years. Yet once girls were given the opportunity, they were able to produce this 'authentic', boy-like sound if that is what the cathedral choir director wanted (Sergeant and Welch, 1997; Howard *et al.*, 2000).

Religion also emerges as an important influence in the opportunity to engage with music for Muslim children. It is extremely rare for Muslim children to study music to examination level or to take part in extra-curricular musical activities (Halstead, 1994). Islamic music is defined by religious caveat, with permitted examples being the religious chant of the Qur'an, music for major festivals and unaccompanied singing for certain activities. Custom and practice in the religious code raises significant challenges to the current configuration of the mainstream school music curriculum, with its continued emphasis on composing.

In general, terms such as 'giftedness' and 'special educational needs' take on a particular significance in music, not least because folk wisdom suggests that the populace is divided into 'sheep' and 'goats' – the musically able or disabled (cf. Mills, 1996). Such a view appears to be supported by studies of musical savants (Miller, 1989), arguments for a particular intelligence dedicated to music (Gardner, 1993) and neuropsychobiological evidence of dedicated cortical areas for music (Carter, 1998). However, although musicians have been reported as having, on average, 25 per cent more of the auditory cortex involved in musical processing, this is biased towards those who began formal music instruction at the earliest age (Pantev *et al.*, 1998). The importance of environmental variables is also evident in studies of high-achieving musicians at a specialist music school (Sloboda and Howe, 1999) and in the development of a strong internal motivation to engage with music across the lifespan (Kemp, 1996). Other non-musical studies support the notion that 'gifted' performance and exceptional skills can be developed (Freeman, 1998).

In summary, the designers of the various national curricula (and the Scottish guidelines) and the UK research community appear to be agreed that, given an appropriately enriching, stimulating and fostering environment, everyone has an opportunity to further develop their species-wide capability for musical behaviour. Yet, unless the statutory curriculum designers seek better collaboration with researchers, the fulfilment of musical potential for the vast majority of children and young people will continue to be elusive.

References

Alexander, R., Rose, J. and Woodhead, C. (1992) *Curriculum Organisation and Classroom Practice in Primary Schools. A Discussion Paper.* London: Department of Education and Science.

Arnot, M., Gray, J., James, M., Ruddock, J. and Duveen, G. (1998) *Recent Research on Gender and Educational Performance.* London: OfSTED/The Stationery Office.

Baily, J. (1995) 'The role of music in three British muslim communities'. *Diaspora*, **4** (1), 77–88.

Baumann, G. (1990) 'The re-invention of *bhangra*: social change and aesthetic shifts in Punjabi music in Britain'. *The World of Music*, **2**, 81–98.

Bray, D. (1997) 'CD-ROM in music education'. *British Journal of Music Education*, **14** (2), 137–42.

Burns, E. M. (1999) 'Intervals, scales, and tuning', in D. Deutsch (ed.) *The Psychology of Music* (2nd edn). London: Academic Press.

Carter, R. (1998) *Mapping the Mind.* London: Weidenfeld & Nicolson.

Carterette, E. C. and Kendall, R. A. (1999) 'Comparative music perception and cognition', in D. Deutsch. (ed.) *The Psychology of Music* (2nd edn). London: Academic Press, pp. 725–79.

Colley, A., Comber, C. and Hargreaves, D. J. (1997) 'IT and music education:

What happens to boys and girls in co-educational and single sex schools?' *British Journal of Music Education*, **14** (2), 119–27.

Cooksey, J. M. and Welch, G. F. (1998) 'Adolescence, singing development and National Curricula design'. *British Journal of Music Education*, **15** (1), 99–119.

Cope, P. and Smith, H. (1997) 'Cultural context in musical instrumental learning'. *British Journal of Music Education*, **14** (3), 283–9.

Cottrell, S. (1998) 'Partnerships in the classroom'. *British Journal of Music Education*, **15** (3), 271–85.

Crozier, W. R. (1997) 'Music and social influence', in D. J. Hargreaves and A. C. North (eds) *The Social Psychology of Music*. Oxford: Oxford University Press, pp. 67–83.

DFE (1995a) *The National Curriculum*. London: HMSO.

DFE (1995b) *Music in the National Curriculum*. London: HMSO.

DfEE (1998a) *Education and Training Statistics for the United Kingdom 1997*. London: The Stationery Office.

DfEE (1998b) *Requirements for Courses of Initial Teacher Training*. Circular 4/98. London: Department for Education and Employment.

DfEE (1999a) *The National Curriculum: Handbook for Primary Teachers in England*. London: Department for Education and Employment/Qualifications and Curriculum Authority.

DfEE (1999b) *The National Curriculum: Handbook for Secondary Teachers in England*. London: Department for Education and Employment/Qualifications and Curriculum Authority.

DfEE (1999c) *All our Futures: Creativity, Culture and Education*. London: Department for Education and Employment.

DfEE (2000) Rt Hon. David Blunkett MP, Secretary of State for Education and Employment. Speech to the North of England Conference, 6 January 2000. [http://www.dfee.gov.uk/speech1/]

Dowling, W. J. (1999) 'The development of music perception and cognition', in D. Deutsch (ed.) *The Psychology of Music* (2nd edn). London: Academic Press, pp. 603–25.

Drummond, B. (1999) 'Classroom music teachers and the post-primary curriculum: the implications of recent research in Northern Ireland'. *British Journal of Music Education*, **16** (1), 21–38.

Durrant, C. (1999) 'The genesis of musical behaviour: implications for adolescent music education'. Paper presented to the British Educational Research Association Conference, University of Sussex.

ERA [The Education Reform Act] (1988) London: HMSO.

Farrell, G., Welch, G. F., Bhowmick, J. and Staunton, J. S. (1999) *Mapping South Asian Music in Britain*. Final Report to the Leverhulme Trust, July.

Finnegan, R. (1989) *The Hidden Musicians*. Cambridge: Cambridge University Press.

Finney, J. (1999) 'The rights and wrongs of school music: considering the expressivist argument'. *British Journal of Music Education*, **16** (3), 237–44.

Freeman, J. (1998) *Educating the Very Able*. London: OfSTED/The Stationery Office.

Gardner, H. (1993) *Multiple Intelligences*. New York: Basic Books.

Green, L. (1999) 'Research in the sociology of music education: some introductory concepts'. *Music Education Research*, **1** (2), 159–69.

Hall, J. (1999) *A Review of Musical Instrument Instruction in Scotland*. Edinburgh: Scottish Council for Research in Education.

Hallam, S. (1998) 'The predictors of achievement and dropout in instrumental tuition'. *Psychology of Music*, **26** (2), 116–32.

Halstead, J. M. (1994) 'Muslim attitudes to music in schools'. *British Journal of Music Education*, **11** (2), 143–56.

Hargreaves, D. J. (1996) 'The development of artistic and musical competence', in I. Deliège and J. Sloboda (eds) *Musical Beginnings*. Oxford: Oxford University Press, pp. 145–70.

Harland, J., Kinder, K. and Hartley, K. (1995) *Arts in their View*. Slough: NFER.

Harland, J., Kinder, K., Haynes, J. and Schagen, I. (1998) *The Effects and Effectiveness of Arts Education in Schools: Interim Report 1*. Slough: NFER.

Harris, N. S. (1989) 'The Education Reform Act 1988: National Curriculum: Framework or straitjacket?' *Education and the Law*, **1** (3), 105–12.

Howard, D. M., Barlow, C. and Welch, G. F. (2000). 'Vocal Production and Listener Perception of Trained Girls and Boys in the English Cathedral Choir'. Proceedings, 18th International Seminar of the ISME Research Commission, Salt Lake City, Utah, USA, 8–14 July 2000, 169–76.

Kemp, A. E. (1996) *The Musical Temperament*. Oxford: Oxford University Press.

Kwami, R. (1998) 'Non-western musics in education: problems and possibilities'. *British Journal of Music Education*, **15** (2), 161–70.

Lecanuet, J.-P. (1996) 'Prenatal auditory experience', in I. Deliège and J.A. Sloboda (eds) *Musical Beginnings*. Oxford: Oxford University Press, pp. 3–34.

Mellor, L. (1999) 'Language and music teaching: the use of personal construct theory to investigate teachers' responses to young people's music compositions'. *Music Education Research*, **1** (2), 147–58.

Miller, L. K. (1989) *Musical Savants*. New Jersey: Laurence Erlbaum Associates.

Mills, J. (1996) 'Starting at secondary school'. *British Journal of Music Education*, **13** (1), 5–14.

Mills, J. (1997) The DfEE/NCET Music/IT Support Project. *British Journal of Music Education*, **14** (2), 109–10.

Mills, J. (1998) 'Music', in G. Clay, J. Hertrich, P. Jones, J. Mills and J. Rose *The Arts Inspected*. Oxford: Heinemann/OfSTED, pp. 59–84.

Modood, T., Berthoud, R., Lakey, J., Nazroo, J., Smith, P., Virdee, S. and Beishon, S. (1997) *Ethnic Minorities in Britain*. London: Policy Studies Institute.

Naughton, C. (1998) 'Free samba: a music and cultural awareness project for teacher trainees'. *British Journal of Music Education*, **15** (3), 287–94.

North, A. C. and Hargreaves, D. J. (1997) 'Music and consumer behaviour', in

D. J. Hargreaves and A. C. North (eds) *The Social Psychology of Music*. Oxford: Oxford University Press.

North, A. C. and Hargreaves, D. J. (1999) 'Music and adolescent identity'. *Music Education Research*, **1** (1), 75–92.

Office for National Statistics (ONS) (1998) *Social Trends 28*. London: The Stationery Office.

OfSTED (1998) *Secondary Education: A Review of Secondary Schools in England, 1993–1997*. London: The Stationery Office.

OfSTED (1999a) *Primary Education. A Review of Primary Schools in England, 1994–1998*. London: The Stationery Office.

OfSTED (1999b) *The Annual Report of Her Majesty's Chief Inspector of Schools*. London: The Stationery Office.

OfSTED (1999c) *Standards in the Secondary Curriculum 1997/98: Music*. London: OfSTED.

OfSTED (1999d) *Special Education: A Review of Special Schools, Secure Units and Pupil Referral Units in England, 1994–1998*. London: The Stationery Office.

OfSTED (1999e) *The Quality of Nursery Education*. London: OfSTED. [http://www.ofsted.gov.uk/pubs/nurserydev.htm/]

O'Neill, S. (1997) 'Gender and music', in D. J. Hargreaves and A.C. North (eds) *The Social Psychology of Music*. Oxford: Oxford University Press, pp. 46–63.

O'Neill, S. and Sloboda, J. A. (1997) 'The effects of failure on children's ability to perform a musical test'. *Psychology of Music*, **25** (1), 18–34.

Pantev, C., Oostenveld, R., Engelein, A., Ross, B., Roberts, L. E. and Hoke, M. (1998) 'Increased auditory cortical representation in musicians'. *Nature*, **392**, 811–13.

Papousek, H. (1996) 'Musicality in infancy research: biological and cultural origins of early musicality', in I. Deliège and J. Sloboda (eds) *Musical Beginnings*. Oxford: Oxford University Press, pp. 37–55.

Paynter, J. (1997) 'The form of finality: a context for musical education'. *British Journal of Music Education*, **14** (1), 5–21.

Pratt, G. and Stephens, J. (1995) (eds) *Teaching Music in the National Curriculum*. Oxford: Heinemann.

QCA (1999) *Early Learning Goals*. London: Qualifications and Curriculum Authority.

Rogers, R. (1998) *The Disappearing Arts?* London: Royal Society of Arts.

Ross, M. (1975) *Arts and the Adolescent* (Schools Council Working Paper 54). London: Evans/Methuen.

Ross, M. and Kamba, M. (1998) *The State of the Arts*. Exeter: University of Exeter.

SCAA (1996) *A Guide to the National Curriculum*. London: HMSO.

SCCC (1998) *Curriculum Framework for Children 3–5*. Edinburgh: The Scottish Office Education and Industry Department.

Sergeant, D. C. and Welch, G. F. (1997) 'Perceived similarities and differences in the singing of trained children's choirs'. *Choir Schools Today*, **11**, 9–10.

Sloboda, J. A. and Howe, M. J. A. (1999) 'Musical talent and individual differences in musical achievement: a reply to Gagné'. *Psychology of Music*, **27** (1), 52–4.

SOEID (1999) *Standards and Quality in Scottish Schools (1995–1998)* Report by HM inspectors of schools. Edinburgh: The Scottish Office Education and Industry Department. [http://www.scotland.gov.uk/library/documents-w5/sqs-00.htm/]

Swanwick, K. (1997) 'Assessing musical quality in the National Curriculum'. *British Journal of Music Education*, **14** (3), 205–15.

Swanwick, K. and Franca, C. C. (1999) 'Composing, performing and audience-listening as indicators of musical understanding'. *British Journal of Music Education*, **16** (1), 5–19.

Swanwick, K. and Lawson, D. (1999) '"Authentic" music and its effect on the attitudes and musical development of secondary school students'. *Music Education Research*, **1** (1), 47–60.

Takeuchi, A. H. and Hulse, S. H. (1993) 'Absolute pitch'. *Psychological Bulletin*, **113**, 345–61.

TES (1998) 'Councils sing the blues'. *Times Educational Supplement*, 31 July, p. 4.

Thomas, R. (1997) 'The music National Curriculum: overcoming a compromise'. *British Journal of Music Education*, **14**, 217–35.

Tommis, Y. and Fazey, D. (1999) 'Musical literacy skills in pre-school children'. *Psychology of Music*, **27**, 230–44.

TTA (1997) *Annual Review 1997*. London: Teacher Training Agency.

TTA (1998) *National Standards for Subject Leaders: National Standards for Headteachers*. London: Teacher Training Agency.

Veblen, K. K. (1996) 'Truth, perceptions, and cultural constructs in ethnographic research: music teaching and learning in Ireland'. *Bulletin of the Council for Research in Music Education*, **129**, 37–52.

Ward, S. (1998) 'Music in primary schools: from the national song book to the national curriculum', in J. Glover and S. Ward (eds) *Teaching Music in the Primary School* (2nd edn). London: Cassell.

Webster, P. R. (1998) 'Young children and music technology'. *Research Studies in Music Education*, **11**, 61–76.

Welch, G. F. (1998) 'Early childhood musical development'. *Research Studies in Music Education*, **11**, 27–41.

Welch, G. F. (2000a) 'Singing development in early childhood: the effects of culture and education on the realisation of potential', in P. White (ed.) *Child Voice*. Stockholm: Royal Institute of Technology, pp. 27–44.

Welch, G. F. (2000b) 'The ontogenesis of musical behaviour: a Sociological perspective'. *Research Studies in Music Education*.

Wiggins, T. (1996) 'The world of music in education'. *British Journal of Music Education*, **13** (1), 21–9.

Conclusions: the international perspective

David J. Hargreaves and Adrian C. North

The authors of our fifteen chapters were invited to write on the basis of some specific topics, suggested by ourselves, under the three broad headings of Aims and Objectives, Contents and Methods, and Student Issues. Inevitably, they varied considerably in the approaches they took, as well as in the issues they chose to emphasize. There were, nevertheless, some unifying issues and common concerns which seemed to arise, irrespective of national or regional background, and we will try to draw these together in this final chapter. They fall under four main headings: historical, political and cultural backgrounds; curriculum issues; aims and objectives; and learning music inside and outside schools.

Historical, political and cultural backgrounds

One simple and obvious fact is that the countries represented in the book vary considerably with respect to physical and demographic character-istics such as geographical size, cultural diversity, population and economic wealth. Some are based on ancient civilizations, with centuries of philosophical tradition concerning questions of moral and personal development and education; some have longstanding musical and cultural traditions, with deep roots in national and political history. Whilst it is beyond our scope to trace the effects of these factors in any systematic or comprehensive fashion, we can, nevertheless, draw upon some examples which have emerged in order to illustrate some specific influences on musical learning and development.

Cheung-shing Yeh, for example, points out that China incorporates 56 nationalities with numerous different languages, and Gerry Farrell that India includes a vast range of political, cultural and musical traditions. South America is another region whose countries suffer from high levels of economic deprivation, and this has an inevitable impact on the school system. The first two of these vast nations have very longstanding philosophical traditions as well as ancient cultures of classical music, whereas the political and historical development of South American music is very different. The popular and 'folk' musics of South America form an integral and vital part of the everyday lives of most of its inhabitants, and Alda Oliveira's account shows that most musical participation and learning is done in these informal contexts rather than in schools.

In contrast, China and India are facing an issue which is of general concern, namely the tension between the preservation of traditional national music and the rise and ubiquity of western (largely Anglo-American) pop music. This is now available to an increasingly large proportion of the world's population as a result of the development of the mass media and internet technology. It is having a powerful effect not only on the musical preferences and purchases of many young people, but also upon more general aspects of youth culture which might include leisure interests, clothing styles, social attitudes and many other aspects of lifestyle. This has been part of the cultural tradition of many western countries for several decades now, as our chapters on the UK, Germany and Scandinavia make clear. It presents a clear cultural challenge in other parts of the world, however, and different countries are responding in different ways.

In China, the world's most populated country, western pop culture appears to have had relatively little impact upon music education. Cheung-shing Yeh explains that the predominant Confucian philosophy emphasizes the role of music and the arts more generally as a means of promoting virtuous moral living, and this also emerges as a significant principle in Korea. In China, this exists alongside a very strong and professional tradition of western-style conservatory-based musical training. The cultural revolution of the 1960s provided an abrupt disruption, however, since many schools were closed. More recent developments have given rise to the development of an official national curriculum which was proposed in 1986: this embraces several ideals which are current in western thinking, such as child-centredness, the accountability of teachers and collaboration between 'stakeholders' in teaching and learning.

A similar tension exists on the Indian and African continents. Gerry

Farrell points out that a wide range of classical, popular, folk and religious musical traditions co-exist in India, as well as the increasingly prominent *filmi* music, which derives from popular (film) culture. Farrell suggests that India is 'at the crossroads' as far as the future resolution of these diverse and sometimes conflicting influences is concerned: it still has been unable to decide, at the dawn of the new millennium, how to adapt to this multicultural diversity. Kathy Primos' account of recent developments in South Africa reveals that there is a similar tension between the western classical tradition, which has been a prominent influence in the past, and African music. She points out that the new 'Curriculum 2005' provides a unique opportunity for cross-cultural interaction, and this represents an exciting challenge for the future.

Russia provides another clear-cut and explicit example of direct historical and political influence upon musical and cultural development. Like China, India and Africa, this is a huge, populous and economically deprived region with very powerful and distinctive cultural traditions. It also has a strong classical, conservatory tradition, and has seen some dramatic political changes over the last century. In the communist USSR, it is well known that composers such as Shostakovich, Prokofiev and Rimsky-Korsakov were subjected to state censorship so as to ensure that their music was congruent with the ideals of the communist regime. In this sense, music and the arts were seen as a more or less direct means of ideological and political control. As Maris Valk-Falk and Marina Gulina point out, the dramatic changes associated with *perestroika* in the later part of the century have changed this to such an extent that western pop and rock music is not only tolerated but even taught in some institutions, although the classical tradition still predominates at most levels of the school system.

The tension between traditional, national musics and cultures on the one hand and western popular culture on the other also occurs in technologically advanced societies. Murao and Wilkins's chapter shows that Japan provides an interesting example of a technologically advanced country that simultaneously incorporates a longstanding tradition of local classical music. The Japanese are currently trying to overcome this potential conflict by conscious attempts to 'fuse' eastern and western musical styles in a number of ways. One has been for Japanese composers to write for children's use in the classroom; and it turns out that this fusion is also occurring spontaneously in children's playground songs. Another development, to be introduced into the National Curriculum requirements in 2002, is that school music teachers will be required to teach Japanese traditional music and to learn a traditional instrument.

Developments in other countries also show very clearly how the long-term historical and political context can have a direct influence upon the development of music and music learning. Some of these can be sudden and abrupt: music education, as such, virtually disappeared in Brazil between 1964 and 1984 as a result of the governing military regime, for example. An even more striking and recent example is that of South Africa, where the results of the 1994 elections led to a sudden and complete re-evaluation of existing practices and paradigms. A parallel can also be seen in the after-effects of the Second World War in Poland: Kacper Miklaszewski and Wojiech Jankowski point out that after years of rule by Russia, Prussia and Austria, specialist music schools were established which served to develop a sense of national culture and identity.

Alda Oliviera's account of longer-term developments in South America shows how religious institutions played a key role in musical learning in Argentina and Peru as well as in Brazil. This was accomplished by the choirs and orchestras in the cathedrals and chapels, and by the work of the missionaries in their fight against slavery. Music thus played an important role in the social and cultural development of an extremely diverse multiracial society. This is parallelled by developments in Portugal: Graca Mota explains that the end of the Portuguese colonization of Africa in 1975 gave rise to an increase in immigration to Portugal of African descent, which infused local musical traditions with new African influences. We might add that mass immigration from particular areas of the world has also had a profound impact on the musical cultures both of France and Britain.

This leads on to the complex issue of multicultural music education. The majority of the countries surveyed in this book would almost certainly emphasize the value of pupils studying musics from a variety of cultural heritages, and Johannella Tafuri discusses this point in some detail in the Italian context. However, they vary considerably in the extent to which they put this ideal into practice. The UK and the USA incorporate many different cultural and racial groups, for example, and so this issue comes to the fore. Gary McPherson and Peter Dunbar-Hall report in detail upon how the music of the Torres Strait Islanders is incorporated explictly into the Australian curriculum, and we have already commented on the Japanese desire to accomplish a fusion between eastern and western musical styles.

Although this issue often raises more heat than light, our international perspective clearly demonstrates its importance, and its resolution will no doubt be accomplished in different ways in different countries. Multicultural education and the nature of national identity are issues which are likely to increase in importance as global communication improves.

Curriculum issues

One clear distinction which can be made in the music education policies of the majority of the countries discussed in this book is that between general and specialist music education: most countries offer both. General music (sometimes called classroom or curriculum music) is, typically, offered at the lower age levels, and is usually taught either by specialist musicians or by general class teachers with extra training in general music. Specialist music education is, typically, offered as an optional or elective subject at the higher age levels within the school system, so that music is not studied by all pupils up to school-leaving age in many countries. Pupils intending to go on to a career in music typically follow additional tuition outside the school alongside that within it.

In some European countries such as the UK, Germany and in Scandinavia, general class music involves activities associated with the 'creativity movement', based on the work of John Paynter, Murray Schaefer and others. However, this is by no means universal: general music education in Russia involves 6–7-year-olds in studying the works of the great Russian composers, for example, with a high expectation of the acquisition of traditional musical skills. Specialist music education is oriented towards the western conservatoire tradition in many European countries such as Poland, Russia, Portugal, Germany, the UK and Italy, as well as in many non-European countries, but once again, this is not universally true. The Australian education system emphasizes a holistic approach at all levels, for example, viewing the processes involved in the development of creativity and self-expression as more important than the technical quality of the products that emerge.

There seem to be two tensions inherent in the balance between general and specialist music education. The first is the question of who is best qualified to teach the former. In the UK, for example, there are many who argue that many specialist musicians are less suited to general than to specialist music in that they tend to emphasize inappropriate standards of excellence in performance and in the products of teaching, rather than general outcomes more related to the process (as in the Australian system). The second, related issue is that specialist music is often too closely associated with the western classical tradition: it is quite possible to carry out specialist teaching in other musical genres. Graca Mota makes both of these points in outlining some of the inadequacies of

Portuguese music education, though these particular problems are compounded by the lack of resources and teaching staff.

Perhaps the clearest example of both of these tensions is in Poland. Kacper Miklaszewski and Wojiech Jankowski structure their whole chapter around what they call the 'two systems' of general and specialist music education. GME involves conventional skills such as the development of ear training, performance skills and reading notation, as well as some creative work, and SME is geared towards very high levels of formal achievement in the western classical tradition. Miklaszewski and Jankowski suggest that the system fails on both counts in practice. Although GME has very ambitious aims, in practice it does not even produce pupils with basic levels of musical skill – and it could well be that these aims are too ambitious, given the available resources. Similarly, the aims of SME are so ambitious and specialized that many young musicians experience high levels of stress and drop out. These authors conclude that that the whole system needs reforming so as to bring the two systems more closely together, and to reorient their objectives.

The other central issue as far as curriculum planning is concerned is that of centralization; practices vary widely between countries with respect to the implementation of a national curriculum. Japan has, perhaps, the most highly prescribed and regulated national curriculum of all the countries represented in this book, and Murao and Wilkins have documented its various revisions over the last decade or two. Other countries with a national curriculum which is specified and regulated in varying degrees include Australia, the UK and India. China and Korea have both introduced a national curriculum relatively recently, and this has represented a marked departure from existing practice. In each case, this has involved a conscious attempt to bring existing practices more into line with those of the western world, as well as a conscious attempt to deal with the clash between local traditional musics and western popular culture, which we discussed earlier.

In other European countries there is less emphasis on centralization, and indeed a conscious move away from it in some cases, such as in Scandinavia. The situation in Germany involves an interesting mixture: Heiner Gembris explains that the sixteen Bundesländer, or regional districts, have autonomous control over their curricula, while there exists simultaneously centralized direction from the Kultusministerkonferenz. This parallels the situation in the USA in some respects. Although all schools are controlled at local level, in particular by school boards set up within each state, there are also national standards to which each state is expected to aspire: and university entrance is based upon national competitive standards.

The effectiveness of centralized and/or decentralized systems in promoting musical learning can only be judged within the specific context of each nation: on local musical tradition and heritage, on other aspects of educational policy and on recent political history in each case. Korea and China have moved towards centralization as a means of organizing and systematizing what was seen as an unacceptably diverse system, and this was also the primary motivation for the recent developments in national curriculum policy in Japan and the UK. In the UK, the level of prescription of course content and method has declined since the original National Curriculum was introduced in 1988. Many of these changes are matters of current national concern.

Aims and objectives

What are music and the arts for? What roles should they play in people's lives? What should be the aims of arts and music education, given these roles? These are not easy questions to answer, especially from the international perspective. We have attempted to formulate a contemporary answer to the first question in a recent paper on the psychological functions of music in everyday life (Hargreaves and North, 1999): the second and third questions also involve social, educational and even moral issues. One of the central questions in many countries today is whether the arts should be an end in themselves, and therefore need no further justification, or whether they should act as a vehicle for other aspects of learning. In his discussion of music education policy in the USA, Rudolf Radocy cites the impact of recent reseach on the so-called 'Mozart effect', which seems to suggest that listening to the music of Mozart can produce direct gains in non-musical domains such as spatial and temporal thinking ability. This is a complex issue which has generated a great deal of heated debate, in the popular press as well as in the research literature.

It is almost certainly premature to formulate educational policy on the basis of research findings that are frequently misinterpreted and misunderstood. Radocy's chapter clearly shows, nevertheless, that the policy implications of the 'Mozart effect' are the subject of serious discussion in the USA. A similar debate has been taking place in the UK in recent years, largely as a result of governmental cuts in the funding of, and time available for, music in the school curriculum. Bodies such as the National Campaign for Music in the Curriculum (NCMC) have been organized to combat these cuts. The NCMC draws extensively on the recent research evidence on the so-called 'transfer' effects of participation in the arts, justifying the importance of the arts in the curriculum in terms of their benefits for other aspects of learning such as reading, spatial skills, language learning, social and emotional development and so on.

While few would want to argue against the case being put forward by campaign groups like the NCMC, their extensive reliance on the evidence for 'transfer' effects may be quite misguided for two main reasons. The first is that the evidence for these effects is by no means overwhelming; the second, more powerful, argument is simply that the arts should be justified in terms of their own intrinsic benefits rather than for their 'spinoffs'. Murao and Wilkins's chapter traces the course of such a debate in Japan, where music education is seen as an end in itself rather than as a means to an end. The emphasis is on 'educating students through music' rather than on 'teaching music to students', although there have been some recent changes in the relative emphasis which is placed upon Japanese musical culture itself.

Our book shows that different countries have formulated very different responses to this basic question. It might be useful to broaden the debate by distinguishing between three main types of rationale that have been put forward in different countries for the inclusion of music in the school curriculum. These range from aims and objectives which are specifically *musical*, through those which involve broader aspects of *personal* development, to those which are primarily *social and cultural*.

We have already mentioned the argument that music exists 'as an end in itself', such that music education should need no further justification. Music education develops certain more or less specific *musical* skills such as sight-reading, singing, ear training, and other performance skills, which are emphasized in the early stages of musical training. However, it also promotes broader, more general musical skills such as emotional expression in performance, musicological understanding, aesthetic appreciation and discrimination, and creativity in improvisation and composition. The balance between the specific and the more general skills varies considerably between countries. In China, for example, the reforms discussed in the 1990s included an emphasis upon musical creativity rather than on the acquisition of traditional skills, and on a child-centred rather than a teacher-centred curriculum: this represents a radical change from the previous, traditional approach.

The broader aspects of musical skill, such as creativity and self-expression, aesthetic perception and emotional expression, lead us on to what we might call *personal* objectives as these go beyond the musical elements themselves. In Australia, for example, the national curriculum framework for the arts emphasizes a holistic view of arts education. This is intended to serve the core goals of education, including the promotion of confident self-expression, creative and innovative thinking, being involved and 'having a go'. Russia provides an interesting and somewhat paradoxical contrast to this. Although there is a strong emphasis on the learning of technical skills, with a fairly narrow focus on Russian classical music, the ultimate aim is, nevertheless, to achieve high levels of emotional expressiveness through music. Technical mastery is an essential prerequisite, but this is seen as serving to promote the expression of feeling, and conceptualizing and interpreting what the composer intended.

Another aspect of personal development through music education is that of character building, moral development and 'virtuous living'. This is seen most clearly in eastern societies, often as a direct result of the influence of Confucian philosophy. In Korea, for example, we have seen that a subject called 'joyful life' was introduced in 1995, and that this combined music with other subjects such as visual arts, social studies and literature. The same influence can be seen in China, where the idea of music as a moral force also surfaces in the emphasis on virtuous living. This eastern emphasis on humility and altruism provides a fascinating contrast with Radocy's view of the 'frontier tradition' which developed in the USA as a result of the survival strategies which individuals were forced to adopt in the early days. The competitiveness and spirit of individual enterprise that derives from this contrasts sharply with the eastern emphasis on social co-operation.

The third group of *social and cultural* objectives of music education see music and the arts as a means of propagating social and cultural values, and even as a vehicle for political and ideological control. In the previous communist countries, for example, the arts specifically served this purpose. The music of some of the most prominent composers was subject to direct political control and censorship, and art that did not conform to the correct political ideologies of social realism and patriotism was considered to be degenerate, and sometimes banned. The same attitudes held in communist China in the last century, where the propagation of the Cultural Revolution dominated official thinking, such that western music was seen to involve 'spiritual pollution'.

Specific social and cultural objectives can be positive as well as negative, however. In the new South African curriculum, as Kathy Primos points out, there is an explicit call for openness to differing paths to music learning, and a willingness to shift entrenched attitudes and thought patterns with respect to existing cultural traditions. It is also worth noting that musical, personal and social/cultural objectives can all, to a certain extent, be included within a single curriculum, as Johannella Tafuri explains when discussing the Italian educational concepts of *educazione, istruzione* and *formazione*.

Social psychological research is increasingly revealing the power of music in people's everyday lives (Hargreaves and North, 1997), and so these aims and objectives of music education deserve serious consideration. It is also instructive to look in more detail at different countries' practices as far as the specific contents of the music curriculum are concerned. There seem to be four broad domains of musical skill that are promoted and encouraged to various degrees in most countries, namely those concerned with *performance*, with *aural and listening skills*, with *understanding and knowledge*, and with *creativity*.

The first three of these are the traditional province of the conservatory, and some countries give them considerable emphasis. Strong western classical traditions predominate in eastern European countries such as Poland and Russia, as well as in China. Although there is a strong emphasis on formal skills within this tradition, the importance of emotional expressiveness and creativity is also stressed in varying degrees.

The relative emphasis that is placed on creativity in relation to pupils' knowledge about and understanding of prescribed music is of considerable interest and international variation. A distinct split between what might be called teacher-centred and pupil-centred approaches has emerged in the book, and the latter is more closely associated with the promotion of creativity. These also seem to be associated with eastern and western approaches to music education respectively, though there are many exceptions to this rule. However, the Indian *guru-shishya* system might be taken as representing the paradigm of the teacher-centred approach. The pupil very clearly works as an apprentice to the guru, spending many months and years learning the traditions and techniques of performance. Interestingly, improvisation is one of the skills which is learnt over this long period, though there are clearly prescribed ways in which this must be done, as Gerry Farrell explains.

'Creative music-making' is given particular emphasis in Australia, in the UK, and in North and South America, and this has been accomplished in some cases by the wholesale importation of the recommendations of music educators such as John Paynter and Murray Schaefer. In the Australian curriculum, Gary McPherson and Peter Dunbar-Hall explain that creative self-expression, or the *process* of music-making, is given more weight than its final products: the process of working and reworking is seen as an integral and valued aspect of 'holistic' music teaching.

These two broad approaches provide an interesting contrast. In a sense, the pupil-centred approach represents the idea that the curriculum should be adapted to the level and specific needs of the child, whereas the teacher-centred approach focuses on pupils adapting to the requirements of the teacher, and to the musical culture. The division between the two is frequently blurred in the methods adopted in different countries, however, and their association with western and eastern cultures is by no means straightforward. Creative music-making is now encouraged in countries such as Poland, Korea, Japan and China, and the division is much harder to conceptualize in African music education. Composition and improvisation exist in many different forms in different musical cultures, and policy-makers have a great deal to learn from this diversity.

Learning music inside and outside schools

As Kathy Primos points out in her chapter, the notion of going to school to 'learn music' is an alien concept in many parts of Africa. Music is an integral part of everyday life, and part of people's social and spiritual welfare: it is a natural part of work, play, rituals, ceremonies and religious and family occasions. The distinction between musical learning and development as a natural result of enculturation, and as the product of specific schooling, or training, is also one with wide international variation.

Alda Oliveira's chapter explains that the South American continent has an extremely rich and multicultural musical heritage, and that a good deal of this is transmitted in informal rather than in school settings. Oliveira describes the bossa nova, tropicalia, marcha-rancho and other musical forms as distinctively South American styles which tend to be created and propagated by key composers and performers within a very active yet informal musical community that exists outside rather than inside the schools. Oliveira suggests that music learning occurs in games, plays, families, inner-city locations, bars, night clubs and on beaches: this provides an interesting and provocative view of the future of music education.

The critical question is whether informal music-making, which occurs in all countries, complements or competes with school music: once again, the answer varies internationally. In Africa and South America, the provision of school music is relatively scarce, so that informal music-making comes to the fore. In the UK, however, there is a very clear divergence and maybe even competition between music inside and outside school, particularly at the secondary-school level. Graham Welch's chapter outlines the evidence from the school inspectors' reports, which clearly show that while music is one of the best taught subjects at primary level, it is simultaneously one of the worst taught in the secondary school: the inspectors see music as being 'ossified and remote from pupils' interests'.

This is very probably because whereas music at primary school is well integrated into pupils' overall programme of study, teenagers, typically, develop very strong interests in certain styles of pop music that are commonly associated with out-of-school activities and leisure interests. There is a growing body of evidence to show that pop music preferences are central to the developing identities of many teenagers. We have ourselves carried out a number of empirical investigations which explore the different functions fulfilled by teenage musical preferences, which constitute a 'badge' of social identity (see North and Hargreaves, 1999; Tarrant, Hargreaves, and North, in press).

This leaves the obvious question as to how secondary-school music provision should approach this issue, and there has been some heated debate in the UK. Ross (1995) has argued that music is one of the least popular subjects in the secondary school because attempts to modernize the music curriculum have failed: that music teachers have stuck to their traditional concerns rather than adapting to new challenges, and that it is unrealistic to teach music as a conventional school subject at secondary level. Our own recent survey of 2465 British 13–14-year-olds (North, Hargreaves and O'Neill, 2000) showed that they perceived the benefits of playing and listening to pop music (including enjoyment, exercising creativity and imagination, relieving tension and stress) as being very different to those for classical music (to please parents and teachers).

On the other hand, many secondary pupils enjoy pop music outside school as well as performing and studying 'classical' as well as pop music within school: there is not necessarily a clear polarity between 'pop' and 'serious' music, nor an association with participation outside and inside school. Practices vary considerably in other countries. We have seen that pop music is also part of the school curriculum in Germany, Scandinavia and even Poland, Russia and India. In spite of this, different forms of popular music are not mentioned explicitly by several of our authors, and its study at higher levels of music education is marginal at best.

However, this is only one aspect of the informal–formal music issue. In many countries there exists a very healthy balance between the two, as well as strong traditions of community-based musical activities. Bengt Olsson describes the strong tradition of municipal music schools in Scandinavia. These take pupils from all ages and levels of ability and form an integral part of local communities. They are similar in many ways to the Japanese 'culture schools' described by Murao and Wilkins, and to the German 'Volkshochschule' described by Heiner Gembris. Murao and Wilkins explain that opportunities for musical instruction are also available from private institutions like the national broadcasting station and the Yamaha and Suzuki schools. As with the karaoke phenomenon, the initial motivation for these was primarily commercial, but they nevertheless now provide a service to the community as whole.

Yet another area of informal music-making which is integral to local communities is represented by Graca Mota's account of the bandas in Portugal. Although these are essentially local amateur groups, the best can attain high standards of professionalism. One of their great strengths is that members are drawn from across generations: men and women of all ages form part of a musical tradition which is passed from grandparents to parents to children in a disciplined manner which can include weekly practice and regular regional competitions. Mota points out that the bandas enable many people to read and write music, play instruments and take part in public events, regardless of age, gender or ability: they provide opportunities which may well not be open to people in the school system. Competitive events are also to be found in Germany, in Japan and in the USA, though attitudes to competition and the reasons for taking part may be very different in each country.

This presents an interesting paradox. Although informal musical activities such as the Portuguese bandas exist outside the school, and clearly benefit the individuals and communities taking part, the ultimate outcome seems to be competitions, which, inevitably, involve external judgement and assessment. Bengt Olsson's analysis of the role of assessment in Scandinavian music education is very helpful in developing a theoretical perspective on this apparent paradox, as well as on the nature of formal and informal music-making. Olsson refers to Saar's (1999) distinction between the pedagogical and musical 'framing' of different musical activities, which provides insight into three other issues, namely the question of authenticity in music, the role of assessment, and the developing identity of the trainee music teacher.

'Pedagogical framing' refers to school-based contextualization of knowledge; it emphasizes 'objective' analysis and the formulation of clear standards of performance. 'Musical framing', on the other hand, is more flexible and less bound by formalized standards: the focus here is upon the creation of new ideas and interpretations. This distinction makes it easy to see that the question of the authenticity of different musical genres and performances is intimately bound up with the extent to which they are defined within one kind of frame or the other.

Authentic performances of pop, folk or world musics are more likely to be framed musically, and, therefore, to occur within informal rather than in formal contexts.

Assessment is an integral part of formal, pedagogically framed music: its value and validity depend very much upon the uses to which it is put. Although 'portfolio' or 'formative' assessment is seen as an integral part of the process of teaching and learning, 'summative' assessments are much more common in music education, and are often used as external evaluations for the purposes of grading or selection. Olsson suggests that assessment can be seen as a vehicle for the control of informal musical activities, by retaining them within a pedagogical frame. The role of the trainee music teacher as either a 'musician' or a 'teacher' is also much more clearly apparent if these are seen as being musically or pedagogically framed respectively, and Olsson elaborates upon how role conflicts can and do frequently occur for individual trainees.

Conclusion: theory and practice

Olsson's analysis is a good point at which to end our review of the main issues in this chapter because it shows how an effective theoretical analysis can serve to explain several practical problems. Generally speaking, few of our authors have been able to show convincing ways in which psychological or educational theory has impinged on teaching practice or curriculum policy in any of the countries we have surveyed. Graham Welch's chapter explicitly laments the fact that this is clearly true in the UK: he identifies several issues where research findings could and should have quite direct influences upon practical decision-making. There are very few explicit attempts to base curriculum plans in psychological accounts of musical development and learning, for example, or to ground their aims and objectives in established research findings.

Rudolf Radocy identifies some of the specific theoretical influences upon North American music education that ought to have had lasting effects upon music-education policy. He concludes, somewhat regretfully, that what he calls a 'bandwagon' mentality has led to American music educators following a succession of fads and fashionable ideas rather than developing a sustained theoretical rationale or consistent policy. Current discussions seem to centre on so-called 'brain-based' education, with a particular interest in the 'Mozart effect' in the case of music, though the influences of behavioural psychology, cognitive and developmental psychology, and Gardner's theory of multiple intelligences are still apparent.

We must conclude, as so often in music psychology and music education, that the gulf between theory and practice remains immense. Our own theoretical aim in compiling this book was to flesh out some of the specific ways in which the social and cultural environment shapes musical learning and development. Taking the international perspective has enabled us to establish beyond doubt that the immense richness and diversity of the world's musical cultures, and the specific historical and political influences which exist in different regions, determine the course of musical learning and development.

The clear lesson to be learned for the future is that our view of the scope and nature of music education needs to be very broad, and certainly more so than is currently the case in many official curricula. The importance of social and cultural contextualization emerges very clearly in our comparison between musical learning in informal as compared with formal contexts. These contexts exert a vital influence upon the nature of music-making as well as on the development of music itself. As the pace of globalization and technological development continue to increase in the twenty-first century, social and psychological studies will assume increasing importance.

References

Hargreaves, D. J. and North, A. C. (eds) (1997) *The Social Psychology of Music*. Oxford: Oxford University Press.

Hargreaves, D. J. and North, A. C. (1999) 'The functions of music in everyday life: redefining the social in music psychology'. *Psychology of Music*, **27**, 71–83.

North, A. C. and Hargreaves, D. J. (1999) 'Music and adolescent identity'. *Music Education Research*, **1**, (1) 75–92.

North, A. C., Hargreaves, D. J. and O'Neill, S. (2000) 'The importance of music to adolescents'. *British Journal of Educational Psychology*, **70**, 255–72.

Ross, M. (1995) 'What's wrong with school music?' *British Journal of Music Education*, **12**, (3) 185–201.

Saar, T. (1999) 'Musikens dimensioner: en studie av unga musikers lärande'. Doctoral dissertation, University of Göteborg: Acta Universitatis Gothoburgensis, no. 133.

Tarrant, M., Hargreaves, D. J. and North, A.C. (in press) 'Social categorization, self-esteem, and the estimated musical preferences of male adolescents'. *Journal of Social Psychology*.

Name index

Subject index